The Best of Boards

Sound Governance and Leadership
for Nonprofit Organizations

11144-359

Marci Thomas, CPA, MHA
Kim Strom-Gottfried, Ph.D.

Notice to Readers

The Best of Boards: Sound Governance and Leadership for Nonprofit Organizations does not represent an official position of the American Institute of Certified Public Accountants, and it is distributed with the understanding that the author and publisher are not rendering legal, accounting, or other professional services in the publication. If legal advice or other expert assistance is required, the services of a competent professional should be sought.

Publisher: Amy M. Stainken
Acquisitions Editor: Robert Fox
Associate Developmental Editor: Whitney Woody
Project Manager: M. Donovan Scott
Cover Design Direction: Clay Porter

About the Authors

Marci Thomas, *CPA, MHA*

 Marci Thomas, CPA, MHA, is an author and discussion leader for Loscalzo Associates, P.A., and also performs quality control and risk assessment consultations for the firm. Ms. Thomas is also a clinical assistant professor at the University of North Carolina at Chapel Hill where she teaches Health Care Consulting and Financial Leadership.

From 1986 through 1999 and again in 2005, Ms. Thomas worked for Deloitte, primarily in the accounting and advisory services department. Most recently, she was Director in Deloitte Consulting in strategy and operations practice in the Atlanta office. While at Deloitte, Ms. Thomas was nationally recognized for her work with managed healthcare, employee benefit plans, and the public sector, including State Employee Retirement Systems and state and local governments. She also worked extensively with organizations required to report under OMB Circular A-133. Ms. Thomas worked with Enterprise Governance including leveraging Sarbanes Oxley Act of 2002 requirements to add value to companies. In the late 90s, she lead the firm's National HEDIS Product Committee and was on the firm's National Regulatory Compliance Task Force, where she chaired the managed care subcommittee.

Ms. Thomas received her Bachelor in Business Administration degree with a concentration in accounting from the Georgia State University and her Master of Health Administration degree at the University of North Carolina at Chapel Hill. She is a frequent speaker at local, regional, and national conferences for groups such as the Healthcare Financial Management Association (HFMA), Healthcare Information Systems Society (HIMSS), Healthcare Compliance Association, and others. She has written articles for publications of the HFMA, HIMSS, and Healthcare Compliance Association and has won numerous awards for her work with those organizations. She is the treasurer of the Adair Estates Homeowners Association and is Vice Chair of the Georgia Society of CPAs Healthcare Section. In addition to writing numerous training manuals for Loscalzo Publishing, she is co-editor and author of a book published by Jossey Bass in 2004, *Essentials of Physician Practice Management*.

Kimberly Strom-Gottfried, *PhD*

Dr. Kim Strom-Gottfried is the Smith P. Theimann Jr. Distinguished Professor of Ethics and Professional Practice at the University of North Carolina at Chapel Hill School of Social Work. She received her BSW from the University of Maine, her MSW from Adelphi University, and her PhD from Case Western Reserve University. She has worked in the nonprofit and public sectors as a clinician, program planner, and trainer.

Dr. Strom-Gottfried teaches in the areas of direct practice, higher education, and human resource management. Her scholarly interests involve ethics, moral courage, and social work education. She is the former chair of the National Association of Social Workers' National Committee on Inquiry and is active in training, consultation, and research on ethics and social work practice. She has written over 60 articles, monographs, and chapters on ethics and practice. She is the author of *Straight Talk about Professional Ethics* and *The Ethics of Practice with Minors: High Stakes and Hard Choices*. Dr. Strom-Gottfried is also the co-author of the texts *Direct Social Work Practice* and *Teaching Social Work Values and Ethics: A Curriculum Resource*. Dr. Strom-Gottfried currently holds an appointment as the University of North Carolina Institute for Arts & Humanities Associate Director for the Academic Leadership Program, which helps prepare and support the next generation of academic leaders.

Preface

We are two professionals concerned about the economic health and viability of nonprofit organizations. Although neither of us currently works in the nonprofit sector, together we have over 40 years of experience with nonprofits in a variety of roles: administering, consulting, auditing, training, and volunteering. Despite our divergent backgrounds (accounting and social work), we share a common belief that too many nonprofits put their missions at risk when they fail to attend to the demands of governance. At the same time, we know that resources are available to assist nonprofits with the tough issues they face, particularly in this time of economic uncertainty and blossoming regulation.

We came together to write this book because we believe that knowledge of laws and regulations is important, and there are chapters in this book dedicated to those topics. But the issues facing boards go beyond the technical components of decision making. Nonprofits and their leaders must distill the facts of any given situation, assess the risks, and ultimately make a proper decision based on those elements. Such decisions are not always clear cut or easy. Ethical, interpersonal, political, and other considerations can affect decision making and the outcomes that result. Thus we focus not only on the laws and policies guiding nonprofits but also on the individual and group dynamics.

This book offers an introduction to the most important things that board members and nonprofit executives need to know. The first chapter sets the stage by helping the reader understand the reasons why the content is important to the governance of the nonprofit. Chapter 2 defines the difference between roles that management and the board hold in the nonprofit and discusses the board's responsibilities in the context of the Independent Sector's good governance model. Suggestions for implementation by smaller nonprofits are a main focus of this chapter.

Chapter 3 discusses the legal and ethical imperatives that the leaders encounter in nonprofit governance and reviews resources for sound decision making. This is followed by chapter 4, which discusses how to resolve the conflict that is bound to arise in nonprofits when management and the board disagree. It identifies a framework for working through those issues.

Boards will have a difficult time governing if they can't read the basic financial statements of a nonprofit. This technical background is essential to understanding the information that is provided to them on a periodic basis as well as the information that may be audited and made available to donors, funding sources, and others. Chapter 5 provides descriptions of the terminology and definitions, illustrated in a set of nonprofit financial statements, that are important to that understanding.

Chapter 6 discusses the uncertainty and risk that nonprofits face as well as methodologies that a board could use to deal with them. This includes the risk nonprofits run related to external forces such as economic markets and the internal risk of fraud, which is prevalent in nonprofits.

Chapter 7 discusses the internal controls that should be implemented to prevent or detect misstatements and fraud. The chapter illustrates the types of fraud to which the nonprofit is most susceptible.

Chapter 8 discusses a variety of issues with which boards should be familiar related to the organization's tax exempt status.

Chapter 9 introduces the concept of moral courage—the capacity of individuals to take unpopular stands and to act in defense of principles. It identified the barriers to moral courage and provides steps and examples to cultivate courage.

Nonprofits that introduce control measures, risk management initiatives, and other structures are undertaking significant change processes. Chapter 10 addresses organizational change and the effects such changes have on the individuals involved. It details the steps in a change process and the strategic decisions needed for successful transformations.

Chapter 11 synthesizes the book's key points and applies them to new cases, creating a platform for application and for continuing conversation.

Throughout this book are tools and templates that organizations and individuals can use to guide essential discussions and to help ensure compliance and, ultimately, the success of the organization. The book is also populated with numerous case examples. Most cases are composites of situations that we have encountered rather than representations of actual organizations. When we do refer to actual nonprofits, we have offered citations that link the case to news reports or other sources describing the situation.

Acknowledgments

The authors are grateful for all the help and support that was given to us by our colleagues, families, and friends as we wrote this book. We particularly want to acknowledge the following:

- The students enrolled in the Public Health Leadership doctorate program at the University of North Carolina at Chapel Hill, who inspired the writing of this book and reviewed earlier drafts
- Charles Walker, for all the time and effort he contributed to editing our work
- Billy Minch, Donarene Steele, Susan Hill, and Wayne Williams from Metcalf-Davis in Atlanta, who contributed their expertise in nonprofit accounting, taxation, and internal controls
- The countless participants in our workshops and seminars who helped us understand the gaps in board knowledge, the challenges facing nonprofits, and the ways this book could help
- Alison Prevost, for managing research and the bibliographic database
- Kay Grinnell, who reviewed the manuscript from the point of view of a board member

Table of Contents

Chapter 1: The Risk is Real; The Time is Now

Chapter 2: Roles of the Board and Management

Chapter 3: Legal and Ethical Imperatives for Leadership

Chapter 4: When Management and the Governing Board Disagree

Chapter 5: Understanding the Financial Statements of Nonprofit Organizations

Chapter 6: Risk Management

Chapter 7: Internal Controls: What Every Executive and Board Member Needs to Know

Chapter 8: Focus on Tax Exempt Status

Chapter 9: The Courage to Lead

Chapter 10: Change Management

Chapter 11: Integration for Action

Chapter 1

The Risk is Real; The Time is Now

There's no doubt about it: nonprofits are going through troubled times. Unemployment is up; the stock market is down. This has wreaked havoc with individual contributions, the life blood of many nonprofit organizations. In addition, when investments decline significantly in value, nonprofits may be doubly affected: (1) they may not have as much available to spend on programs, and (2) the foundations another hefty chuck of their support may not have as much to give. Contributions from individuals and corporations and grants and gifts from foundations were responsible for approximately 43 percent of nonprofit revenue in 2005.[1]

A GuideStar Survey taken from March through May 2009[2] noted that approximately 52 percent of nonprofit organizations saw a drop in their contributions, approximately 36 percent of grantors gave nonprofits less money over the 3 month period and 8 percent of the 2,279 nonprofits that responded to the survey are in danger of shutting down.

Never before has it been more important for nonprofits to put their best foot forward. Donors, foundation and government grantors, and other funding sources are looking for nonprofits that do good work and support causes that they value. In other words, donors and grantors expect that the nonprofits they support will spend the money on the programs that the funding sources want to support. Allegations have been made over the past several years of fraud against nonprofits, for example, theft of assets by employees and even by executives and board members. When this happens, the cash that would have helped the nonprofit's constituents is gone, and, in addition, the organization's reputation may be damaged.

One fairly recent example of the loss of reputation involves the United Way of the National Capital Area (UWNCA). The organization has yet to fully recover. Oral Suer, the executive director of the organization, stole approximately $500,000 over a period of approximately 10 years. On May 14, 2004, a federal judge sentenced Oral Suer to 27 months in prison, which was the maximum sentence possible for his theft from the organization.[3]

---

1 Kennard T. Wing, Thomas H. Pollak, and Amy Blackwood, *Nonprofit Almanac* (Washington DC: Urban Institute Press, 2008).

2 "The Effect of the Economy on the Nonprofit Sector, March–May 2009" (GuideStar USA, Inc: 2009).

3 Ian Wilhelm and Brad Wolverton, "D.C. United Way Leader Pleads Guilty to Fraud," *Chronicle of Philanthropy*, May 18, 2004.

Although the amount stolen is relatively small given the size of other frauds and the size of UWNCA, the damage he did to the reputation of the organization still lingers in 2009. In 2001, before the fraud came to light, the organization raised more than $90 million in contributions. During 2003 and 2004, private donations declined to $38 million. This resulted in the termination of almost 65 employees. And in 2008, 6 years after the fraud was identified, the organization raised only $38.3 million.

In January 2008, the IRS issued its new Form 990. The new form was, in part, redesigned to respond to the suggestions of the U.S. Senate Finance Committee. The new form asks over 50 questions, throughout the core form and supporting schedules, about business arrangements that the IRS may find troublesome as well as various policies, procedures, and processes designed to prevent or detect fraud and noncompliance with laws and regulations. Many of these questions require detailed explanation. The answers to these questions serve to highlight the degree to which nonprofits have appropriate governance. There is also a question requiring nonprofits to disclose whether they have experienced theft or other diversion of assets during the year. With such scrutiny coming from regulators, funding sources, and even the public, it is doubly important for nonprofits to evaluate their internal governance practices.

But the harm fraud does to nonprofits is not limited to just internal wrong doing. In 2008, a massive ponzi scheme came to light that resulted in a loss of over $50 billion to nonprofits nationwide. How did the ripples of the Madoff scandal affect these nonprofits? Depending on the extent to which a given nonprofit relied on the foundation's financial support, the ripple could have been a tsunami, resulting in the deferral or cancellation of important programs or even outright closure. Nonprofit leaders have been vocal about the distress caused by this single scandal and the damage created for the communities and individuals that rely on nonprofit agencies' services or research. The following paragraphs describe the effects on several nonprofits.

The Elie Wiesel Foundation for Humanity was established in the 1980s to foster dialogue and support programs that promote acceptance, understanding, and equality across the globe. Although distinct in its connection to Holocaust survivor, author, and Nobel-laureate Elie Wiesel, the foundation is in many ways indistinct from other foundations that selflessly aspire to create social change, and in doing so touch the hearts and lives of millions.

In late 2008, the following appeared on the foundation's website:

> To Our Friends:
>
> We are deeply saddened and distressed that we, along with many others, have been the victims of what may be one of the largest investment frauds in history. We are writing to inform you that the Elie Wiesel Foundation for Humanity had $15.2 million under management with Bernard Madoff Investment Securities.
>
> This represented substantially all of the Foundation's assets.
>
> The values we stand for are more needed than ever. We want to assure you that the Foundation remains committed to carrying on the lifelong work of our founder, Elie Wiesel. We shall not be deterred from our mission to combat indifference, intolerance, and injustice around the world.

> At this difficult time, the Foundation wishes to express its profound gratitude for all your support.

The Elie Wiesel Foundation for Humanity[4]

They were not alone. According to the Chronicle of Philanthropy,[5] approximately 150 nonprofit organizations were affected by the Madoff Ponzi scheme, and 105 of them lost 30 percent or more of their assets. Of course, the real damage of this sort of far reaching scandal is not limited to the investors. As previously discussed, when a foundation loses its assets, the other nonprofits to which it donates lose as well. For example, the Lappin foundation closed after losing all of its assets—8 million dollars—and the Chais Family Foundation, which gave over 12 million a year to Jewish causes abroad, ceased operation in December 2008. The Picower Foundation lost $1 billion in the Madoff scandal and has closed its doors. Since its creation in 1989, the Picower Foundation had given over $268 million to the Massachusetts Institute of Technology, Human Rights First, the New York Public Library, the Children's Health Fund, and countless other programs like the University of Pennsylvania's Center for Neurodegenerative Disease Research, for work on drug discoveries to treat Parkinson's disease and other conditions.

Unfortunately, the Madoff scandal is not a singular event. A decade ago, the 11,000 investors in the Baptist Foundation of Arizona lost over $570 million when it went bankrupt after its real estate investments collapsed. As will be discussed in chapters 8 and 9, the methods by which fraud is perpetrated come in many forms. Although few cases of embezzlement, mismanagement, and fraud in the nonprofit sector rise to the level of the Madoff scandal, individually and collectively they create fear and cynicism in donors and regulators. Is it any surprise that benefactors, foundations, federal and state governments, and other stakeholders want more emphasis on transparency and accountability? They rightfully ask "Why were the indicators of trouble overlooked? How did nonprofits' leaders and directors let this happen on their watch?"

Clearly, some players are downright corrupt or inept. In other cases, lapses in accountability come from an overemphasis on mission at the expense of attention to organizational processes and structures. When this imbalance occurs, agencies fail to

- create and uphold internal controls,
- evaluate risks to the business,
- identify where theft could occur,
- understand and comply with laws and regulations and contract and grant provisions, and
- identify financial warning signs that would encourage organizational changes to streamline resource allocation.

Why does the imbalance occur? Why do paid and volunteer leaders fail to attend to these important aspects of management? Although in hindsight it may appear that many leaders

---

4 Retrieved from www.eliewieselfoundation.org/madoffupdate.aspx on April 16, 2011.

5 Niki Jagpal and Julia Craig, *Learning from Madoff: Lessons for Foundation Boards*, (Washington DC: National Committee for Responsive Philanthropy, 2009).

and board members are fiscally irresponsible and negligent in their fiduciary duties, the more likely explanations are that leaders and board members

- are unaware of the laws and regulation they need to follow.
- are unable to analyze the organization's financial statements.
- operate the organizations with very few resources and with pressure to use them on programs instead of administration.
- are committed to the mission of the nonprofit and the constituents served, perhaps at the exclusion of other priorities and responsibilities.
- trust the motives and activities of their fellow board and staff and view checks and balances as a formality, or even a sign of distrust.
- are preoccupied by the daily administrative demands and unable to take the time or space to examine systems.

To anyone who has ever served as a volunteer board member or a harried nonprofit leader, these are no doubt familiar reasons for lack of oversight. But, in the eyes of the IRS, funding sources, donors, and the general public, there are no good reasons for such lapses, and there is no margin for error. Because the resources of a nonprofit belong to the community, nonprofits are accountable for what they do with them. And when grantors, whether federal, state, or foundation, are involved, compliance is a condition of funding.

Beyond these understandable, if dangerous, rationales for poor compliance, there is the issue of those who know the rules but choose not to follow them. The 2008 *Health Care Industry Developments* Audit Risk Alert[6] notes that the Department of Health and Human Services' Office of the Inspector General (OIG) and the U.S. Department of Justice are aggressively pursuing those institutions that are noncompliant with rules relative to time and effort reporting. This noncompliance generally takes the form of improper charges to grants for direct labor, fringe benefits, and related indirect costs. Because these are generally the largest costs in a grant, institutions may, for example, move time of employees from one grant to another grant that can absorb the cost even though the personnel did not work on the program. Behavior such as this is justified on the basis that the grant was "the researcher's," and so, therefore, was the money. Another common rationalization is that the both grants belong to the institution, so it's not hurting anyone. However, these interpretations are at odds with funding agreements and, in the case of federal money, the law. As will be more fully discussed in chapter 9, the Office of Management and Budget created cost and administrative circulars prescribing the rules that those organizations receiving grants and contacts must follow. Therefore, claims for money improperly spent are, in fact, fraudulent claims.

Since 2003, Johns Hopkins University, the Mayo Clinic, Cornell University, Northwestern University, and the University of Alabama at Birmingham have all come under fire by the National Institutes of Health and have been charged multimillion dollar settlements and paybacks. In 2003, a physician filed a sealed civil complaint against Weill Cornell Medical College, asserting that it used funds from a $23 million dollar grant to subsidize patient care in the facility rather than for its intended purpose (to study diseases in children). Although Cornell University settled for $4.4 million, it did not admit to wrongdoing.[7]

---

6 *Health Care Industry Developments*, (New York: American Institute of Certified Public Accountants, 2008) p. 5.

7 Bernard Wysocki Jr., "As Universities Get Billions in Grants, Some See Abuses," Wall Street Journal Online, August 16, 2005. Retrieved from psychrights.org/research/Digest/Science4Sale/WSJPhantomStudies.htm on April 16, 2011.

The financial penalties, reputational damage, and even jail time associated with these adverse findings aren't limited to large targets like the Mayo Clinic and Johns Hopkins University. The OIG reports that in 2008, an Ohio man who ran a nonprofit agency that contracted with counties in Ohio to provide foster care services was sentenced to 27 months in prison and had to pay over $557,000 back to the government for stealing state grant money from the nonprofit and funneling it into for-profit businesses that he personally owned. He claimed that money was being paid for foster care services when it was actually being routed to his own personal investment accounts.[8]

In North Carolina, former Congressman Frank Ballance was sentenced to prison in 2005 after pleading guilty to funneling tax dollars into the nonprofit John A. Hyman Memorial Foundation that he operated to help poor people fight drug and alcohol abuse and to using $100,000 for himself and his family.

In some cases, even members of the board of directors are involved. Thom Randle of Chico, California, was indicted for embezzling $693,000 from the Columbian Retirement Home, a nonprofit retirement facility. He was on the board of directors and served as the vice president of finance. He opened unauthorized bank accounts and used a computer to transfer the funds from the retirement home's accounts to those he opened and controlled in their name. The thefts took place over a 2 year period. He used the stolen funds to pay for personal expenses.

As these cases illustrate, risk and ruin in nonprofits can come from both *malfeasance* (the intention to defraud or harm) and from *nonfeasance* (failing to carry out expected responsibilities). In either scenario, though, the buck stops at the top: these situations all call into question the role of nonprofit leaders and boards. A main function of paid and volunteer leadership in nonprofits is to set the tone from the top and communicate the organization's commitment to integrity, ethical values, financial transparency, and accountability, as well as compliance with laws, regulations, and provisions of contracts and grants. Knowledge and capacity are important but insufficient ingredients in organizational compliance. Administrators and board members must also have the courage to act responsibly.

When most of us think of courage, we think of people who risk life and limb to save others or who put their well-being at risk for a greater good—the firefighter or the whistle-blower, for example. But there are other, potent forms of courage required for assuring organizational integrity, and you'll learn about them throughout this book. Could the destruction wrought by Bernie Madoff have been avoided or contained if more people had been willing to confront his conflicts of interest, question his investment methods, or resist the pull of unsustainable returns? Could people of courage have bolstered and supported those who *did* speak out about Madoff's methods? We'll never know. We can't rewrite the past, but we can provide the tools to avert future catastrophes.

To be effective as a nonprofit these days, it takes more than a passion for the mission. It takes the knowledge, skills, and courage to
- identify factors in the environment that affect the entity,
- read and analyze financial information,

---

8 Retrieved from www.oig.hhs.gov/fraud/enforcement/criminal/2008/0308.asp on April 16, 2011.

- understand the laws, regulations, and provisions of contracts and grant agreements so the organization will be in compliance, and
- assess the risk to the organization.

After evaluating the circumstances facing the organization in light of those factors, the leaders and the board need to have the courage to make the right decisions and the skills to act on that courage.

Call to Action

Nonprofit leaders and their boards certainly have cause to be overwhelmed with the tasks before them. Endowments are down, and donors' discretionary spending is squeezed. Record unemployment diminishes tax collections and workplace fundraising. Governmental resources are scarce and competitors more plentiful. The National Center for Charitable Statistics[9] states that currently there are more than 1.5 million nonprofit charities, foundations, churches, and other nonprofits. They are all in some way vying for public, philanthropic, or governmental support. Funders are moving toward targeted giving, choosing to give larger amounts of funding to a smaller number of organizations. An April 2009 report from the Foundation Center noted in a survey it conducted in January 2009, with 1,243 foundations responding, that 43 percent of them expected to reduce the overall number of grantees, and 46 percent expected to decrease the number of new grantees they will fund in 2009.[10] Foundations have been discouraged with the level of accuracy in reporting in their less administratively and financially well managed grantees. In a more competitive environment, amid increased demands for transparency, compliance, and financial accountability, nonprofits will increasingly find themselves with less money to devote to new initiatives and infrastructure.

Success in this environment demands creativity, efficiency, and information. The remaining chapters of this book are designed to provide nonprofits and their boards with the practical knowledge and guidance, as well as with the electronic tools and templates, they need to make sense of the regulations, to implement strong internal controls, and to cultivate the courage to act on that knowledge.

In today's volatile and uncertain environment, a nonprofit organization needs strong leaders and a strong board to successfully fulfill its mission. We like to think of it as

Mission = Compliance = Courage

or

$$M = C^2$$

---

9 Retrieved from www.nccs.urban.org/statistics/quickfacts.cfm on January 25, 2009.

10 *Foundation Growth and Giving Estimates* (New York: Foundation Center, 2009).

Conclusion

There is no doubt that the risk is real and that the time is now for nonprofit executive management and their boards to commit to placing increased emphasis on governance-related issues. Yet board members are frequently selected based on their interest in and knowledge about the organization's mission; they may have less focus on internal governance issues, believing that mission is more important than governance. In the new environment in 2011, the focus on governance by regulators and funding sources is unmistakable. Organization leaders and board members must realize that organizational process and structure, far from detracting from the mission, are irreplaceable ingredients in effectively accomplishing its program goals. In the new environment, neglecting these structural issues is no longer an option. Along with increased oversight, as discussed in this chapter, penalties for noncompliance have increased. Further, board members have accepted a legal *duty* for proper management of the organization's affairs, and good intention is not an excuse for lapses. Succeeding chapters will equip nonprofit executive management and board members with the knowledge and skills to better discharge their responsibilities in the nonprofit environment in 2011 and beyond.

Chapter 2

Roles of the Board and Management

Karen Lee, board chair of a small social service nonprofit, sat in a roundtable meeting sponsored by the North Carolina Center for Nonprofits. The participants were there to discuss the role boards should play in nonprofit organizations. Karen was eager to hear how other boards were run but worried that she would be asked to step into a board role for which she was unprepared. Around the table were the board and audit committee chairs from organizations of varying size and complexity: a state community college, several charities, and a United Way affiliate.

The first participant to speak was Howard, the board chair from a large charitable organization with $191 million dollars in support and revenue. "Our board has 30 members. We have several active committees including an audit committee. We have made some improvements in governance as a result of all of the press around transparency and accountability. We want to be the organization that is above scandal. The board takes its fiduciary responsibility very seriously. We see our role as one of strategy and oversight. We approve the operating budget and listen to recommendations of management for new programs and changes or significant modifications to programs. We review and approve the compensation of the executive director and perform an evaluation of her each year. We also help the organization raise funds. We understand that we have a fiduciary responsibility to the organization and this is discharged through our oversight, vested particularly in the audit committee. We have a code of ethics that includes a conflict of interest policy."

The board chair from the private community college spoke next. "We have a much smaller board. There are seven board members. Each of our board members represents a different area of the state. Because of our membership constraints, we do not have a financial expert on the board. There are business people on the board but none has the experience to prepare not-for-profit or governmental financial statements. The board cares passionately about higher education, and we have doubled our enrollment over the last five years. We take a more hands-on approach than Howard was describing, and the President of the College accuses us from time to time of usurping her role. Our board has an investment committee to oversee the endowment. We also approve the compensation for the President and each year review her progress. I am very interested in learning more about governance and that's why I volunteered to participate in this group."

(continued)

(continued)

Other participants described what they saw as the function of the board at their organizations. It seemed to Karen that all of the organizations were much larger than hers. She finally spoke up. "I feel a little embarrassed about being here. My organization is very small. We have a little over $300,000 in revenue. Our board is made up primarily of people in the community interested in mental illness. We have 12 board members, and none of us would qualify as a financial expert. The thing that makes our board different is that we actually participate in some of the operations because there is not enough paid staff. One board member serves as the treasurer and signs checks to segregate duties a little more than would be possible using only the executive director and the employees. The board raises money, sometimes opens the mail, provides legal services, and even cuts the grass. We have a financial statement audit because we get allocations from the United Way, and our auditors have made us aware of our control deficiencies. That's one reason why I'm here. We really do want to "do the right thing."

The group was quiet for a few minutes. Then the moderator spoke up. "Nonprofits come in all sizes and have varying degrees of complexity. A smaller organization will not be able to do some of the things that larger ones can. But that doesn't mean that it can't follow the principles of good governance. It just needs to adapt the principles to its circumstances."

Governance in the 21st Century

State law requires corporations to have a governing body or board whether they are commercial entities or nonprofits. There are very few rules as to how the governance function should be carried out, providing the organization with flexibility. However, Form 1023, which is used to apply for tax exempt status from the IRS, requires the nonprofit to list its governing board so that the IRS can evaluate whether the governance function is sufficient. But these are legal and compliance reasons; they do not get at the heart of why governing bodies are important.

Part of the reason for the focus on governance over the last decade comes from high profile corporate failures that gained national attention. The majority of these were related to public companies such as Enron and WorldCom. In 2002, an enterprise governance study was performed by the Chartered Institute of Management Accountants and the International Federation of Accountants in response to these failures, which examined the concept of governance.[1] The study covered 27 international organizations in a variety of industries and looked for the reasons for the corporate failures of some and for best practices in others. This report identified lack of attention and oversight by the board of directors as a key element in the corporate failures. These are important tenets of governance.

The term *governance* is widely used and, depending on the context, can have different meanings. *Enterprise Governance: Getting the Balance Right* uses the definition of *governance* set forth by the Information Systems Audit and Control Foundation (ISACF). Governance

---

1 Chartered Institute of Management Accountants and the International Federation of Accountants, *Enterprise Governance: Getting the Balance Right* (New York: International Federation of Accountants, 2004).

is defined as "the set of responsibilities and practices exercised by the board and executive management with the goal of providing strategic direction, ensuring that objectives are achieved, ascertaining that risks are managed appropriately and verifying that the organization's resources are used responsibly."[2] This definition applies to corporate governance whether it relates to a large multinational public company or a small nonprofit.

In October 2007, the Panel on the Nonprofit Sector published a report titled "Principles for Good Governance and Ethical Practice: A Guide for Charities and Foundations." The paper identifies 33 principles of good governance recommended by the panel (the Good Governance Model). It has significance because it was published in an ongoing effort to help nonprofits retain the ability to self-govern. The public and legislators, most notably Charles Grassley of the Senate Finance Committee, already had a heightened awareness of fraud in public companies. The spirit of the principles codified in the requirements of the Sarbanes Oxley Act of 2002 was assumed to apply to nonprofits even though most of the provisions of the law did not. As discussed in chapter 1, several nonprofit frauds came to light in the early 2000s, and the Panel on the Nonprofit Sector was created in 2004 to find ways to strengthen governance, transparency, and ethical standards.

The Panel on the Nonprofit Sector defines the term *governance* through 13 of its principles that outline the requirements of boards.[3] The principles are meant to be adapted to the type, size, and complexity of the organization. As will be discussed later in this chapter, the principles operationalize the ISACF definition by suggesting the activities that should be conducted by the governing board.

Because governance is a shared responsibility between executive management and the governing board in most organizations, it is important to define the role of the board for two primary reasons. First, the board plays an important role in being a check and balance on management who are involved in the day-to-day activities of the nonprofit. The second, more practical reason for defined roles is that duplication of effort is neither efficient nor effective.

Purpose of the Governing Board

Governing boards can have several names depending on the type of nonprofit organization, such as a board of directors, board of trustees, or board of regents. No matter what it is called or whether its members are elected or appointed, the objectives of the governing board are to
- assume responsibility for the organization's compliance with laws and regulations and provisions of funding source agreements.
- set strategic objectives to be accomplished.
- create policies to guide the implementation of activities designed to assist the organization in meeting its strategic objectives.

---

2 Gertz, Michael, ed. *Integrity and Internal Control in Information Systems V.* Massachusetts: Kluwer Academic Publishers, 2003.

3 "Principles for Good Governance and Ethical Practice: A Guide for Charities and Foundations," Panel on the Nonprofit Sector, October 2007.

- serve as content matter experts and a sounding board for the chief executive.
- hire the chief executive and monitor his or her progress toward meeting strategic objectives.
- set its own governance processes and assess its performance in meeting its objectives.

A nonprofit may also create other types of boards when the number of board members becomes excessive. One very prevalent category of board is the advisory board. These board members may have specific content expertise that is helpful to the nonprofit organization. Another is a fund-raising board. These board members are called on not only to provide financial resources, as all board members should, but also to use their contacts and community position to raise money or in-kind donations for the nonprofit organization. These functions are not the primary responsibility of the governing board. From this point forward in this text, all references to "the board" refer to the governing board.

Board Committees

Boards may also have committees to do the work that may be too detailed for the entire board to manage. Committee members are generally selected for their content expertise. Committees are particularly helpful when the organization does not have certain expertise in house.

A description of the function of the most frequently used board committees including the percent of organizations that used those committees from the 2008 Grant Thornton Board Governance Survey follows in table 2-1.

Table 2-1

Committee	Function	Percent Boards Reporting Such a Committee*
Executive committee	Acts on behalf of the board when it is not necessary or possible to have a meeting of the full board. The full board should always validate the executive committee's decisions at the next meeting.	87%
Finance committee	Supports the development of the annual budget, monitors the spending against the budget, monitors the level of cash and determines the level of necessary reserves. Provides commentary on the "financial health" of the organization to the board. This committee provides input to the strategic plan.	81%
Audit committee	Monitors the effectiveness of internal controls over financial reporting and compliance with laws, regulations and contracts and grant agreements, if any. Discusses the quality of significant accounting and reporting principles, practices, and procedures with the external auditors and obtain their feedback. Reviews the scope of the external auditors' annual audit including inquiry as to any limitations placed on the external auditors by management. Reviews the audit fee annually. Inquires about the independence of the external auditors and ask them to disclose any outside relationships between the auditors and management. At the conclusion of the audit, reviews the financial statements and the letters prepared related to internal control deficiencies. Monitors the implementation of any corrective action needed to remediate internal control deficiencies. Reviews Form 990. Recommends the selection, retention, or termination of the external auditors to the board.	74%

Committee	Function	Percent Boards Reporting Such a Committee*
Development (fund raising committee)	Monitors the funds raised against the development plan. Oversees all relationships with professional fundraisers. This committee can also encourage board involvement in fund raising. The actual fundraising is management's responsibility.	57%
Investment committee	Oversees the investment policy and monitors investment returns. Performs due diligence on outside investment managers and especially monitors the types and levels of alternative investments.	50%
Program committee	Ensures that a community needs assessment is performed. Monitors fulfillment of the organization's progress against its program goals.	40%
Governance committee	Determines the skills necessary for board members. Recruits and orients new board members. Responsible for the annual self-assessment. Monitors attendance at meetings. Evaluates board member participation and contribution.	37%
Compensation committee	Oversees the compensation of highly compensated individuals and ensures that appropriate measures have been taken to determine that it is comparable to the compensation of other organizations of similar size and scope. Ensures that appropriate documentation is maintained to support compensation decisions.	36%
Strategic planning committee	Oversees the development of the strategic plan and communicates recommendations to the board.	34%
Human resources committee	Monitors management's adherence to state and federal employment laws and regulations that This committee may also monitor the salaries of highly compensated individuals to ensure they are comparable to those in other, similar organizations. This may also be a function of the compensation committee that could act as a subcommittee of the human resource committee. The human resource committee also monitors that performance evaluations are completed, that each employee has a current job description, and that the appropriate training, development and career path planning takes place.	23%

* 2008 National Board Governance Survey, Grant Thornton.

Legal Responsibilities of the Board

Nonprofits serve the public and, as a result of their tax exempt status, derive a benefit by relief from taxes or the ability to issue tax-exempt debt. In addition, many nonprofits receive support in the form of grants from federal, state, and local governments and foundations. Other support comes from corporate and individual donors. So regardless of the type of activities conducted by the nonprofit, the public benefit is there. Those exercising the governance function, by law, are designated to protect the organization by assuming overall responsibility and liability for it. The legal responsibilities of the members of the governing board are often referred to as the duty of care, duty of loyalty, and the duty of obedience.[4] These will be explained with examples below.

The **duty of care** instructs the board to conduct the affairs of the nonprofit in the way that a prudent person would.

4 Bruce R. Hopkins, *Legal Responsibilities of Nonprofit Boards* (Washington DC: BoardSource, 2003).

Lesson Learned

It is likely that the board violated its duty of care by not acting in a prudent manner. The governing board should have evaluated whether this was the right move for the organization given the external conditions. The board should think independently and not be swayed by a chief executive's hopes. More due diligence should have been conducted and the funds raised prior to making any commitments.

The **duty of loyalty** instructs the board to be loyal in its dealings with the nonprofit and to put the organization's needs above its own. The board should not have any conflicts of interest, and the members should keep all the information they learn about the organization or its stakeholders and constituents confidential and not use it for private gain.

In 2008, the United States was in a recession. Many nonprofits were badly hurt through a decrease in funding from state sources, foundations, and donors. These trends were evident throughout the country and particularly evident in the city served by Healthy Start, a nonprofit agency serving mothers with children birth through age five. The board of Healthy Start approved a budget that contained provisions to expand the organization's reach. It also gave approval to the executive director's proposal to lease additional space and hire new employees. The board believed the executive director who assured them that a fund-raising effort would be successful. Six months later, the nonprofit had depleted its reserves, and the board was not sure that it would survive because the additional contributions did not materialize.

Lesson Learned

The board member has violated his or her duty of loyalty by using the organization for the purpose of self-enrichment by churning the account. Although related party transactions are not always improper, they need to be approved by the board and would also need to be disclosed in the Form 990 and in the financial statements. The board should consider how its constituents would view dealings with related parties prior to allowing them to occur.

The **duty of obedience** instructs the board that it should be faithful to the mission of the organization. This means that the actions taken by the board should support the mission; this extends to the purposes identified by donors for which their restricted contributions are to be used.

A board member of a charity with a large endowment fund wanted to provide investment management services for the organization. The board approved the contract with the board member and documented that it believed the commission that would be charged by the board member for trades would be competitive. At the end of the year when the independent auditor was reviewing the investment transaction fees for the endowment, the amount appeared higher than expected. When the auditor reviewed the investment statements, it was apparent that the board member was making excessive purchases and sales.

Lesson Learned

The duty of obedience has been violated because using restricted contributions for unrestricted purposes violates the trust between the donor and the organization. The organization should have gone back to the donor to seek release from restriction. The temptation may be tempting to justify this by saying it is for the good of the organization and will be paid back, but is not sufficient.

Of the 33 principles set forth in the Panel on the Nonprofit Sector's Good Governance Model, only 6 are legal requirements:

1. Have a governing body responsible for reviewing and approving the organization's mission, strategic direction, annual budget, key financial transactions, compensation practices, policies, and fiscal and governance policies.

2. Abide by federal, state, and, if applicable, international laws and regulations.

3. Maintain complete, current, and accurate financial records.

4. Institute policies and procedures to ensure the appropriate investment and management of institutional funds.

5. Use contributions for purposes consistent with donor intent.

6. Provide donors with acknowledgements of donations consistent with IRS requirements.

Sheltering Arms is a nonprofit whose mission is to serve the homeless. It owned 2 buildings, which were used to provide program services to homeless women and their children. The organization received $25,000 in restricted contributions to remodel the kitchen of one of the facilities in January 2009. In May 2009, the organization was experiencing cash flow problems, and the board voted to sell one of the facilities and to use $15,000 of the restricted contributions to meet operating expenses. The profit from the sale of the building was used to start a thrift store in hopes of generating additional income for the organization. The board did not seek permission from the donor to use the restricted money for unrestricted purposes.

IRS Form 990 and Governance

Most tax-exempt organizations are required to file an informational tax return, Form 990, each year. Beginning with the 2008 tax year, tax-exempt organizations were asked not only to provide information on their financial position and activities for the year but also to answer a series of questions about governance, policies and procedures, and events that took place during the year, such as whether there was a material diversion of assets. This is due to the emphasis that federal and state governments, funding sources, and the IRS are now placing on transparency and greater accountability. The IRS is using the questions on the new Form 990 not only to obtain additional qualitative information from nonprofits but also to correlate sound governance practices with compliance with tax laws and effective utilization of charitable assets. Because Forms 990 are provided to and published on Guidestar.org, the increased disclosure should also serve to shine a bright light on those organizations that have good governance policies and procedures and alert donors to the ones that do not. Although more robust discussion of the tax issues for nonprofits can be found in chapter 8, the governance policies and procedures highlighted in the new Form 990 should be considered when implementing any of the frameworks for good governance discussed in the following section.

A comparison of key objectives of the board of directors with the good governance model and questions from IRS Form 990 can be found in appendix A at the end of this chapter.

Frameworks for Good Governance

Governance models provide a framework or guided process for accomplishing the objectives of governance. Perhaps the most widely respected governance model in the literature today is the Carver Policy Governance® Model (the Carver model), which was described in John Carver's book *Boards that Make a Difference*.[5] The model applies to commercial organizations, governments, and nonprofits. The model requires that boards of directors step up to the plate and govern as the voice of the organization. Nonprofits do not have owners. They have constituents or stakeholders that include the beneficiaries of the mission, donors, funding sources, and members of the community in which the organization is situated.

Carver presents a model based on the concept of servant leadership, which was developed by Robert Greenleaf in 1977.[6] The board can only lead after it is servant. This means that the board must understand the judgments and values of its stakeholders as defined by the organization's mission. Although the board is made up of individuals, the board speaks with one voice to those inside the organization and to the outside world. Therefore, the board has total authority and also accountability.

The board does not run the day-to-day operations of the organization. However, it is accountable for the organization's actions. This means that it must effectively supervise the chief executive, who will then delegate a part of his or her assigned responsibilities to others within the organization. If the delegation of responsibility to the chief executive is not clear then the results will be less effective, and it will not be possible to properly evaluate the performance of that person.

Carver presents the concept of ends and means to describe the definition of the success. The ends are the eventual goal to be accomplished (not the methods by which the goals or the impact on the constituents are accomplished). And the ends are not necessarily spelled out in the mission.

---

5 John Carver, *Boards That Make a Difference*, 3rd Ed. (San Francisco: Jossey Bass, 2006).
6 Robert Greenleaf, *Servant Leadership* (New York: Paulist Press, 1977).

> **Mission Statement:** Wheeling Aging Center is committed to providing quality home care to the elderly residents of Wheeling, WV, at the lowest possible cost, enabling them to live in their homes longer.

The ends are the outcomes by which the organization's success is measured. How it gets there are the means. Because the board is accountable for the organization, it is accountable for the ends and the means. The board, after obtaining input from constituents, staff, and outside professionals, demonstrates its accountability by developing policies about the

- ends or outcomes.
- limitations or parameters for the chief executive (the chief executive can decide how to accomplish the ends within the parameters or limitations).
- delegation and measurement (how authority is passed from the board to the chief executive and how it is measured).
- governance processes (the manner in which the board conducts its activities and carries out its leadership role).

In the Carver model, the board lets the chief executive do his or her job within the parameters established.

Area	Board Sets Parameters	Staff Functions	Board Monitoring
Financial accountability	Increase donations by 20%	Development	Quarterly
	Spend amounts as prescribed by funding source	Establish effective internal controls	Quarterly
	Increase number of constituents served by 15%	Expand program reach within budget	Quarterly
	Monitor spending so as not to overspend budgeted expenses in total	Focus on variance analysis and determining the most cost effective delivery of service	Monthly
	Investments should be diversified according to the investment policy	Evaluate investment professionals against the policy	Quarterly
	Timely filings of all government and funding source reports	Establish effective internal controls to establish accurate, timely reporting	Quarterly

The board should set the work plan and agenda for the year and for its meetings; determine what it needs for development and succession planning; establish limits for the chief executive in the areas of budgeting, compensation, programs, and other issues; establish the results that are expected; and monitor the achievement of the results.

The Carver model is most difficult to implement when it comes to smaller organizations because in those organizations, the board is often expected to function as staff.

Panel on the Nonprofit Sector Framework— Good Governance Model[7]

The Panel on the Nonprofit Sector's principles also serves as a framework for governance. In addition to the 6 legal requirements noted, there are 27 other principles that nonprofit boards should consider when forming policies for the organization. The principles are divided into 4 important categories:

- **Legal compliance and public disclosure.** These principles deal with polices that should be developed to comply with legal and regulatory requirements and to enhance transparency and accountability to the public.
- **Effective governance.** These principles deal with policies and procedures related to effective oversight of the organization.
- **Strong financial oversight.** These principles deal with discharging the fiduciary responsibilities of the organization, evidencing good stewardship of the organization's resources.
- **Responsible fund-raising.** These principles deal with policies and procedures that the organization should have in place to deal with soliciting funds for its support from the public.

Where the Carver model is more concerned with the division of responsibility, this model is concerned with meeting legal and regulatory requirements. The Good Governance Model spells out the specific elements the board should address and assumes that the board will cause these outcomes to occur. The model does not concern itself with whether the actions are taken directly by the board or, where possible, delegated to the chief executive. Therefore, it is easier to adapt this model to smaller, less complex organizations.

In the following pages, the Good Governance Model's principles are summarized followed by a discussion of the principle or principles and suggestions for practical application.

Legal Compliance and Public Disclosure

Summary of Principle: Laws and Regulations	Discussion
The board is responsible for ensuring compliance with provisions of laws and regulations.	Although this may sound like there is an expectation that every board should have an attorney, it really means that the board should be aware of the applicable laws and regulations and identify any red flags in dealings or potential dealings so that legal counsel or other specialists can be consulted. The IRS website (www.irs.gov) contains many helpful resources related to tax law for exempt organizations, and the website www.stayexempt.org has a several interactive tutorials on tax issues. Many of the laws with which nonprofits need to comply are state specific. State associations for nonprofits will have helpful resources. For example, the North Carolina Center for Nonprofits publishes a resource that contains a list of websites where board members could go to obtain synopses of state and federal employment law, charitable solicitation laws, and laws relating to lobbying and advocacy (www.ncnonprofits.org/conference/handouts/2010/ChangingLandscape/Heinen_Resources_NCLawsforNonprofits.pdf). The National Council of Nonprofits' website contains a list of state associations for nonprofits (www.councilofnonprofits.org/salocator).

---

7 "Principles for Good Governance and Ethical Practice: A Guide for Charities and Foundations," Panel on the Nonprofit Sector, October 2007.

Summary of Principle: Code of Conduct	Discussion
Nonprofits should have a formal code of conduct or code of ethics including a conflict of interest policy.	This is one of the most important policies that an organization can have. In fact, the Form 990 specifically asks if the organization has a written conflict of interest policy, asks whether it is consistently monitored and enforced, and asks for a description of how this is done. A code of ethics should outline the conduct that is expected of the organization's governing board, executives, staff, and volunteers. In some organizations, this even extends to key contributors. When the governing board embraces the code of ethics and conflict of interest policy, it sets an important tone from the top and demonstrates that the organization is serious about conducting business in a forthright and ethical manner. The code of ethics, though, is not enough in and of itself. The way that the policy is implemented is even more important. Staff, volunteers, and new board members should receive training on the code of ethics. Some organizations require an annual certification that the code has been and will continue to be followed and that all incidents of noncompliance of which the individual is aware on the part of him- or herself or others have been reported.

The conflict of interest policy ties into the duty of loyalty discussed in this chapter. Every board member and executive, as well as employees in financial and procurement positions, should be required to sign a statement that declares any conflicts of interest or asserts that they have none. Conflicts of interest may be present in fact or in appearance. Both are important because board members, especially, should be seen to be without blemish. If an issue arises in which a board member has a conflict of interest, he or she should recuse him- or herself from any discussions about that issue and not participate in any vote. |

Summary of Principle: Whistleblower Policy	Discussion
Nonprofits should have a whistleblower policy that states that the organization will not retaliate against any person coming forward with information about fraud, illegal acts, or violation of the organization's policies.	Although it is important to try to protect the confidentiality of whistleblowers, this is not always possible when conducting an investigation. Title 11, Section 1107 of the Sarbanes Oxley Act of 2002 prohibits retaliation against whistleblowers. It states that anyone who intends to retaliate and takes action against a whistleblower including interfering with his or her employment will be fined or imprisoned for up to 10 years, or both. This portion of the act is applicable to all organizations. Form 990 asks whether the organization has a whistleblower policy.

Joseph T. Wells, founder and chairperson of the Association of Certified Fraud Examiners (ACFE), discussed some of the findings in the ACFE "2010 Report to the Nations on Occupational Fraud and Abuse" in an article published in the *Journal of Accountancy* in June 2010. He stated that tips and complaints are the number one method of fraud detection. An effective whistleblower policy, training for employees on when and how to use the organization's reporting mechanism, and effective follow-up are all key features to fraud prevention and detection. The board should consider the most appropriate mechanism for the size, complexity, and budget of the organization. Hotline companies are effective but so are less expensive mechanisms such as using a law firm to receive and investigate complaints or reporting directly to a designated board member. More important than the mechanism is the support and credibility that the board lends to the policy. |

Summary of Principle: Document Retention and Destruction Policy	Discussion
The nonprofit organization should have a document retention and destruction policy to protect the records of its governance, finance, and administration.	Protection of the records will also help to prevent allegations of wrongdoing on the part of the board and employees. The document retention policy should address the length of time that records are to be kept, appropriate methods of destruction, and prohibition against concealment or destruction of records when an official investigation is underway. Document retention policies should also address electronic files and voicemail. Many nonprofits are unaware that electronic documents and voicemail are given the same status as hard copy files in litigation cases. Because electronic files are backed up on a regular basis, the document retention policy should also cover archiving documents and back-up procedures. It is important that if a nonprofit is involved in any official investigation that no documents be destroyed. Otherwise, the organization could face criminal obstruction charges. Form 990 asks if the organization has a document retention and destruction policy.

The National Council on Nonprofits has a guide for document retention on its website www.ncna.org.

One only has to look back to March 2002 when the Justice Department indicted Arthur Andersen, formerly one of the Big 5 accounting firms, to appreciate the gravity of document retention. The main reason for the demise of the firm was the claim that employees on the Enron account shredded records once the company revealed the extent of the misstatement of the company's financial statements. All large firms have been involved with clients who committed accounting fraud, yet this action was the beginning of the end for Arthur Andersen. Its other clients and its employees began leaving the firm in large numbers. Even though the firm was exonerated in 2005, the damage was done.[8] |

Summary of Principle: Protection Procedures	Discussion
Nonprofits should have procedures in place to protect property, financial assets and information, human resources, and program content, as well as their reputations.	The board is responsible for having an understanding of the risks facing the nonprofit and addressing and monitoring those risks on a periodic basis. Risk management is an important part of the board's responsibilities. The level of risk assessment will vary based on the size and complexity of the organization.

Board members can be held personally liable for certain violations of law such as the failure of the nonprofit to remit payroll taxes to the IRS, approval of excess benefit transactions (discussed in chapter 8), or any kind of self-dealing. Board members do have some protection, though, in the Volunteer Protection Act of 1997. Under the act, if a volunteer's actions result in any harm while operating in the capacity of a volunteer, he or she is not personally liable unless there was willful or reckless misconduct or gross negligence. The nonprofit could be held liable though. The interpretation of this law varies state by state, and board members can always be sued. Therefore, the board should ensure that the governing documents include indemnification protections for them as well as reimbursement for any expenses they incur in litigation related to their governance roles.

The board should also assess the organization's need for insurance on assets, liability coverage for incidents that might occur on its properties or during events, and directors' and officers' liability insurance. Risk management also extends to good internal controls to protect against damage to the organization's reputation. This topic will be discussed in chapter 7. |

---

8 "Enron and the Fall of Arthur Andersen," National Public Radio Podcast, Scott Horsley reporting, May 26, 2006. Retrieved from www.npr.org/templates/story/story.php?storyId=5435092 on November 6, 2010.

Summary of Principle: Public Disclosure	Discussion
Disclosure of information related to the organization's governance, finances, and program activities should be available to the public.	Because transparency is presently such a big focus for the IRS, Senate Finance Committee, state charity officials, and other organizations that scrutinize nonprofits, the board should ensure that all interested parties have access to important documents. The Form 990 asks for a description of how the organization makes its governing documents, conflict of interest policy, and financial statements available to the public. Disclosure of the work that the nonprofit does in the community is also good public relations and is attractive to donors. This information could be posted on the organization's website. The organization should consider making the following available: • List of board and staff members • Financial information, financial statements, and Forms 990 for the past 3 years • Program services and accomplishments • Mission, vision, and values statements • Code of ethics and conflict of interest policy • Whistleblower policy

Effective Governance

Summary of Principle: Mission	Discussion
The governing body is responsible for setting the nonprofit's mission and its strategic direction.	Among the things the board should oversee are the annual budget, compensation policies and practices, and fiscal and governance policies. Management should draft the policies. Management and the staff of the organization are informed about the limitations of the organization's resources and may be in a better position to make recommendations and to inform the board if its budget and staffing constraints prohibit certain activities from taking place as the board may wish. In addition, the board should select the chief executive and evaluate his or her contributions to the organization. This may include termination if the stated objectives are not met. Some smaller nonprofits may not have staff, so board members may be expected to occupy more hands-on roles. Although this is not ideal because it is difficult for the board to monitor and challenge its own activities, it is a reality for some smaller organizations. Where paid staff is available, the board should function as policy setter and advisor and monitor the work of the chief executive and staff.

Summary of Principle: Functions	Discussion
The board should meet regularly to perform its assigned functions.	Boards can identify certain individuals with content expertise to meet more frequently in committees and report back to the board, which meets less frequently. Board meetings do not have to be face to face. More often with organizations whose board members are not in one city, conference calls or web calls are held. With today's technology, board members can meet face to face with the aid of a webcam on their computers.

(continued)

(continued)

Summary of Principle: Functions	Discussion
	The Better Business Bureau (BBB) has a program that evaluates and provides accreditation to charities without charge. Organizations are judged on how well they meet the BBB's 20 standards for charity accountability. In the Governance and Oversight category, the minimum requirement is for the board of directors to have at least 3 evenly spaced meetings per year of the full governing board. The majority of members should be present in person for at least 2 of the meetings.[9] The Panel on the Nonprofit Sector also agrees that, generally, at least 3 meetings should be held. However, in the case of foundations that only make grants once a year or other types of organizations with widely dispersed board membership, 1 or 2 meetings a year may be sufficient.[10] In June 2007, BoardSource conducted a survey of over 2,100 board members and executives of nonprofit organizations. Among those organizations surveyed, boards met an average of 6.9 times a year.[11]

The advantage of face-to-face meetings is that they promote team building, which is very important to boards. When board members live in locations that are not conducive to face-to-face meetings (such as those representing a national organization), supplementing face-to-face meetings can be one way to encourage participation and prevent board burnout. It is important, however, to ensure that virtual meetings do not violate state laws. Addressing these issues up front may go a long way toward ensuring compliance:[12]

- The legal status of the organization (trust, corporation, or unincorporated association) may make a difference
- Generally, the location in which the nonprofit is incorporated, not where it is located, determines the state law that applies to the organization. However, this is not always true. For example, the California Integrity Act of 2004 requires foreign corporations that do business or hold property in the state of California to comply with this state law.
- Determine if the law has any kind of prohibition to virtual meetings. Many states require that board members be able to hear one another simultaneously
- Some states, for example California and Illinois, permit boards to meet in any way they choose as long as they can communicate with one another. The term *communicate* is different than *hear*.

In addition, boards should ensure that their by-laws permit virtual meetings. It is also important to have written policies that guide the frequency and conduct of virtual meetings.

9 Standards for Charity Accountability, Better Business Bureau, Wise Giving Alliance. Retrieved from www.bbb.org/us/ Charity-Standards/ on November 8, 2010.

10 "Principles for Good Governance and Ethical Practice: A Guide for Charities and Foundations," Panel on the Nonprofit Sector, October 2007, p. 13.

11 Nonprofit Governance Index 2007 (Washinton DC: BoardSource, 2007).

12 "Virtual Meeting Attendance: Not Present, But Still Here" (Washington DC: BoardSource, 2009) p. 6–7.

Summary of Principle: Size and Structure	Discussion
The board should review its size and structure so that there are sufficient members to allow for good deliberation and diversity in point of view. Unless the organization is small, the Panel on the Nonprofit Sector recommends at least five members.[13]	Grant Thornton, a national accounting firm, conducts board governance surveys on the practices of nonprofit organizations every year. The last published survey in 2009 showed that 39 percent of the respondents surveyed had between 16 and 30 board members, 37 percent had between 6 and 15 members, and 15 percent had larger boards with 31 to 50 members. Only a few (6 percent) of organizations had more than 50 board members.[14] It should be noted that the majority of the 465 respondents to the survey had annual revenues less than $50 million.

Summary of Principle: Construction	Discussion
Diversity of expertise, background, skills, genders, race, and ethnicities are very important in the construction of a board.	Some boards serve a narrow band of constituents, and this may guide how the board is constructed. For example, if the nonprofit is a trade group for pediatricians, then the members of the board are most likely to be pediatricians. However, if a nonprofit is related to a cause such as a heart association, then the members of the board should represent various ages, genders, ethnic groups, races, and occupations, such as physicians, that are affected by the disease.

A nonprofit dealing with issues on aging served the state of Oregon. To ensure that all areas of the state were represented, the board by-laws required that 4 of the board members be selected from prescribed areas of the state. In addition, to ensure that varying points of view were considered when developing and funding programs, members were to be drawn from different age, gender, race, and ethnicity groups. This resulted in 10 of the 15 board slots being filled with the best qualified members available that represented those categories. The other 5 slots were available for content experts, including a person with financial expertise.

It is important that at least one and preferably more board members have financial expertise. This is critical in that the board has a fiduciary responsibility to the organization and its constituents. Financial literacy begins with the ability to read and understand nonprofit financial statements and the IRS Form 990. Some smaller organizations may have a difficult time finding a board member with financial expertise. The state associations of nonprofits mentioned earlier can frequently assist the nonprofit in its search, and organizations such as Atlanta Women's Foundation provide training for women to serve on nonprofit boards.* If the organization is still unable to find a qualified member with financial expertise, another strategy could be to solicit pro bono help from an accounting firm that is not the organization's external auditor.

* Atlanta Women's Foundation, www.atlantawomen.org/

---

13 "Principles for Good Governance and Ethical Practice: A Guide for Charities and Foundations," Panel on the Nonprofit Sector, October 2007, p. 14.

14 "National Board Governance Survey for Not for Profit Organizations" (Chicago: Grant Thornton, 2009) p. 10.

Summary of Principle: Characteristics	Discussion
The majority of members that are on a nonprofit board should be independent. The Panel on the Nonprofit Sector believes that 2/3 of the members should not only be independent but should also not be compensated as employees or independent contractors or receive material financial benefits from the organization except as a member of the charitable class that is served.[15] They should also not be related to management of the organization. This principle would not apply to private foundations or organizations such as churches that may be required to have related parties or paid representatives of the organization on its board. If board members are paid, then appropriate comparability data should be used to determine the amount paid along with the rationale for the compensation. This information should be disclosed to any party that requests it.	Independence may seem to be a straightforward concept, but the IRS requires that a board member only be considered independent if he or she meets three tests. These tests will be more fully discussed in chapter 8. The IRS does not require that board members be independent. It asks the preparer of Form 990 to enter the number of voting members of the governing board that are independent. In addition, there is a requirement to disclose compensation information related to payments made to board members on the core Form 990 and its Schedule J.

Most people tend to think of board members as volunteers who are willing to give of their time to serve the cause. In addition, many professional service firms and larger companies expect their employees to serve on nonprofit boards. The firm or company then benefits by being seen as a responsible corporate citizen. In addition, donors and other funding sources want their contributions to be spent on program rather than on administration; for that reason, compensating board members might adversely affect the organization. Form 990 requires identification of amounts paid to board members, so this information is publicly available.

There are others who believe that board members will not serve to the best of their ability unless they are compensated. For example, compensating board members might assist those who would otherwise not be able to contribute the time to serve, which could promote diversity. Paying board members might stimulate better attendance at meetings. It might attract more qualified members and promote professionalism.[16]

Paying board members is not illegal. However, the Federal Volunteer Protection Act of 1997 defines a *volunteer* as "an individual performing services for a nonprofit organization or governmental entity who does not receive compensation other than reasonable reimbursement or any other thing of value in lieu of compensation, in excess of $500 per year."[17] Therefore, paying board members may affect protections under the act. The organization's by-laws should be specific as to any compensation to be paid.

According to the BoardSource Governance Index Survey, only about 3 percent of nonprofit organizations compensate board members, and 11 percent of those organizations had budgets greater than $25 million. |

---

15 "National Board Governance Survey for Not for Profit Organizations" (Chicago: Grant Thornton, 2009) p. 15.

16 "Should Board Members of Nonprofit Organizations Be Compensated?," Center for Association Leadership, November 2006, www.asaecenter.org/Resources/whitepaperdetail.cfm?ItemNumber=22981.

17 Federal Volunteer Protection Act of 1997, Public Law 105–19—June 18, 1997, Section 6, A &B.

Summary of Principle: Responsibilities	Discussion
The board has a responsibility to hire the chief executive, determine compensation, and conduct an evaluation of that individual and any changes to compensation other than for cost of living.	As discussed in this chapter, the board is responsible for the conduct of the organization. The board will put policies in place that include specific parameters and then delegate the responsibility of the day-to-day operations to the chief executive. Therefore, it is critically important that a qualified person be recruited to join the organization. Compensation is a very important issue and is a significant focus of the IRS and other watchdog agencies. One of the questions on Form 990 asks if the process for determining compensation for the chief executive (as well as other officers and key employees of the nonprofit) included a review and approval by independent individuals using comparability data and whether there was contemporaneous documentation of the discussions and decision. Excessive compensation could result in an excess benefit transaction. The instructions to Schedule L of Form 990 state that an excess benefit transaction is one in which a tax exempt organization (501 c3 or c4) directly or indirectly provides a benefit to a disqualified person that exceeds the value of the consideration, or in this case services of the employee, given by the person. The chief executive is in a position to exercise substantial influence over the organization, and, therefore, is a disqualified person. This concept will be more fully explored in chapter 8.

Summary of Principle: Positions	Discussion
The positions of board chair, board treasurer, and chief executive should be separate. If the nonprofit does not have paid staff, then the board chair and treasurer should be separate.	This is an important segregation of duties and should help to prevent conflicts of interest in fact and appearance.

Summary of Principle: Training	Discussion
Board training is very important. The board should establish a process for providing education and communication to its members about the programs and activities of the organization as well as about their legal and ethical responsibilities. The board should receive and review information related to financial activities on a timely basis.	This will ensure that the members have the tools to carry out their duties. Board orientation and training should include discussion of the by-laws, conflict of interest policy, code of ethics, roles and responsibilities, financial information (including the most recent financial statements, audited financial statements, and Form 990), and information about directors' liability and insurance. Periodically, the board should receive updates on issues relating to nonprofits. There are several good sources that can be tapped for this sort of information. One very good one is *The Nonprofit Times*, a periodical that is available monthly in print or online. The periodical can be accessed online at www.nptimes.com. The AICPA produces a good yearly risk alert for nonprofit organizations. It can be purchased at www.cpa2biz.com. Larger accounting firms, such as Grant Thornton, also publish a number of nonprofit surveys and white papers dealing with governance, accounting, and tax issues.

Management should provide the board with monthly financial information so that the members can monitor the financial position and results of operations of the organization. This monitoring may be delegated to an audit committee. In these cases, the board should still receive financial information but perhaps not as much. This is a decision that should be made by the board and not by management. The board or audit committee should monitor. |

(continued)

(continued)

Summary of Principle: Training	Discussion
	• metrics related to programs so that performance can be assessed against the mission and strategic plan. • financial information related to the organization's liquidity, financial position (assets and liabilities), reserves, activity (revenues and expenses), compliance with donor restrictions, endowment, and other investment information especially concerning investments that are not publicly traded (alternative investments). • hot line calls and disposition and significant issues affecting internal controls. • fundraising efforts. A dashboard could be created to provide the information in sufficient detail to monitor but not so much detail that board members become overwhelmed. A sample dashboard for monitoring nonprofit activity can be found in appendix B at the end of this chapter.

Summary of Principle: Performance Assessment	Discussion
Boards should assess their own performance at least once every three years and should have policies in place to remove board members who are no longer carrying out their responsibilities. The board should establish clear policies on the length of terms, review the governing documents at least once every five years, and regularly review the organization's mission and goals and its progress toward those goals.	The board should create a set of documents that outlines the roles and responsibilities of board members, including their responsibility for attendance at meetings, requirements for advance preparation, and norms for contributions to the discussion. The documents should also set out expectations for raising money and board members' monetary contributions to the organization. The documents should also address the committees of the board and the responsibilities of committee members. These items are important for periodic self-assessment, but perhaps even more important is how the board believes it is doing with the more subjective items such as • understanding of the mission and vision of the organization and how this understanding is used in evaluating the strategic plan and in making decisions. • agreement on management responsibilities versus board responsibilities as well as the shared roles. • financial needs assessment and progress toward meeting those goals. • understanding of needs of the community and progress toward meeting those needs. • quality and contribution of expertise supplied by the board members. • its ability to enhance the reputation and visibility of the organization. • its role in assessing the risks related to the organization and how they can be mitigated (through insurance). • quality of its monitoring, review of financial information, resource allocation, and review of the chief executive. • its process for evaluating the strategic plan and making modifications. • evaluation of committee structure and committee performance. • quality of board diversity. • quality of skills present on the board that are necessary to meet the organization's goals and objectives. • effectiveness of board leadership. • quality of relationship with chief executive. • quality of meetings (written agenda, board package sent out in sufficient time to review, time productively used, healthy debate on issues, and the like). There are a variety of self-assessment tools that can be purchased from vendors such as BoardSource and various state associations of nonprofits. Many of them are in electronic form and are very comprehensive. Given the size and complexity of the organization and the board's willingness to self-assess, the board may not wish to assess all of the aspects that are included in the various tools. The board should determine which are the most relevant and important factors for self-assessment and select those. Additional factors can be added over time. A sample tool is included in appendix C at the end of this chapter. Survey Monkey provides an excellent mechanism for anonymous board self-evaluation that can be constructed at no or very low cost to the organization (www.surveymonkey.com/). Giving board members the ability to perform the self-assessment anonymously encourages honesty. The aggregate results can be used for discussion. Survey Monkey can also be used to provide feedback on an individual board meeting or committee activities.

Summary of Principle: Loans and Transactions	Discussion
The organization should not provide loans or loan guarantees or other related transactions such as relieving debt or lease obligations to directors, officers, or trustees.	This is a very important principle and should not be ignored. Many states prohibit this type of activity. From time to time, the organization may find it necessary to provide a loan to an employee, but this should not extend to substantial contributors, board members, executives, or related parties. Any of these types of loans are required to be disclosed on Form 990.

Summary of Principle: Resources	Discussion
The organization should spend a significant amount of its budget on the mission. However, it is important to provide resources for administration and, if applicable, fundraising.	The amount spent on administration is necessary to ensure that the organization's objectives are carried out in the appropriate fashion. It is important to recruit and retain talented people to run the organization; design, implement, and monitor effective internal controls; manage volunteers; raise money; promote the reputation and programs of the organization to the public; and ensure legal compliance. These activities have a price. Some watchdog agencies recommend that nonprofit charitable organizations spend at least 65 percent of their funds on programs. In 2004, the Center on Nonprofits and Philanthropy at the Urban Institute reported on the Nonprofit Overhead Cost Project. It reported that nonprofits in various sectors of the industry had average administrative and fundraising cost ratios as follows:[18]

Type of Organization	Percent Fundraising and Administrative Expenses	Percent Program Expenses	Percent Spending Less Than 65% on Programs
Human services	20	80	14
Arts, culture, humanities	28	72	28
Education	20	82	15
Health	21	79	15
Environment and animals	22	78	18

Charity Navigator is a well known organization that rates charities based on their *organizational efficiency* and *organizational capacity* using financial ratios. The intent is to show donors or potential donors how efficient the charity is in using dollars currently and how likely the charity is to grow its programs and services over time. Charity Navigator's statistics[19] show that approximately 90 percent of the charities rated spent at least 65 percent of their budget on programs and services. And 20 percent of those spent at least 75 percent of their budget on programs and services.

One way that the program expense ratio is decreased is when the organization uses fund-raising organizations. Accounting principles require nonprofits to report the gross amount of funds raised as a contribution and the amount paid to the professional fund-raiser as fund-raising expense. In addition, when donors designate a beneficiary in their contributions to United Way, United Way takes a percentage for an administrative fee. The percentage varies by location. This is also considered fund-raising expense to the nonprofit. When United Way allocates funds to a nonprofit, no administrative fee is charged to the nonprofit. Therefore, the entire amount is considered a donation. Nonprofit boards need to be aware of such issues and evaluate the contracts before the nonprofit enters into agreements with professional fund-raisers. At issue are the terms, minimums, and percentages that the fund-raising organizations require. The board should question whether the arrangements are really worth it.

---

18 Mark A. Hager and Ted Flack, "The Pros and Cons of Financial Efficiency Standards," Brief No. 5 (Washington DC: Urban Institute, Indiana University, 2004).

19 Statistics retrieved on November 9, 2010, from Charity Navigator website: www.charitynavigator.org/index.cfm?bay=content. view&cpid=48.

Summary of Principle: Reimbursement	Discussion
Nonprofits should have written policies describing the types of reimbursements that can be made to employees and board members for travel expenses.	Travel and entertainment expenses are some of the most abused areas in nonprofits. EduCap and its Loans for Learning Program is a high profile example of egregious abuse. In 2006, allegations of impropriety and abuse were raised against the chief executive of Educap, Catherine Reynolds, by *Higher Ed Watch*, the United States Senate's tax committee, the IRS, and the Government Accountability Office.[20] In 2007, the organization significantly reduced its operations. A CBS News report focused on the usage of Educap's $31 million jet, which the chief executive allegedly used for personal travel for herself, family, and friends. The investigation of the organization identified other abuses as well.[21]
	The IRS focuses on travel and entertainment as a possible source of abuse, and nonprofit organizations are now required to disclose information related to companion travel and first-class or charter travel (among other reimbursed items) on Schedule J for officers, directors, trustees, and certain key and highly compensated employees. This disclosure will help the IRS to identify possible abuses for investigation.
	Nonprofits should not provide reimbursement for individuals, such as spouses or dependents who accompany the organization's employees or board members, unless they are also conducting the business of the nonprofit. There could be an exception for dinners to which the nonprofit representative is invited to bring a guest.

Summary of Principle: Solicitation	Discussion
Nonprofit solicitation materials should be truthful and clearly identify the organization. Contributions should be used consistent with the donor's intent. The organization must provide donors with specific acknowledgments of contributions in accordance with IRS requirements. The organization should adopt policies to determine whether accepting certain types of gifts could compromise ethics, financial circumstances, program focus, or other interests. Employees and volunteers that solicit gifts should be trained and supervised so that they understand the laws and regulations governing solicitation.	The Federal Trade Commission (FTC) estimates that approximately 1 percent of charitable gifts is collected using fraudulent techniques or is used inappropriately. It estimates that for 2005 and 2006, misrepresented or misused donations were between $2.6 to $3 billion. The FTC shines a bright light on the issue, but the regulations governing charitable solicitation are enacted by the states. There are only 9 states that do not have statutory requirements. A standardized form, which is accepted by the majority of states, has been created by the National Association of State Charity Officials (the Uniform State Registration Statement) for reporting under the state solicitation laws. But most states require that this annual form be supplemented with additional information. The state requirements apply to solicitations over e-mail and the internet as well as by mail or telephone. It is important for boards to be aware of the requirements and also to know other related state requirements. A helpful summary for state contacts, requirements, and fees can be found at the Center for Public Policy and Administration, University of Utah.[22]

---

20 Paul Fain, "U.S. Senator Broadens Inquiry Into Spending by Nonprofit Lender EduCap," *Chronicle of Higher Education*, July 24, 2007.

21 Sharyl Attkisson, "Loan Charity's High-Flying Guests Exposed", CBS Evening News, March 3, 2009, www.cbsnews.com/stories/2009/03/03/eveningnews/main4841768.shtml?tag=contentMain;contentBody.

22 Jamie Usry, "Charitable Solicitation Regulation for the Nonprofit Sector: Paving the Regulatory Landscape for Future Success," July 30, 2008, www.imakenews.com/cppa/e_article001162331.cfm#_ftnref2.

Summary of Principle: Solicitation	Discussion

In response to issues surrounding abuse of donor relationships, the Association of Fundraising Professionals, the Association for Healthcare Philanthropy, and the Council for Advancement and Support of Education developed a donor's bill of rights.[23] The principles, which are listed below, have been endorsed by numerous nonprofit organizations and appear on the websites of many nonprofit trade groups and charities:

1. To be informed of the organization's mission, of the way the organization intends to use donated resources, and of its capacity to use donations effectively for their intended purposes
2. To be informed of the identity of those serving on the organization's governing board and to expect the board to exercise prudent judgment in its stewardship responsibilities
3. To have access to the organization's most recent financial statements
4. To be assured their gifts will be used for the purposes for which they were given.
5. To receive appropriate acknowledgement and recognition
6. To be assured that information about their donation is handled with respect and with confidentiality to the extent provided by law
7. To expect that all relationships with individuals representing organizations of interest to the donor will be professional in nature
8. To be informed whether those seeking donations are volunteers, employees of the organization, or hired solicitors
9. To have the opportunity for their names to be deleted from mailing lists that an organization may intend to share
10. To feel free to ask questions when making a donation and to receive prompt, truthful, and forthright answers

One of the risk areas in nonprofits is that in times when cash is tight, restricted contributions may be used for unrestricted purposes. Although the nonprofit may consider this to be borrowing, in reality, without the donor's agreement (preferably in writing), it is misuse of funds. The board should set a clear tone in this regard and monitor the use of restricted donations. This is true for endowment funds that are permanently restricted, the use of income and appreciation from endowment funds that may carry donor restrictions, and also gifts, whether solicited or unsolicited, that are restricted as to timing of use or purpose.

Schedule M of Form 990, which relates to noncash contributions, asks "Does the organization have a gift acceptance policy that requires the review of any non-standard contributions?" Nonprofits may, from time to time, receive gifts that could put them at risk for environmental remediation obligations, gifts of partnership interests, or interests in assets that might give rise to unrelated business income or other noncash gifts. The donor's expectations for those gifts might be that the organization will use (not sell) the assets, which would result in a larger tax deduction. A gift acceptance policy with clear guidelines will enable the organization to be prepared to evaluate whether a noncash gift should be accepted. Generally, it is not a good idea to accept gifts unrelated to the mission unless the donor is willing for it to be sold. The board has responsibility for creating this policy and should be notified if the organization receives an offer of such gifts so that it can determine whether to accept them.

---

23 Donors Bill of Rights. Retrieved from the Association of Fund Raising Professionals website on November 10, 2010: www.afpnet.org/ethics/enforcementdetail.cfm?itemnumber=3359.

Summary of Principle: Privacy	Discussion
The organization should always respect the privacy of donors. At least once a year, donors should be provided with an opportunity to refuse to have the organization sell their names or make use information about them or their donations.	This is not only an important practice from a legal standpoint, it is also important to preserve donor trust and loyalty. Donors, especially large donors, may wish to give more to organizations with missions that dovetail with their interests to the exclusion of other organizations. This is especially true in economic hard times. Preferring to concentrate on organizations that have greater meaning to them, these donors likely do not want to be solicited by other organizations that may assume that a donor has the resources to make additional contributions. Some donors may not wish to be acknowledged on the organization's website, programs, or collateral materials or even in conversation. It is important to note that although donors may not wish to be publicly acknowledged, the information required for Schedule B of Form 990 (name, address, and aggregate contributions per donor) must be provided to the IRS. This information should not appear in any public place such as Guidestar.org because the information is removed prior to publishing the Form 990s on the Guidestar website.

Conclusion

Governance is a shared responsibility between executive management and the governing board, and it is important to define the role of the board for two primary reasons. First, the board plays an important role in being a check and balance on management who are involved in the day-to-day activities of the nonprofit. The second and more practical reason for defined roles is that duplication of effort is neither efficient nor effective.

The board and its members are responsible for the overall protection of the organization through the exercise of their legal duties of care, loyalty, and obedience. Their responsibility is to ensure legal, regulatory, and funding-source compliance; set strategic objectives; create policies to guide the implementation of those objectives; monitor the implementation thereof; serve as content matter experts and as a sounding board for the chief executive; hire the chief executive and monitor performance; set its own governance processes; and assesses its performance in meeting its objectives.

The chief executive's job is to run the day-to-day operations of the organization, implementing the policies and strategies set by the board. The distinction is that although that the board does not run day-to-day operations, it is accountable for the organization's actions; it must think independently and not be unduly influenced by the chief executive. The organization's ability to carry out its mission is effectively reduced when management and the board do not work hand in hand in their respective roles.

Appendix A
Comparison of Key Objectives of the Board of Directors With the Good Governance Framework and Questions From IRS Form 990

This chart illustrates how the 33 principles of the Good Governance Framework support the key objectives of the board of directors and how the questions on IRS Form 990 reinforce the importance of the 33 principles.

Key Board Objective—Thomas and Strom-Gottfried	33 Principles of the Panel on the Nonprofit Sector	Form 990 Question
Assume responsibility for the organization's compliance with laws and regulations and provisions of funding source agreements	1. Compliance With Laws and Regulations	N/A
Create policies to guide the implementation of activities designed to assist the organization in meeting its strategic objectives	2. Code of Ethics	Question on Form 990 relates to conflicts of interest
Create policies to guide the implementation of activities designed to assist the organization in meeting its strategic objectives	3. Conflicts of Interest	Part VI, lines 12 and 19
Create policies to guide the implementation of activities designed to assist the organization in meeting its strategic objectives	4. Whistleblower Policy	Part VI, line 13
Create policies to guide the implementation of activities designed to assist the organization in meeting its strategic objectives	5. Document Retention and Destruction Policy	Part VI, line 14, and Schedule E
Create policies to guide the implementation of activities designed to assist the organization in meeting its strategic objectives	6. Protection of Assets	N/A
Create policies to guide the implementation of activities designed to assist the organization in meeting its strategic objectives	7. Availability of Information to the Public	Part VI, lines 19 and 20
Set strategic objectives to be accomplished	8. Review and Approve Mission, Strategic Direction, Budget, Key Financial Transactions and Policies, and Fiscal and Governance Policies	N/A
Set its own governance processes and assess its performance in meeting its objectives	9. Board Meetings	Part I, line 3, and Part VI, lines 1a and 8
Set its own governance processes and assess its performance in meeting its objectives	10. Sufficient Meetings	N/A

(continued)

(continued)

Key Board Objective—Thomas and Strom-Gottfried	33 Principles of the Panel on the Nonprofit Sector	Form 990 Question
Set its own governance processes and assess its performance in meeting its objectives	11. Board Diversity	N/A. Questions on diversity relate to faculty, administrative staff, and students.
Set its own governance processes and assess its performance in meeting its objectives	12. Board Independence	Part I, line 4, and Part VI, line 1b
Monitor the progress of the chief executive towards those objectives	13. CEO Evaluation and Compensation	Part VI, line 15, and Part VII
Set its own governance processes and assess its performance in meeting its objectives	14. Separation of CEO, Board Chair, and Treasurer Roles	Part I, line 4, and Part VI, lines 1b, 2, and 3
Set its own governance processes and assess its performance in meeting its objectives	15. Board Education and Communication	N/A
Set its own governance processes and assess its performance in meeting its objectives	16. Evaluation of Board Performance	N/A
Set its own governance processes and assess its performance in meeting its objectives	17. Board Member Term Limits	N/A
Set its own governance processes and assess its performance in meeting its objectives	18. Review of Governing Documents	Part III
Set strategic objectives to be accomplished	19. Review of Mission and Goals	Part I, line 1, and Part 3, line 1
Set its own governance processes and assess its performance in meeting its objectives	20. Board Compensation	Part VI, line 15, and Schedule J
Set strategic objectives to be accomplished	21. Financial Records	N/A
Set strategic objectives to be accomplished	22. Annual Budget, Financial Performance, and Investments	Part IV, line 10, and Schedule D
Create policies to guide the implementation of activities designed to assist the organization in meeting its strategic objectives	23. Loans to Directors, Officers, and Trustees	Part IV, line 26, and Schedule L
Set strategic objectives to be accomplished	24. Resource Allocation for Programs and Administration	Part I and Part III
Create policies to guide the implementation of activities designed to assist the organization in meeting its strategic objectives	25. Travel and Other Expense Policies	Schedule J
Create policies to guide the implementation of activities designed to assist the organization in meeting its strategic objectives	26. Expense Reimbursement for Nonbusiness Travel Companions	Schedule J
Create policies to guide the implementation of activities designed to assist the organization in meeting its strategic objectives	27. Accuracy and Truthfulness of Fundraising Materials	N/A

Key Board Objective—Thomas and Strom-Gottfried	33 Principles of the Panel on the Nonprofit Sector	Form 990 Question
Create policies to guide the implementation of activities designed to assist the organization in meeting its strategic objectives	28. Compliance With Donor Intent	Schedule D
Create policies to guide the implementation of activities designed to assist the organization in meeting its strategic objectives	29. Acknowledgement of Tax Deductible Contributions	Part V, lines 6 and 7
Create policies to guide the implementation of activities designed to assist the organization in meeting its strategic objectives	30. Gift Acceptance Policy	Schedule M, line 31
Create policies to guide the implementation of activities designed to assist the organization in meeting its strategic objectives	31. Training and Oversight of Fundraisers	N/A
Create policies to guide the implementation of activities designed to assist the organization in meeting its strategic objectives	32. Fundraiser Compensation	Part 1, line 16a, Part IV, line 17, and Schedule G
Create policies to guide the implementation of activities designed to assist the organization in meeting its strategic objectives	33. Privacy of Donors	N/A

Appendix B
Example Dashboard for Board Evaluation

Following is an example dashboard that could be provided to the board by management to use as a tool for monitoring. The board would choose the metrics that were most important to their monitoring responsibilities and determine the frequency with which the metric should be reported.

Purpose: To assist the board in evaluation of the organization, including its programs and their impact on the community, financial position and results of operations, compliance and risk management, fundraising, human resources, and governance.

Category 1: Program Service Efforts and Accomplishments			
Metric	Target	Current Status	Prior Quarter
Number of clients served in adult daycare programs (quarterly)			
Attendance at awareness classes (quarterly)			
Videos on working with the elderly sold (quarterly)			
Signatures for petitions to congressional representative (quarterly)			
Number of volunteers serving meals to the elderly (quarterly)			
Results of client satisfaction survey (yearly)			
Category 2: Financial Position and Results of Operations			
Metric	Target	Current Status	Prior Quarter
Number of days cash on hand (quarterly)			
Number of days pledges in current receivables (quarterly)			
Pledges written off as uncollectible (quarterly)			
Days in accounts payables			
Grants funding received vs. budgeted			
Operating margin			
New individual donors by type (individual, corporate, foundation)			
Donations against budget—unrestricted (quarterly)			

Category 2: Financial Position and Results of Operations			
Metric	Target	Current Status	Prior Quarter
Donations against budget—restricted (quarterly)			
Restricted donations spent (quarterly)			
Investment return on endowment funds (quarterly)			
Expenses greater than budget (quarterly)			
Category 3: Compliance and Risk Management			
Metric	Target	Current Status	Prior Quarter
Met deadline on payroll withholding and benefit plan remittances (report monthly)			
Numbers of workers compensation claims (quarterly)			
Percentage of calls to hotline investigated and resolved (quarterly)			
Financial statements delivered to bank, covenants met (quarterly)			
Form 990 filed on timely basis (yearly)			
Category 4: Human Resources			
Metric	Target	Current Status	Prior Quarter
Number of training classes attended by management and staff (quarterly)			
Number of accidents (quarterly)			
Numbers of days employees were absent from work (quarterly)			
Results of employee satisfaction survey (yearly)			
Percentage of performance evaluations written and delivered to employees (yearly)			

(continued)

(continued)

Category 5: Board of Directors			
Metric	Target	Current Status	Prior Quarter
Attendance at board meetings (monthly)			
Time spent evaluating financial position, operations, risk to the organization from external environment and internal controls, including the risk of fraud (quarterly)			
Time spent evaluating strategic direction (yearly)			
Time spent with external auditors (yearly)			
Time spent evaluating the executive director (yearly)			
Audited financial statements reviewed and approved			
Form 990 reviewed and approved			

Appendix C
Sample Board Self-Assessment Document

This is an example of a form that could be used by the board to assess its effectiveness. The form could be given to board members and the results compiled by the organization's staff. It could also be automated using a tool, such as Survey Monkey, for anonymous results. The results could be used to facilitate discussion among the members and create action plans for improvement.

Purpose: To assist the board in evaluating its performance during the year. Evaluate your perception of the board's performance by selecting 1–5 as follows:

1. Poor
2. Average
3. Good
4. Very good
5. Exceptional

Category 1: Size, Structure, Independence, Diversity, Orientation, Training, Meetings	1	2	3	4	5
Board has an appropriate number of members for the size and complexity of the organization. Membership is sufficiently diverse in order to include different points of view and stimulate discussion.					
Board has sufficient committees with technical expertise to facilitate good governance.					
Board has sufficient independent members (recommendation 2 and 3).					
Board has the appropriate policies and procedures to answer affirmatively to Form 990 questions.					
Board has members with sufficient training to facilitate monitoring (financial, program, regulatory compliance).					
Meeting time is used productively.					
Board agenda and package is sent sufficiently in advance so members can prepare.					
Board package contains the right amount of information at the right level of detail.					
An atmosphere of trust and cohesiveness exists among the board members.					

Category 2: Board Responsibilities	1	2	3	4	5
Board members set the tone for the organization for integrity, ethical values, and moral courage.					
Board members proactively reach out to the community to build awareness for the mission of the organization and solicit the community's needs.					
Board understands the potential areas of risk and considers plans to mitigate them.					
Board should identify and assess the risk of fraud in the organization.					
Board understands its obligations as it relates to the duties of care, loyalty, and obedience.					
Board views itself as accountable to the community and regulatory bodies for the actions of the organization.					
Board annually reviews the performance and compensation of chief executive.					
Monitoring of compliance with laws and regulations is performed quarterly.					
Board annually approves the budget for the year and sets effective parameters for the chief executive to follow relating to revenue, expenditures, investments, and other important financial aspects of the organization.					
Board annually reviews Form 990.					

(continued)

(continued)

Category 2: Board Responsibilities	1	2	3	4	5
Board annually reviews its financial statements.					
Board meets at least annually with the independent auditors.					
Board annually reviews the strategic plan.					
Board chair ensures that individual directors are evaluated either by each other or by the board chair.					
Board chair ensures that conflict of interest statements are signed.					
Board monitors its own performance by completing and discussing the results of the self-assessment.					
Board members all contribute to the organization.					

Chapter 3

Legal and Ethical Imperatives for Leadership

WholeHealth is a nonprofit health system operating hospitals, specialty clinics, home health, and hospice services. WholeHealth was among four finalists submitting bids for a multimillion dollar contract to provide health services to the state's employees. During a lunch break in the bidders' conference, an executive assistant tidying the room found, in plain sight, the figures submitted by the three other competing health providers. Acutely aware of the significance of the contract for WholeHealth, the assistant alerted her boss, the vice president of medical care management, who instructed her to copy the paper and return it to the conference room. He reasoned that WholeHealth might or might not want to use the information, and having the information would keep all of their options open. When he met at the end of the day with Helen, the CFO, to brief her about the negotiations, he also told her about obtaining the competitor's data. Shocked, she held up her hands and said, "Have you looked at them?" "Of course I skimmed them. We're definitely in the ballpark, but not the lowest bid at this point." Helen interrupted, "Stop right there. I don't want to know any more until I've had a chance to talk with Hal (WholeHealth's COO).

The dilemma facing Helen and Hal involves both legal and ethical issues. Is it legal to have taken and copied a proprietary document? Is it legal to obtain a contract by dishonest means? Having obtained the information, what is the ethical thing to do?

Should WholeHealth admit the mistake and risk losing this contract, its reputation, and future business with the state (and possibly with others)? Loss of this or other contracts would have devastating effects on the organization's programs and workforce.

Should WholeHealth acknowledge the situation and blame it on the workers who copied the bids? Separating the organization's ethics from the individuals' might spare WholeHealth from censure, but would this be a fair and just action? What message would it send to the rest of the workforce?

Should WholeHealth use the advantageous, if ill-gotten, information? The vice president argued that the ends (a big contract, good health care for state employees, and financial stability for WholeHealth) justify the means by which the bid was gotten and suggested that the information may have been intentionally left in the hope that WholeHealth would use it to get the inside track or in order to entice and entrap the organization in wrongdoing.

(continued)

(continued)

Should WholeHealth destroy the competitive information and place a firewall between individuals with the information and those who will take part in subsequent negotiations on the bid? This option would not permit WholeHealth to benefit from the information. Is that sufficient?

Whether in the public, corporate, or nonprofit sector, individuals in administrative and leadership positions face unique challenges as they strive to balance competing demands, values, and constituencies. With such responsibilities also comes great power. It is easy to identify leaders who have used their positions to improve communities and create healthy and effective workplaces. Unfortunately, it is perhaps easier to identify administrators whose decisions were personally ruinous as well as destructive to employees, customers, and other constituencies of their organizations. This chapter examines the ethical and legal standards that impinge on the paid and volunteer leaders of nonprofit organizations (NPOs) and suggests strategies for ensuring ethically and legally sound decisions.

Legal Accountability

The passage from the Book of Luke, "From those to whom much has been given, much will be expected," aptly captures the position of NPOs in the United States. Voluntary and philanthropic organizations benefit society by addressing fundamental human needs; contributing to civic well-being through education, conservation, arts and music, and interpersonal associations; and acquiring and allocating resources. In light of these honorable aims, individuals contribute time and money to nonprofits, and governments acknowledge the role of nonprofits though tax exemptions. In exchange for these benefits, nonprofits are expected to be careful stewards of their resources, to be trustworthy in carrying out their missions, and to be responsible for self-regulation through trustees and governing boards. "Those who presume to serve the public good assume a public trust."[1]

The most fundamental level of accountability is legal. Nonprofits are expected to abide by local, state, and federal statutes. These laws pertain to a vast array of issues such as

- governance,
- solicitations and other financial transactions,
- personnel matters,
- representation of mission and activities,
- delivery of services, and
- zoning and property management.

Unfortunately, there are abundant examples of illegal behavior on the part of nonprofits, including

- excessive executive compensation,
- embezzlement,

---

1 Independent Sector, *Obedience to the Unenforceable: Ethics and the Nation's Voluntary and Philanthropic Community.* (Washington, DC, 2002) p. 11.

- diversion of charitable funds,
- investment fraud,
- mismanagement,
- kickbacks,
- "sweetheart" contracts with friends and relatives,
- money laundering and conspiracy,
- telemarketing scams,
- fraudulent solicitation,
- sexual misconduct, and[2,3]
- misappropriation of funds for personal uses.[2,3]

The penalties for illegal conduct vary, depending on the violation and determinations about the degree to which the error was incidental, accidental, or volitional. Punishments can include fines, restitution, placement in receivership, consent agreements governing future conduct, withdrawal of tax-exempt charitable status, and imprisonment. Nonprofit scandals also extract other prices, including the destruction of individual and organizational reputations, the erosion of trust, shame, and even suicide.

Legal compliance is a complex and far-reaching element of nonprofit leadership. Despite that, it is only the baseline for accountability and trustworthiness. It is not enough for an organization to behave legally; it must behave ethically as well.

Ethical Accountability

Like laws, ethics involve determinations between right and wrong. However, although laws specifically stipulate or forbid particular actions, ethics can either be specified (in professional standards or ethical codes), or they can exist as values and principles that must be interpreted and applied by individuals and organizations.

In the first instance, ethics take the form of rules for conduct. They are set forth by professional associations, accrediting agencies, and individual organizations to communicate expectations of behavior. For example, a profession's code of ethics may have standards addressing conflicts of interest with patients, an accrediting agency's code might address confidentiality and the proper handling of electronic records, and an individual organization's code might address the process for respectfully resolving disputes or effectively diversifying the staff and clientele. Some ethical standards are ideal—that is, they exist to articulate an organization's highest aspirations and to create norms of behavior that live up to those ideals. Other standards are enforceable rather than merely aspirational. Like laws, they can be used to set forth firm expectations and penalties for violations of those expectations. For example, a code of ethics that forbids exploitive relationships with a nonprofit's donors or clients would lay the foundation for censure of employees and trustees who behave unethically.

---

2 Margaret Gibelman and Sheldon R. Gelman, "Very Public Scandals: Nongovernmental Organizations in Trouble," *Voluntas: International Journal of Voluntary and Nonprofit Organizations*, vol. 12, no. 1 (New York: Springer, 2001) p. 49–66.

3 Margaret Gibelman and Sheldon R. Gelman, "A Loss of Credibility: Patterns of Wrongdoing Among Nongovernmental Organizations," Voluntas: International Journal of Voluntary and Nonprofit Organizations, vol. 15, no. 4 (New York: Springer, 2004) p. 355–381.

In contrast to the ethics that are codified, ethics are also "the rules you carry around with yourself." Each of us has a sense of right and wrong that is cultivated by our upbringing, our moral and faith traditions, and our experiences and values. Is it acceptable to lie on a resume? Is it okay to download copyrighted material? Or, is it okay to "borrow" a bidding sheet to get a competitive advantage for a state contract? Deciding what is ethical means looking at questions such as these and arriving at a yes or no answer based on principles such as honesty, integrity, trustworthiness, fairness, and responsibility. But even when a group of people embraces those principles, each may not apply them in the same way. Herein rests the complexity of ethical decision-making.

One school of thought about what is "right" takes the stance that if something is wrong, it is wrong in all conditions. Known as rule-based decision-making or deontology, this perspective would suggest that if it is ethical to be honest, one should be honest in all conditions. In viewing the case at the beginning of the chapter, deontologists would say that if taking and using the bid is right, then we should permit everyone to do it in all circumstances.

An alternative to rule-based decision-making is the utilitarian perspective. It maintains that what is "right" depends on the outcome or consequences. Sometimes this view is embodied in the notion that we should do what brings the greatest good for the greatest number of people. If the consequence of getting the competitors' information is that it advantages WholeHealth, its employees, and patients, would that be a right decision, even if the way it was obtained was "wrong?"

A third perspective on ethics is a care-based approach, which would hold the good of the relationship as the defining characteristic of a "right" decision. Applying this view means that one must consider the effect a choice will have on the relationship involved in the dilemma and choose the path that preserves and honors the relationship. Preserving the trust of state contractors and fellow providers would take precedence in a care-based perspective over outcomes or rules.

Still another approach focuses on the principle of justice. It suggests that what is right is whatever one would choose to do without knowing what position he or she might hold in the matter. Under this model, what would be right for WholeHealth would be the option that they would choose if they didn't know whether they would be a competing agency, themselves, or the state contractor. From this "veil of ignorance,"[4] WholeHealth would probably choose not to use the bid information; perhaps they would even admit to the error in taking it.

This is typically the point where readers pull out their hair and scream about hating ethics. Some just shrug and say, "If there are different ways to decide what's right, does it make any difference what I choose?" Others conclude, "Look, I know what's right and wrong. I don't need to analyze it and I don't need to worry about anybody else but myself." All of these are understandable and commonly held positions. Although it is possible to empathize, these myths cannot stand unchallenged. Why?

---

4 John Rawls, *A Theory of Justice*, (Cambridge: Belknap, 1971).

Society, communities, groups, and organizations need ethics to function effectively. Common principles and standards of right and wrong bind us and guide us through complex decisions. They help us avoid the anarchy and chaos that arise when everyone acts according to individual standards and self-interest.

That said, ethical decisions fall along a continuum. Some choices are clearly ethical or unethical. Others present dilemmas in which principles conflict and analysis and discussion are needed to discern the proper path. Taking and copying proprietary information is unethical. Deciding what to do about it is a dilemma of competing principles. Honesty and trustworthiness would compel disclosure of the theft; fairness to other bidders and responsibility to WholeHealth's wellbeing would argue for nondisclosure but also for destroying the stolen information so as not to unfairly advantage WholeHealth in the bidding. Both choices then, are "ethical," so discussion involves which is the better, more principled choice between two acceptable alternatives.

Understanding different philosophies for determining what is right is indispensable for effective, open discussion of ethical dilemmas. Care-based, rule-based, outcome-based, and justice-based perspectives may lead to different choices, but their real gift is in illuminating the pros and cons of different options and emphases. Too much focus on outcomes means those in the minority always lose out to the majority. Too much emphasis on rules fails to account for the context in which rules are applied. Too much emphasis on the relationship may privilege loyalty over fairness. Too much emphasis on justice may mean sacrificing one's well being for the least compelling option.

For nonprofits, ethical behavior is essential to public trust. NPOs and those affiliated with them are held to a higher standard than the law and a higher standard than other sectors of society. Ethical accountability is a business imperative.

Management, employees, contractors, volunteers, and directors are all responsible for the integrity of the organization. It is not sufficient to be doing the right thing while standing aside in the presence of unethical behavior. As citizens and nonprofit leaders, we must constantly wrestle with the tension between respecting the rights and prerogatives of others and the need to uphold organizational and community standards. Chapter 11 addresses this tension, examining when and how we act to support ethical principles.

Accountability in nonprofits means being both ethical and legal. Neither standard alone is enough: some things that are legal are not ethical. For example, it is legal for nonprofit executives and board members to fly first class and enjoy lavish meals and accommodations, but it is not an ethical use of funds for the small and struggling NPO. It is legal for a nonprofit to feature clients' pictures and stories in fundraising appeals, but it is not ethical to reveal their private information in that way. It is legal to compensate the director of development by awarding bonuses based on funds raised, but such arrangements are considered potentially risky conflicts of interest. In light of their public trust, NPOs must operate in ways that are above reproach. Even behaviors that can ultimately be justified may alienate donors, clients, and other important stakeholders. When faced with ethical gray areas, management and boards should consider how news accounts, IRS Form 990 reporting, and other accountability mechanisms might view their choices. Finally, some actions are both illegal and unethical, for example, fraudulent reporting on the Form 990, intentional accounting misstatement, discriminatory treatment of patients and employees, preferential jobs for family members, and diversion of funds from their intended programs. These should not constitute ethical and legal dilemmas; however, the NPO must still be assiduous in identifying and addressing them when they occur.

Who is Accountable for Accountability?

Given the high accountability bar for nonprofits, who is responsible for staying on top of ethical and legal practices? Ultimately, everyone associated with an organization is accountable for his or her own actions and those of the group as a whole. The board of directors, however, holds particular legal responsibility for the direction and integrity of the nonprofit. This fiduciary responsibility, or position of trust, is both a legal and an ethical imperative for board members. The failure to ably carry out this role puts the entire enterprise in jeopardy.

Examinations of nonprofit scandals reveal several common symptoms of governance failures, including "failure to supervise operations, improper delegation of authority, neglect of assets, failure to ask the 'right questions,' lack of oversight of the CEO, failure to institute internal controls, absence of 'checks and balances' in procedures and practices, and isolation of board members from staff, programs and clients."[5, 6] Although board members can't know everything, they must have the systems and norms in place to ensure ethical and legal conduct. And they must have the capacity to seek and evaluate information and not simply to avoid scandal but to ensure that the nonprofit lives up to the trust bestowed upon it.

Outside the organization, other groups strive to assist in transparency and accountability. The IRS and other regulatory agencies, credentialing bodies such as the Council on Accreditation, and The Joint Commission conduct periodic, in-depth reviews and place a seal of approval on worthy organizations. Watchdog programs such as Guidestar, the Better Business Bureau Wise Giving Alliance, and The American Institute of Philanthropy provide benchmarks, ratings, and data to help prospective administrators, volunteers, and donors evaluate NPOs.[5] [6]

How to Instill Ethical and Legal Accountability

There are many strategies for ethical and legal accountability in nonprofits. None alone will suffice, but each is a step in the right direction. In the coming chapters, we address many of these key strategies in detail, but let's review each briefly here.

Honest Communications

Board members, executive management, and staff have and use communication mechanisms to raise concerns, share observations, ask questions, and respectfully deliberate even

---

5 Margaret Gibelman and Sheldon R. Gelman, "Very Public Scandals: Nongovernmental Organizations in Trouble," *Voluntas: International Journal of Voluntary and Nonprofit Organizations*, vol. 12, no. 1 (New York: Springer, 2001) p. 49–66.

6 Margaret Gibelman and Sheldon R. Gelman, "A Loss of Credibility: Patterns of Wrongdoing Among Nongovernmental Organizations," Voluntas: International Journal of Voluntary and Nonprofit Organizations, vol. 15, no. 4 (New York: Springer, 2004) p. 355–381.

when they disagree. This means that people put the well-being of the organization above their personal interests so that conflicts do not result in divisiveness, sabotage, or backstabbing. The communication mechanisms facilitate thorough and forthright appraisal of problems, opportunities, options, and consequences. The ability to communicate facilitates organizational innovation and growth, helps avoid legal and ethical quagmires, and promotes constructive dialogue about difficult legal, moral, or strategic issues.

Strong Relationships

The board, executives, and staff should be linked by knowledge of and respect for each other.[7] Individuals need to know those with whom they interact most often—their interests in the nonprofit, backgrounds, activities, talents, weaknesses, interpersonal styles, and the like. Building these reciprocal ties allows a deeper understanding of individual approaches and motivations and creates cohesion that facilitates trust, cooperation, communication, accountability, and even confrontation when needed. Building social capital among the staff and leadership helps NPOs celebrate successes, make wise decisions, weather tough times, and keep the organization's needs in the forefront.

Internal Controls

Internal controls refer to an organization's systems for managing and monitoring resources, detecting fraud, and promoting accountability. Internal controls involve a variety of processes, linked to the organization's objectives, that ensure that those objectives are met in an efficient and effective manner and that requirements for financial and legal compliance are met. As such, most of the individuals and elements in an NPO bear responsibility for some or all of these processes.

Clear Expectations

Clear expectations are inherent in internal controls, but they go beyond processes and procedures to shape behavior in other ways. Successful, ethical organizations set forth clear expectations for board members, executives, and staff that are communicated in the form of position descriptions, orientations, policies, board and staff development activities, and periodic evaluations. Healthy NPOs have a clear organizational direction that is linked to the mission and strategic planning or other objective-setting activities. They have well articulated expectations for outcomes, and these are used to evaluate management, assess efficacy and efficiency, make programmatic decisions, and serve as benchmarks for growth. Further, there are clear expectations for behavior, set and modeled from the top, that indicate the NPO's commitment to transparency, integrity, honesty, and other ethical principles. These expectations can be conveyed in written or electronic documents (such as a code of conduct, policies, and procedures) and in daily interactions wherein the norms are part of the dialogue in committee and board meetings, personnel evaluations, and trouble-shooting sessions.

---

7 Jim Brown, *The Imperfect Board Member: Discovering the Seven Disciplines of Governance Excellence* (San Francisco: Jossey-Bass, 2006).

Skilled Boards

Boards of directors or boards of trustees have significant responsibility for the direction and well-being of their NPOs. In perhaps its most important function, the board hires and evaluates the CEO who is then responsible for leadership decisions that permeate the rest of the organization. Selection of a person with the skills, integrity, commitment, and vision to lead a complex organization sets the stage for the practices that will follow.

Involved and Informed Boards

Proper governance requires having the right people around the table. Often boards seek members with expertise in accounting, law, or the organization's niche or mission (health care, the arts, or domestic violence, for example). Often NPOs seek members whose financial wherewithal or connections may benefit the organization. Board membership should reflect a mix of abilities and backgrounds, but all members should be united in their willingness to commit time and talents to governance of the NPO. Board members should be dedicated to the nonprofit's mission and familiar with its operational environment. They should be objective and inquisitive. Although the board's role is not to serve as a micromanager, it must avoid the other end of the continuum: a hands-off or rubber stamping function that may allow unethical or illegal activities to go unchecked.

Financial, Document, and Ethics Audits

At their essence, audits are periodic tests to determine whether an organization's practices are in keeping with accepted standards. Therefore, financial audits examine and assess an organization's financial statements, records audits examine patient files and treatment notes, and ethics audits review compliance with ethical standards. These and other assessments can be done internally or externally; some are voluntary (ethics audits), and others are mandatory (financial audits) or required as part of larger accreditation procedures (records audits). Audits should result in an objective appraisal of the organization's compliance. As executives and board members receive the findings, they bear responsibility for action to address areas of weakness or failure. Audits can serve as early warning signs of dysfunction, incompetence, or corruption; it is incumbent on the leadership to act on the warning offered.

Compliance Officers

Most nonprofits have at least one individual tasked with responsibility for monitoring ethical and regulatory compliance. In some organizations, this may be part of a position's larger portfolio of duties, or it may be the primary responsibility for a Chief Compliance Officer (CCO). Depending on the organization, the CCO might interpret and monitor compliance with federal privacy laws, serve on the audit committee, devise and oversee harassment policies, or consult with the board and other members of the management team.[8] The CCO plays a role that is both proactive and reactive in regard to organizational integrity. He or she designs policies, educational programs, and structures to prevent and identify unethical or illegal behavior and offers mechanisms to encourage reports, investigating, and intervening

---

8 Chief Ethics & Compliance Officer (CECO) Definition Working Group, *Leading Corporate Integrity: Defining the Role of the Chief Ethics & Compliance Officer (CECO)* (Washington, DC: Ethics Resource Center, 2007).

as circumstances require. Compliance programs are not simply intended to avoid scandal but rather to foster trust and streamline communications so that all members of the organization see ethics as their responsibility.

Resolving Dilemmas

How should NPO staff, executives, and trustees determine the "right" course of action when principles are in conflict? Numerous variations exist, but the fundamental ethical decision-making model requires individuals or groups to consider and weigh the options available, striving to maximize "goods" and minimize harms in choosing a course of action. One example of a decision-making model follows a useful and memorable ABCDE format:[9]

A. Assess options

B. Be mindful of process

C. Consult

D. Document

E. Evaluate

The steps can be applied in any order—they do not need to be performed in a linear A to E fashion—and they can be applied either prior to arriving at a decision or retrospectively in determining whether an urgent or spontaneous decision was sound.

Assessing options means generating and weighing various possibilities, as indicated in the WholeHealth case at the outset of the chapter. Some options may be mutually exclusive; others might be combined or employed in a stepwise fashion. The key is to get as many alternatives on the table as possible and to avoid narrow, dichotomous thinking. It is rare that there are only two possibilities.

The next step is to consider the merits of each option. Which choices are legal? Which are congruent with ethical theories and with principles such as integrity, trustworthiness, responsibility, and fairness? Which are aligned with organizational and professional policies, values, and standards? What facts of the case are relevant for various choices? What information is needed to better understand the pros and cons of the various options?

As a result of this process, some alternatives will be ruled out as illegal, unethical, or not feasible. Others will be brought into sharper perspective. This step may be revisited a number of times in the decision-making process as new information and ideas are brought to bear on the dilemma.

Being mindful of process means considering not simply *what to do* but *how to do it*. What strategies are available for carrying out the options? Sometimes, considering the process for enacting an alternative makes it more viable or compelling—or *less*. Who should carry the message? Should communications be in person or in writing? Attention to process involves considering the time, place, participants, approach, and even the words in carrying out an ethical decision. Considerations of process also help rule out some strategies as illegal, unethical, or unsound. For example, it would be inappropriate to go to the media about an organizational problem without first considering or attempting established internal reporting

---

9 Kim Strom-Gottfried, *The Ethics of Practice with Minors: High Stakes, Hard Choices*, (Chicago: Lyceum Books, 2008).

or problem solving procedures. Deception, threats, and other such tactics are also ill-advised in that they undermine the very integrity that the individual is trying to achieve.

Consultation speaks to the benefits of dialogue and discussion. Seeking supervisory guidance, professional expertise, or peer feedback helps in the identification and evaluation of options, the evaluation of past decisions, and the generation of strategies or processes for action. Consultants may be in-house; current or former board members; part of local professional or nonprofit networks; affiliated with national NPO associations; or ad hoc resources with legal, financial, or other specialized expertise. And consultation is not just limited to people. Vast resources exist to guide board members and executives. Books and articles, best practice summaries, interpretive guidelines, and other tools are available commercially and through national nonprofit affiliates and associations. Resources such as these are also valuable in building an NPO's capacity for identifying and addressing ethical challenges *before* specific dilemmas arise.

On occasion, individuals and organizations resist consultation in the name of patient privacy, proprietary interests, or other confidentiality concerns. Certainly confidential sources of assistance exist, and beyond those, individuals can seek advice without divulging the specifics of a situation. Valuable input can be obtained simply by sharing the broad outlines of a dilemma and the nature of the principles in conflict. Privacy, embarrassment, shame, pride, and fear are all understandable reasons to resist obtaining input in solving leadership dilemmas. However, the failure to seek and use expertise is negligent because the individual's comfort is put ahead of the organization's needs.

Documentation is an essential element of risk management. The old adage "if it isn't written down, it didn't happen" applies here. Personal notes, meeting minutes, and case records are all venues for recording the options considered and discarded, advice received, and processes used in reaching a decision in an ethical dilemma. When cases are precedent-setting, such records help create the foundation for congruent future decisions. If decisions come under scrutiny or litigation, contemporaneous documentation demonstrates that thoughtful processes were used to come to or reflect upon an ethical dilemma. It spells out the tradeoffs and principles brought to bear in choosing one direction over another. Reluctance to keep records and supporting documentation about a decision, its rationale, and the process by which it was made raises red flags about integrity and transparency. The principle of publicity asks the decision maker "Would you be comfortable if others knew about your decision—could it withstand the light of day?" Decisions that can't withstand the principle of publicity should raise red flags.

Evaluation involves attention to the intended and unintended consequences of an ethical decision. Was the outcome what was expected? If so, to what can that be attributed: luck, the decision process, execution? If the outcome was not what was expected, can anything be done to remedy the situation and prevent a recurrence? Because ethical dilemmas sometimes involve a choice among multiple objectionable alternatives, evaluation cannot rest on the quality of the outcome alone. It must also address process. Were the right people involved? Were relevant facts and viewpoints weighted appropriately? Were consequences accurately anticipated? Were harms mitigated and benefits maximized? Were strategies for carrying out the decision used effectively?

Evaluation, documentation, and consultation go hand-in-hand. They not only address the immediate dilemma, but they also build capacity for more easily addressing future dilemmas.

Sometimes, the use of models such as this will identify an ideal solution to the dilemma at hand. At other times, though, the result is improved clarity rather than consensus. That is, the process generates options and illuminates the risks and benefits of each, but, ultimately, it is incumbent on the users to weigh the pros and cons to select and implement the one that they judge best. The model supplies the support and rationale for the given choice but not the choice itself.

What About WholeHealth?

At the outset of the chapter, we identified four options for Hal and Helen in ethically dealing with the improperly obtained bid information, though savvy readers may generate still other possibilities. Two choices involve acknowledging the error; one of these would place the blame on the worker who took the data, and in the other, the organization takes responsibility. In the third option, WholeHealth would destroy the information and exclude those who possess the information from further bid negotiations. The final alternative would have WholeHealth use the information for their strategic advantage.

How do the options stack up when weighed by ethical principles and standards, policies, and laws? The fourth choice, using the information, is clearly the least desirable. Although the organization may value competitiveness and financial success, it should not come at the cost of integrity, honesty, and legality. The message sent (of winning at any cost) would have destructive consequences for WholeHealth if applied to any situation, and the use of the bid itself could be ruinous to the organization if the act were ultimately revealed.

Similar concerns apply to the decision to admit the mistake but attribute it to the workers involved. Certainly, those involved in taking and copying the information should be held accountable, but making them the scapegoats to save the organization violates principles of fairness, honesty, and trustworthiness. We don't know enough about WholeHealth to determine if such censure is congruent with the organization's values or policies. Blaming the individual workers may send a message that WholeHealth does not tolerate deceit, but it may also send a message that the agency will not stand behind its workers when they are doing something in good faith that they believe coincides with the agency's interests.

If WholeHealth admits that the documents were taken and copied, it would certainly be upholding principles of honesty, fairness, and trustworthiness. It might be exposing itself to legal sanctions for theft of the information, but it certainly would better position itself by being forthright in revealing the misdeed. The consequences of acknowledging the bid copying are hard to judge. Revealing it may damage WholeHealth's reputation and jeopardize receipt of the current and future contracts, to the detriment of staff, patients, and the organization as a whole. On the other hand, forthrightness may play into WholeHealth's favor, identifying them as an organization willing to take the moral high road, admit errors, and do what is needed to correct those errors. In this, it might renew or strengthen the confidence of funders, patients, and the public. It would also send employees a powerful message from the top about the company's values.

Deciding not to reveal the information, but rather to mitigate the damage, presents advantages and disadvantages. It upholds the principle of fairness in the bidding process while not being wholly truthful or trustworthy in doing so. It protects WholeHealth from the damage that might arise from revealing improper behavior. As long as it remains a secret, the misuse of the bid and efforts to address it would have no effect on WholeHealth's employees, patients, or reputation. However, keeping a secret is difficult. As often happens in scandals, efforts to contain the information may create greater damage than the initial error. If the bid copying is revealed at a later date, it could cast doubt on WholeHealth's integrity and on whether the organization *really* avoided using the ill-gotten information. Legal and financial penalties might ensue, and it would be too late for WholeHealth to regain the high ground.

Assessing the options reveals that all have pros and cons, though some have greater disadvantages than others. The process for implementing the selected path should be part of future discussions: If the theft is to be revealed, who should be told? How? When? By whom? Hal and Helen must begin their consultation with the CEO, who should then involve the board chair. The two predominant leaders will likely relieve Hal and Helen from responsibility for the decision but might well seek their input throughout the process. The CEO and president should also consult with legal counsel, other board members, and staff responsible for communications and marketing. These discussions will help identify the legal implications of taking the bid, add new dimensions in weighing options, identify new options, and devise a strategy for rolling out (or containing) any information about the ethical dilemma. Individuals involved in the case may also seek personal advice and assistance from legal experts, spiritual leaders, mentors, or other trusted consultants. This is particularly vital if those charged with making the decision disagree about the direction to take. Dissent about the ultimate decision may create an irretrievable breach among those involved. Sometimes these fissures heal with time, but in other instances, people "vote with their feet" and leave rather than accede to a direction they find unwise or morally bankrupt.

The individuals involved should keep personal records of their conversations, advice, and inclinations in the case. Similarly, all should be involved in evaluations of the ultimate outcome, examining the wisdom and durability of the decision, the strategy employed for carrying it out, the intended and unintended consequences, and the lessons learned. Even cases that end in tragedy and scandal can be instructive to other leaders and NPOs that aspire to ethical and successful management.

Conclusion

NPOs, their board members, executives, and staff are governed by an array of legal and ethical obligations. Failure to adhere to these obligations can put individual careers and the enterprise as a whole at risk. Each NPO should promulgate a code of conduct and designate a compliance officer to ensure adherence to policies and laws. In addition, each individual must bear responsibility for personal integrity, sound judgment, and fair dealing. NPOs can enhance the adherence and ethical action by promulgating a systematic process for decision-making. One such framework is suggested and applied in this chapter. Numerous resources exist for increasing ethical and legal capacities at NPOs. These are discussed in chapter 11 and on our website, www.nonprofitboardresource.com.

Chapter 4

When Management and the Governing Board Disagree

Martin is an investment banker. His firm encourages partners to become involved in the local nonprofit community and in service projects. Because of this and his interest in eradicating child abuse, he agreed to his nomination for the board of a local family violence prevention agency. The nonprofit was excited, too. The executive director and board president were eager to bolster the "money know-how" on the board and anticipated that Martin might be willing to serve as treasurer in the future. In the meantime, they assigned him to the Finance and Investments Subcommittee (FIS). At the first meeting of the FIS, Martin was astonished to find that the agency had exclusively allocated its investments to highly restrictive socially responsible funds. Although his plan had been to be a silent "learner" until he got more familiar with the board, he could not contain his discomfort. "Look, I'm all for socially responsible investing, but you also have to look at return on investment and diversification. You are missing a lot of opportunities for income that you sorely need. It seems irresponsible to stick with this investment plan."

Martin's lecture was met with silence, but the air was filled with the unspoken reactions of others around the table. One committee member thought, "Who the hell does this guy think he is, coming in here and telling us what to do?" Another thought, "This is the classic corporate patriarchy! I don't know why we keep recruiting these people for our board. They just don't get what we're about." Still another thought, "Good luck, buddy. I've already tried that. It's like hitting your head against a wall." The executive director and subcommittee chair both winced. They privately agreed with his position but knew he was taking on a sacred cow that had consumed the board's deliberations for over a year. On the other hand, maybe his position would help tip the scales toward change that had eluded the FIS thus far.

As in most areas of life, opportunities for conflict abound in the nonprofit sector. Board members may disagree with one another about CEO candidates, new initiatives, or assuming a particular level of financial risk. Members of the management team may clash with each other about strategic directions, budget priorities, or recessionary cuts. Board members and paid staff may conflict over fundraising prospects, organizational growth, or the cultivation of new board members. "Conflict may be defined as a struggle or contest between or among individuals with opposing needs, ideas, beliefs, values, or goals.... Conflict exists even if only one person perceives it."[1]

Although there are limitless possibilities when it comes to the parties and issues that give rise to disputes, the strategies for dealing with them follow only a few well-worn paths:

- Concerns go unaddressed but are raised in private conversations, creating distrust and subterranean alliances. These coalitions and disingenuous communications affect group functioning in the short term and can create lasting schisms that affect team performance.

- Conflicts are avoided, but then they erupt in new forms unrelated to the issues at hand. The group then focuses on the immediate issue and misses (or avoids) the chance to address the deeper, underlying conflict.

- Difficult issues are raised but are belittled, papered over, or discussed at length with no apparent resolution. The spokesperson is eventually marginalized as a malcontent, idealist, stick-in-the-mud, bleeding heart, or partisan.

- In an effort to maintain harmony, conflicts are avoided. Members focus on areas of consensus and avoid difficult decisions. There is a superficial feeling of comfort often to the detriment of the organization.

- Difficult questions and topics are raised in the proper time and setting, issues are aired, members are heard, options are considered, and decisions are made in keeping with the board's agreed-upon practices.

How can organizations such as Martin's move from conflict avoidance to conflict management? How can difficult conversations be initiated to foster the best possible outcome in the event of disagreements? And ultimately, what options exist to address schisms that arise between elected and appointed nonprofit leaders? This chapter draws on the literature on intrapersonal and interpersonal perspectives on conflict to help the reader weigh options and strategies for successfully resolving governance conflicts. The dilemma facing Martin may also be construed as one of strategic change management, inviting the use of other concepts and tools for resolution. These strategies are introduced and applied in chapter 10.

The Head Game

Why are conflicts so often avoided or mismanaged? To paraphrase the comic strip Pogo, "sometimes the enemy is us." Most of us are simply conflict averse. Conflicts create friction and tension when we would much prefer friendliness, warmth, and ease in our relationships. Conflicts are uncomfortable. They create stress, trigger fear, and ignite our competitive urges. Addressing conflicts head on can invoke negative stereotypes and labels: the complainer, the nit- picker, the contrarian, the person who just couldn't leave well enough alone. Although the title of this chapter is "When Management and the Governing Board Disagree,"

---

1 Nancy E. Algert and Christine A. Stanley, "Conflict Management," *Effective Practices for Academic Leaders*, vol. 2, iss. 9 (Stylus Publishing, 2007) p. 1–16.

at their essence these are disagreements between *people*, and thus they are unavoidably personal and laden with meaning. The classic response to conflict is "fight or flight,"[2] though Algert and Stanley cite research that indicates women may be predisposed to a "tend and befriend" response instead. Conflicts cannot be avoided, and even with outstanding skills, they may persist. The key is to develop the mindset and abilities needed to manage them and keep them from exacting a destructive toll on the work of the organization or unit.

Beyond acknowledging the ways in which conflict itself is a deterrent to action, a second part of the head game involves understanding our individual responses to conflict. Thomas and Killman developed a classic instrument for appraising conflict management styles across axes of assertiveness and cooperation.[3]

Most individuals have a dominant or preferred approach for addressing conflict, and those approaches tend to cluster in one of five styles. Each style presents particular strengths and weaknesses, suggesting that we should consciously select and use a style for a particular situation, rather than default to the one that comes most naturally. For example, a *competitive* approach, in which one "pulls rank" or forthrightly states a position and stalwartly defends it, is most appropriate for high stakes conflicts or unpopular decisions.[4] At the other end of the continuum, *avoidance* may be the preferred strategy for insignificant issues, "no-win" situations, or instances when the timing is not right to take a stand. It is distinct from *accommodation*, in which one party concedes a point to keep the peace or to achieve a higher purpose or a longer term objective. *Compromise* involves a give and take, in which common ground is sought and each party settles for less than he or she might have hoped. In contrast, *collaboration* builds upon each party's wishes and ideas, creating an outcome that is greater than the sum of the original positions.

Finally, beyond being aware of the antipathy toward conflict and the preferred style for managing it, each of us must be attuned to our own hot buttons and biases. Hot buttons are those statements and situations that trigger a disproportionate emotional response in us. Biases are our prejudices, presumptions, and preferences (some examined, some not) that influence the positions we take and the meaning we give them. The perceived put down, the loaded issue, the colleague who grates on our nerves, and the subordinate for whom we are willing to go the extra mile are all artifacts of our experiences, and they play themselves out in the present.

Self-regulation starts with self-understanding. Be attuned to the moments that incite intense reactions in you and examine their deeper meaning. What rests behind your response? What does the incident symbolize? Are you prone to attribute negative motives to others? Do you see any patterns in your reactions—distrust, sympathy, harsh judgments, rescuing, or pessimism? Next, enlist the help of others. Who among your trusted others (mentor, colleague, supervisor, partner, pastor, coach, or therapist) would be forthright in sharing insights about your blind spots and helpful to you in working on them? Develop a repertoire

---

2 Nancy E. Algert and Christine A. Stanley, "Conflict Management," *Effective Practices for Academic Leaders*, vol. 2, iss. 9 (Stylus Publishing, 2007) p. 1–16.

3 Kenneth W. Thomas and Ralph H. Kilmann, *The Thomas-Kilmann Conflict Mode Instrument* (Palo Alto: CPP, Inc., 1974).

4 Nancy E. Algert and Christine A. Stanley, "Conflict Management," *Effective Practices for Academic Leaders*, vol. 2, iss. 9 (Stylus Publishing, 2007) p. 1–16.

of alternative responses when you feel a bias creeping in or a button being pushed: count to 10, breathe deeply, manage physiologic responses, remind yourself that the outcome matters, or recite a mantra like "Calm. Connected." Conflicts are often, by their very nature, high stakes situations. To effectively handle them, we must be at our best to call upon and use our skills and strategies to reach an effective resolution.

Communication

Effective communication skills are necessary to bridge the gulf that divides individuals in conflict. Although persuasive arguments or compelling oration are fine abilities, other communication abilities are more important for managing difference. These include active listening, reflection, empathy, inquiry, and self-involving statements. These can then be bundled into models to facilitate difficult discussions.

Most people speak better than they listen (and *more than* they listen). Even when we think we are listening, we are often constructing our reply or playing a tape ("I *knew* that's how he'd react" or "If she thinks I'm buying that excuse again, she's mistaken"). Both responses keep us from truly hearing what the other person is saying. *Active listening* requires open posture, attentive eye contact, and careful listening, both for what is said and for what is not said. It means creating the space of time and silence to allow people to get past the superficial to the meaningful. It requires patience to let others' positions, concerns, and feeling unfold without interruption.

Active listening is demonstrated and augmented by reflection, empathy, and inquiry. *Reflection* involves restating what you heard the other say, thereby checking for accuracy and demonstrating attention. "So you see investing in socially responsible funds as an expression of our mission for social change." *Empathy* involves hearing the other's underlying message and feelings and being able to put them into words. It is akin to putting yourself in the other's shoes. "It sounds like you worry that FIS is being hypocritical by investing in goods that contribute to the injury of women." Active listening is also advanced by earnest *inquiry*. Questions are used to enhance dialogue and expand understanding. In this, open-ended questions are more generally more effective than closed (yes or no) questions, which can seem accusatory ("What industries would you rule out for investments?" versus "Do you object to investing in corporations that make alcohol?"). The communication skill of *confrontation* differs from the typical definition, which implies anger and argument. In this context, confrontation is a form of inquiry. It means calmly presenting contrasting messages in an effort to seek clarification ("You've said you are worried about the stability of our endowment, and you've also said you want high risk, low yield investments"). A final salient skill is the use of *self-involving statements*. In these, the speaker owns a position, concern, or feeling. "I'm discouraged that we keep revisiting this topic at each meeting without progress" or "I'm worried that we're violating our fiduciary responsibility in making this decision without current data."

It is crucial to note here the importance of regulated emotions and, related to them, tone of voice. Conflicts incite intense physiologic reactions. The failure to manage these, along with the emotions and cognitions that give rise to them, will undermine effective, constructive communications. And of course, tone is everything. You can summarize a position in a snappish tone or in a tentative one. A question can be posed in a curious tone or as a cross-examination. Empathy can be sincere or superficial. Self-involving statements can be offered with humility or domination. Confrontation can be curious or, well, confrontational.

A number of excellent texts are available to help leaders master high stakes interpersonal communications. They address the internal and external elements of conflict resolution and offer memorable frameworks for successfully utilizing communication skills. One example is "Situation-Behavior-Impact."[5] This strategy requires description of the event, the behavior observed, and the effect it had on others. For example, "When we were discussing investment options, you turned away and started checking messages on your phone, and the rest of us felt disrespected and dismissed." An alternative recommended by Patterson, et al., is "Content-Pattern-Relationship."[6] In this, an event is linked to past events and the future health of the relationship. "This is the third meeting in a row in which we have discussed the investments without any progress. I'm concerned that people are checking out of the conversations and losing their confidence in the board." These techniques are used to greatest effect when linked to change strategies,[7] which are addressed in depth in chapter 10.

A final significant element in communication requires avoiding detrimental communication skills. This involves more than simply eschewing incendiary statements and postures. Scott identified five errors,[8] commonly made with the best of intentions, that diminish the power of the message and the success of the sender. The first error is beating around the bush instead of calmly and clearly addressing the concern. Asking, "How do you think things are going between us?" rather than saying, "I'm concerned that you and I seem unable to agree on anything in our meetings" presents a false and deceptive opening that masks the true intentions of the conversation. In the second error, "the sugarcoated spitball," the key issue is sandwiched between two compliments.[9] This both obscures the central concern and demeans all future compliments as simply a prelude to complaint. Similarly, with "too many pillows," the message is softened to the point where the intent is lost.[10] In the fourth error, the speaker is so consumed by internal dialogue and expectations about how the conversation will proceed that he or she responds to that script instead of the conversation itself. As a result, statements are mechanistic or defensive in anticipation of reactions that have yet to occur. In the final scenario, "Machine Gun Nelly" unloads on the listener as a result of anxiety or a pent-up series of grievances, which fails to differentiate concerns or allow for reaction or damage control.[11]

---

5 Sloan R. Weitzel, *Feedback That Works: How to Build and Deliver Your Message* (Center for Creative Leadership, 2003). Retrieved from www.ccl.org/leadership/pdf/publications/readers/reader405ccl.pdf.

6 Kerry Patterson, Joseph Grenny, Ron McMillan, and Al Switzler, *Crucial confrontations: Tools for talking about broken promises, violated expectations, and bad behavior* (New York: McGraw-Hill, 2004).

7 Kerry Patterson, Joseph Grenny, David Maxfield, Ron McMillan, Al Switzler, *Influencer: The Power to Change Anything* (New York: McGraw-Hill, 2008).

8 Susan Scott, *Fierce conversations: Achieving Success at Work & in Life, One Conversation at a Time* (New York: Berkeley, 2004).

9 Susan Scott, *Fierce conversations: Achieving Success at Work & in Life, One Conversation at a Time* (New York: Berkeley, 2004) p. 143.

10 Susan Scott, *Fierce conversations: Achieving Success at Work & in Life, One Conversation at a Time* (New York: Berkeley, 2004) p. 144.

11 Susan Scott, *Fierce conversations: Achieving Success at Work & in Life, One Conversation at a Time* (New York: Berkeley, 2004) p. 147.

Constructive Norms

Successful conflict resolution in nonprofit organizations (NPOs) involves more than effective individual communications. It also requires a climate that supports respect, transparency, and straightforward treatment of differences. Several strategies help to foster positive norms in regard to conflict. Orientation for new board and staff members should address the organization's values; policies regarding respect, diversity, and other matters; the expectations associated with various roles in the organizations; the short-term and long-range goals of the organization; and the processes for change.

Some organizations have articulated codes of ethics that specify expectations for employee and volunteer conduct. These documents serve multiple purposes. They set forth an expectation of integrity and fair practices, mitigate risk, enhance public image, create a culture set on "doing the right thing," and provide guidance about steps to take when violations occur.[12, 13] Regardless of whether an organization has such a code, individual units can adopt standards or ground rules for their operations. Algert and Stanley offer one such "Code of Cooperation for the Management Team:

1. Remember that every member is responsible for the team's progress and success.
2. Listen to and show respect for the contributions of other members.
3. Criticize ideas, not persons.
4. Do not allow hidden agendas.
5. Do not allow collusion.
6. Strive for consensus.
7. Resolve conflicts constructively.
8. Pay attention; avoid disruptive behavior.
9. Avoid disruptive side conversations.
10. Allow only one person to speak at a time.
11. Ensure that everyone participates and that no one dominates.
12. Be succinct; avoid long anecdotes and examples.
13. Understand that pulling rank is not allowed.
14. Attend to your personal comfort needs at any time but minimize team disruption..."[14]

Boards, teams, departments, and other groups can also create their own ground rules. Rather than simply offering a list of guidelines and asking for the group's endorsement, thorough conversation about the rules and how they will be implemented can help members consider and internalize the expectations. For example, what does "confidentiality" mean? Does it mean that no one on the board talks about the organization outside the meetings? That seems draconian and at odds with the role of the board as ambassadors of the NPO. Does it mean that no one will discuss what happens in meetings? How then will decisions and context be explained to new members or those who missed a given

---

12 Steven Barth, *Corporate Ethics: How to Update or Develop Your Ethics Code so That it is in Compliance With the New Laws of Corporate Responsibility* (Boston: Aspatore, 2003).

13 Patrick E. Murphy (Ed.), Eighty Exemplary Ethics Statements (Notre Dame: University of Notre Dame Press, 1998).

14 Nancy E. Algert and Christine A. Stanley, "Conflict Management," *Effective Practices for Academic Leaders*, vol. 2, iss. 9 (Stylus Publishing, 2007) p. 1–16.

meeting? Will viewpoints be shared without attribution? Will members be encouraged to share their personal insights and viewpoints outside the meeting but not those of other members? Might this lead to inappropriate communications about proprietary or sensitive information affecting the NPO? In any given group, the individual interpretations of confidentiality could vary along these lines. Systematic and detailed discussion clarifies divergent viewpoints and encourages buy-in.

After such rules are set, the group should revisit them regularly to avoid drift and evaluate the extent to which practices actually conform to the group's intentions. Some boards will highlight their code or ground rules by posting them or having a distinct (laminated) sheet in each member's packet. Others review the guidelines at the end of each meeting and ask for written, verbal, or electronic feedback about the climate and content of the meeting.[15]

A final element in creating constructive norms about conflict has to do with the actions of those in power. Leaders (both formal and informal) play a role in both shaping the organizational culture and sustaining it. That is, by their actions they create a safe place for disagreement, model civil discourse, and remind others of the values and ground rules that guide the group. They can make observations about the communications taking place in the group and shape the *process* of discussions as well as the *content*. When leaders neglect this role or, worse, act in a contrary manner, they still shape group culture but in a manner in which conflict is mishandled.

Negotiation

Fisher, Ury, and Patton[16] offer several recommendations for successfully negotiating the end to conflicts. The first is to avoid positional bargaining. When disagreeing parties stake out entrenched positions, it is difficult to then move toward agreement because any compromise is perceived as a loss. Further, the outcome or agreement may be achieved at the expense of the ongoing relationship and future cooperation.

The second step in successful bargaining is to "separate the people from the problem." This involves separating the relationship or interpersonal issues from the substantive differences between the parties. To be successful, a negotiator must listen well and put himself or herself in the other's place, perceiving the situation from that perspective without making presumptions based on his or her own fears and biases. This may be accomplished by inquiry and by seizing opportunities to defy negative expectations. If a veteran board member anticipates being challenged by the newcomer about the investment policy, the adept newcomer would empathize with the difficulties in crafting an investment strategy and ask the veteran his or her ideas about making it a less arduous process in the future. "Imbedded in this strategy are the skills of being in touch with one's own emotions, not reacting defensively when others express strong emotions, and communicating in a non–judgmental and non–inflammatory manner. When dealing with difficult people over difficult problems, the temptation is to avoid them at all costs. Symbolically, this raises difficulties in bridging

---

15 Ron Charan, *Owning Up: The 14 Questions Every Board Member Needs to Ask* (San Francisco: Wiley, 2009).

16 Roger Fisher, William Ury, and Bruce Patton, B. *Getting to Yes: Negotiating Agreement Without Giving In.* (New York: Penguin, 1991).

the emotional barriers between the parties, and it raises practical difficulties because people are naturally suspicious if they feel they haven't had sufficient input into a given plan. When the urge is to withdraw, the best strategy is to reach out."[17]

The third step involves moving from positions to interests. This requires taking proactive steps to find existing areas of agreement, uncover different but complementary needs, and recognize multiple interests so that areas of disagreement are minimized and a greater range of possible, mutually satisfying outcomes can be reached. It involves looking behind the positions of each participant and behind the emotions and statements to ask the questions *why* and *why not*. "Why is it important to invest in socially responsible funds?" "Why won't she support other investments?" "What interests of hers stand in the way of saying yes to my suggestion?" "If she agrees to my request, what are the possibilities for her? What if she says no?"

A deeper look behind Martin's position might reveal his concern for the costs of selective investing and the poor rate of return, especially for a small agency with few resources and such a vital mission. The veteran board member's interests may reveal that she fears FIS will appear hypocritical if it supports violent and unhealthy industries, and that she thinks scarce resources shouldn't be used to invest in industries that harm, on a large scale, the women FIS serves. In this case, the concern for FIS's clients is shared by both parties. Both are also interested in wise use of scarce resources. Based on these mutual and complementary interests, they might agree to look at data on the different funds available to see if any maximize return while avoiding troubling industries. They might also consider other ways for FIS to exercise its social change ideals apart from its investment strategy. Perhaps the additional dividends from a better performing fund could be used to support social change efforts. These might ultimately have a greater impact than withholding a meager endowment from a particular mutual fund.

The fourth step in the negotiation process involves inventing options for mutual gain and avoiding premature solutions. This does not mean that mutually acceptable agreements should be deferred but that it is dangerous to offer premature criticism and premature closure. As Fisher, et al., put it, "Judgment hinders imagination."[18] The discomfort of disagreement can lead either party to accept the first viable option, if only to draw the conflict to a close. Agreeing to forestall a decision and to make a concerted effort to generate a range of possibilities helps keep participants from viewing the negotiation as a zero-sum game and allows innovative, mutually beneficial options to emerge.

The fifth element in negotiating conflicts involves the selection and use of objective criteria with which to evaluate the options generated. A board member and CEO may be in disagreement about the appropriate deployment of endowment funds, but such impasses can be unblocked if the parties can agree to external standards to determine their course of action. For example, they might agree to research the investment recommendations of similar agencies, their local coalition of providers, or their national association and consider those in

---

17 Kimberly J. Strom-Gottfried, "The use of conflict resolution techniques in managed care disputes," *Social Work*, vol. 43, 1998, p. 393–401.

18 Roger Fisher, William Ury, and Bruce Patton, B. *Getting to Yes: Negotiating Agreement Without Giving In.* (New York: Penguin, 1991) p. 58.

making FIS decisions. In light of the varied holdings of multinational corporations, it might be difficult to achieve the purity in social investments desired by some on the board. Therefore, the board might agree to a balance between a reasonable rate of return and an acceptable type of investment. Discussing and setting these tolerance thresholds externalizes the benchmark away from individual board members and places it on agreed upon standards.

A final suggestion in difficult negotiations involves the use of "negotiation jujitsu,"[19] wherein one negotiator embraces the other's positions rather than resisting them. In some ways this strategy is the culmination and integration of all the preceding recommendations. The skills for this step include asking questions, being open to correction, using silence, looking behind opposing proposals, and inviting criticism of your own proposal. Martin might approach the reviewer in the following ways (and remember that tone is everything!):

> "I appreciate your concern that FIS support social causes congruent with our mission."

> "I agree that it's important to be true to our organizational values in everything we do. Are there some areas besides investments in which that is difficult to do?"

> "What do you see as the shortcomings of more robust investments?"

> "I'm concerned about FIS's finances, as I know you are. How did that play in to the investment strategy?"

> "Can we agree on a plan that will maximize the use of our funds without betraying our mission?"

Beyond the steps in conflict resolution process, Fisher, et al., recommend that each party develop his or her BATNA ("best alternative to a negotiated agreement"), which serves as a basis by which to evaluate options.[20] Establishing a BATNA requires thinking carefully about what will happen if the parties can't reach a negotiated agreement and simultaneously serves as an impetus to engage in a process to reach such an agreement. Thus, establishing a "no agreement" position involves analyzing the alternatives at one's disposal if agreement isn't reached and anticipating what the other side's default position might be.[21] If Martin and the others fail to find a mutually agreeable alternative, what are each person's best possible options? For Martin, it might be to accept the investment plan limitation for the time being and work on it as a longer term change process. Alternatively, he may feel that the decision is so flawed that he can no longer serve on the board. The BATNA for board members who favor socially responsible funds is that status quo. Clearly, not reaching an agreement hurts Martin more than the veteran board members. This illustrates the fact that the better one's "no agreement" alternatives are the more power they have in the dispute. In fact, the quality of one's BATNA may determine whether he or she is willing to negotiate at all.

It is important to recognize that BATNAs are not static. Negotiators can take steps to improve their options and shift the balance of power. For example, if Martin decides to defer

---

19 Roger Fisher, William Ury, and Bruce Patton, B. *Getting to Yes: Negotiating Agreement Without Giving In.* (New York: Penguin, 1991) p. 193.

20 Roger Fisher, William Ury, and Bruce Patton, B. *Getting to Yes: Negotiating Agreement Without Giving In.* (New York: Penguin, 1991).

21 David A. Lax and James K. Sebenius, *The Manager as Negotiator: Bargaining for Cooperation and Competitive Gain* (New York: Free Press, 1986).

the battle over investments to a later time, in the interim he may accrue more legitimacy as an important, knowledgeable contributor to the board. His increased stature may move others to his position or make the risk of his resignation a more troubling prospect. External conditions can also alter non-cooperative alternatives. Failing endowments, court cases alleging NPO boards with lax financial oversight, and other events may shift the power to Martin's position and away from the status quo. The issues of power and power differentials are addressed at length in chapter 10.

Assisted Resolution

Sometimes, conflicts are so entrenched or serious that they require assistance from an outside party for successful resolution. Alternative dispute resolution (ADR) refers to options that rest outside of the legal system and are alternatives to legal remedies. The two most common strategies are mediation and arbitration. Participation in either can be compulsory or voluntary, and their results can be binding or nonbinding. In both models, a neutral third party gathers data, hears positions, and identifies common goals. Mediators may also address the emotional elements of the dispute and help the parties to better communicate, thus facilitating better conflict resolution in the future. Some mediators may suggest novel solutions to entrenched problems and encourage the parties to do the same. The primary difference in the ADR models is that the mediator's role is to help the disputants find common ground and a mutually acceptable outcome. Arbitration results in a ruling or decision by the third party rather than by the individuals in conflict.

There are a number of advantages in ADR; perhaps foremost among them is the effort to preserve the relationship between the parties while crafting a practical outcome that is responsive to their respective interests. The disadvantages can arise when one party is not behaving honestly or sharing all pertinent information. ADR is also compromised when one party is passive or easily intimidated by the other.

NPOs may engage third parties to assist with a variety of challenging issues with the hope of avoiding or addressing conflict. Consultants may assist leadership with strategic planning, compensation studies, merger and acquisition decisions, and other matters. An ombudsman's services may be invited to deal with ethical issues, interpersonal frictions, or staff-management disputes. Some consultants and ombudsmen can facilitate negotiations and mediate disputes, or the NPO may retain specially trained mediators to assist with conflicts.

Conclusion

Despite his best intentions, Martin may have violated committee norms from the outset by speaking up forcefully as a newcomer on the board. As such, he may have alienated other, powerful members and discouraged possible allies from speaking up. If his intent is to encourage the committee to reconsider its investment plan, he must begin by healing the rift from his initial meeting. Many of the skills and strategies advised in the preceding paragraphs would serve him well. First, he must apologize, acknowledge that the other committee members have a far deeper history with the issue than he, and adopt a stance of inquiry to learn about the positions of others and the options they have considered in the past. He should also allow time for the committee members to get to know him. As they understand his concerns, intentions, expertise, and dedication to FIS, his input will have more value. If Martin's concerns about the investment priorities continue, explicit change strategies (chapter 10), negotiation, or mediation may be required in order to bring the conflict to a successful end.

Martin may also face a common question that plagues conflict resolution: "Is it worth it?" To answer this, one must consider the alternatives. Conflict resolution strategies are well regarded for use in a variety of situations in which the emotional, financial, and personal stakes are high, such as divorce, child custody, and victim and offender confrontations. The alternatives to attempting collaborative agreement are unpleasant: harboring feelings of anger, frustration and powerlessness, having to invest further energies as disputes crop up in another form, or withdrawing from disagreements altogether and just "doing time." The last option is a dangerous precursor to burnout and an abdication of the individual's ethical and legal responsibilities to the organization. As a volunteer, Martin has the option of resigning entirely from the board. This may seem like an easier path than addressing conflict or being a passive member of the board. Unfortunately, leaving in the midst of a dispute may prove unsatisfying and ultimately more troubling than staying to work it out. If he resigns, can Martin really let go of his concern for FIS's decisions? Even if Martin can resign with a clear conscience, quitting may be in his interests but not in FIS's. Conflict is a part of everyday existence. Family life, corporate life, and civic life all rely on the ability to bridge differences of opinion and the willingness to try. Sometimes, it is necessary to vote with one's feet, but resignation at the first sign of resistance diminishes the individual and the systems of which he or she is a part.

Chapter 5

Understanding the Financial Statements of Nonprofit Organizations

Lauren Gibbs put down the phone and smiled. After her retirement, one of her goals was to become involved with a nonprofit organization whose mission was preserving the environment. And this call gave her a golden opportunity. A nonprofit with such a mission asked her to be the chair of its audit committee. Lauren looked at this as an opportunity to contribute to her favorite cause, and the nonprofit looked at her as the ideal board member. Lauren had an MBA and until her retirement was an executive in a consulting firm. In addition, she had a depth of knowledge about the environment and a passion for excellence.

The problem was that she knew very little about nonprofits and the legal, regulatory, and other issues facing them in 2010. She also was not familiar with nonprofit financial statements. She thought a few minutes about the responsibility she had taken on. Just because she wasn't an expert in these areas didn't mean she couldn't become one. All she needed was a little guidance. She picked up the phone again and called a friend to ask for help.

A nonprofit organization needs focused expertise in its executives and on its board of directors. Frequently, those people who serve as executives and board members have a passion for the mission but less enthusiasm and interest in the financial, legal, and regulatory side of the organization. Although it is commendable that nonprofits exist to provide services to those in need and that board members make contributions in their various areas of expertise, it is also important to remember that a nonprofit has a fiduciary responsibility to its funding sources and the community to be a prudent steward of those resources. This will require executives and board members to spend the time, effort, and financial resources to obtain the necessary expertise and to implement systems to ensure regulatory compliance, accurate financial reporting, and good stewardship of the organization's assets. This chapter addresses these challenges by providing a look at the basic information that a board member or non-financial executive needs to know.

Characteristics of Nonprofits

Nonprofit organizations vary in their missions but share three characteristics that are present in varying degrees and that distinguish them from investor-owned entities or entities like credit unions and similar membership organizations:

1. They receive contributions of resources.
2. They provide goods and services, or both, for reasons other than to make a profit.
3. There are no ownership interests (other than as a subsidiary of another nonprofit).

The absence of ownership interests is by far the most important condition of its tax exempt status. As defined by the Internal Revenue Code, "no part of the net earnings of the organization may inure to the benefit of any private shareholder or individual...."[1] Because nonprofits do not have shareholders in the general sense, the regulations define the term as "a person having a personal and private interest in the activities of the organization."[2] Effectively, this covers anyone who has anything other than an arm's length relationship with the nonprofit.

Nonprofit organizations range from cemeteries to zoological societies. Many of them are charitable, educational, cultural, or religious organizations. The accounting and reporting for these organizations are very similar. The accounting and reporting are somewhat different for nonprofit health care organizations that provide medical services because these organizations are frequently compared to commercial entities.

Responsibility for Financial Information

Management is responsible for the content of the organization's financial information including adopting sound accounting policies. In addition, it should establish and maintain controls over the authorization, recording, processing, and reporting of transactions and events. The board of directors or trustees is responsible for management oversight. The degree of oversight depends largely on the size, complexity, and resources of the organization. Smaller organizations with fewer and less knowledgeable employees may require more oversight, and those organizations with more knowledgeable employees may require less. It is important to note that the oversight responsibility remains the same regardless of the individual characteristics of the organization.

The Committee of Sponsoring Organizations (COSO) is a voluntary private-sector organization originally established in 1985 to sponsor the National Commission on Fraudulent Financial Reporting in response to the Foreign Corrupt Practices Act. Its mission is to provide guidance to executives and boards on ethics, governance, internal control, fraud, and financial reporting. To do this, COSO created a framework that organizations can use for designing and implementing policies and procedures to safeguard the assets of the organization and prevent or detect misstatement of financial information, whether due to fraud or error. This helps not only to provide a vehicle for executives and board members to execute

---

1 Retrieved from www.irs.gov/irb/2005-42_IRB/ar11.html on April 16, 2011.
2 Treas. Reg. §1.501(a)–1(e).

their fiduciary responsibilities, but also to protect the assets, including the reputation, of the organization.

Understanding how to do the follow will provide nonfinancial executives and board members with the tools to effectively carry out their respective roles. In this and subsequent chapters, we address each of these competencies:

- Read financial statements
- Analyze the information and assess risk in the organization **(described in detail in chapter 6)**
- Evaluate the **organization**'s internal control structure for financial reporting **(described in detail in chapter 7)**
- Protect the organization's tax exempt status **(described in more detail in chapter 8)**

Basis of Presentation for Financial Information

Financial statements are prepared using accounting principles. These principles spell out the accounting for transactions and dictate the required disclosures in published financial statements. Most nonprofits will use the

- cash basis of accounting (which reports the flow of cash in the organization),
- modified cash basis of accounting (which generally mirrors the informational tax return), or the
- accrual basis of accounting.

Funding sources may dictate the basis of accounting.

Cash Basis of Accounting Versus Accrual Basis

Accounting principles that are generally accepted in the United States of America are referred to as generally accepted accounting principles (GAAP). GAAP consists of accounting pronouncements that for commercial entities and nonprofits were promulgated by the Financial Accounting Standards Board (FASB).[3] The accrual method, as prescribed by GAAP, requires that revenue be recorded when earned and expenses when incurred. Nonprofits earn revenue when they provide goods or services for a fee. The fee may or may not be the price that could be charged in a commercial environment. They also are considered to have "earned" revenue when they receive contributions or a promise to receive contributions. This is not an earnings process like one would see in a commercial entity because contributions are nonreciprocal. However, contribution revenue is recognized when donations are made. Contributions will be more fully discussed subsequently in this chapter.

However, not all financial statements are prepared on a GAAP basis. Some smaller nonprofits prepare their statements on the cash basis of accounting. This means that revenue is recorded when it is received and expenses are recorded when they are paid. This method does not take into consideration that an organization may earn revenue but not have

---

3 Governments are subject to the accounting principles promulgated by the Governmental Accounting Standards Board as well as certain Financial Accounting Standards Board pronouncements.

received the cash or that an organization may be obligated for expenses that have not yet been paid and, therefore, does not present an accurate picture of the financial position of the organization. The notes to the financial statements will disclose the basis of accounting.

A charitable organization was on the cash basis of accounting. It had the following transactions during the year.

Contributions made by donors	$100,000
Of the $100,000, the amount of contributions actually received in cash	$ 75,000
Expenses incurred by the organization during the year	$ 95,000
Of the $95,000 in expenses, the amount actually paid out in cash	$ 80,000

Financial results on the cash basis of accounting are shown in the following table.

Contributions	$ 75,000
Expenses	(80,000)
Decrease in net assets	(5,000)

On the cash basis, the charitable organization would have a decrease in net assets. However, on the accrual basis, a different story emerges.

Contributions	$100,000)
Expenses	(95,000)
Increase in net assets	5,000

The true picture that best represents the service level and accomplishments of the organization is that it received the contributions even though $25,000 were in the form of pledges. And it really incurred $95,000 in expenses even though it still owed $15,000, so cash paid out was $80,000.

Basic Financial Statements

Nonprofits have three or four basic financial statements depending on the type of organization. These statements must be read together to have a complete picture of the organization:

1. **Statement of Financial Position** (also referred to as a balance sheet). This statement reports the organization's assets, liabilities, and net assets at a point in time. This point in time is usually at the end of the organization's fiscal year (most commonly March 31, June 30, September 30, or December 31). The statement of financial position focuses on the organization as a whole and is required to present its net assets, which is the difference between the assets and liabilities, by classification (unrestricted, temporarily restricted, and permanently restricted). The concept of net asset classification will be addressed in this chapter.

2. **Statement of Activities.** This statement reports the results of operations (revenues and expenses) and change in net assets for the year. The change in net assets must be presented in total and also by net asset class as described in the preceding.

3. **Statement of Cash Flows.** This statement provides information about the cash receipts and disbursements of the organization that result from operating activities, financing activities, and investing activities. The statement is a bridge from accrual-based accounting to the flow of cash. If the organization is on a cash basis, this statement is unnecessary. The cash flow statement also includes a summary of noncash activities such as contributions of in-kind items.

4. **Statement of Functional Expenses.** This statement provides information about the organization's expenses by function and by natural classification. An organization's functions are broken out by program services and supporting services. Supporting services are further identified as management or general and fund-raising. This information is valuable to the users of the financial statements when judging how a nonprofit's resources are used. Examples of natural classification are salaries, occupancy, depreciation, and repairs and maintenance. All organizations are encouraged to present a statement of functional expenses. However, the statement is only required of voluntary health and welfare organizations. If comparative (two years) financial statements are issued, the statement of functional expenses should also be comparative.

An organization should also produce financial information more frequently (preferably monthly) for internal purposes. Certain funding sources or lending institutions may require quarterly information. It is very helpful to also provide the board with a balance sheet on a monthly basis. Smaller organizations, however, are less likely to provide that information more often than yearly because many of them operate on a cash basis during the year and convert to accrual only at year end. A funding source may require a complete set of financials that would include the balance sheet and cash flow statement or may require only a statement of activities. Some may only require information pertinent to the budget and actual expenditures for their programs.

Footnotes to the Financial Statements

Footnotes are an integral part of the financial statements. They provide the user with a description of the organization, its significant accounting policies, and information about important aspects of its account balances and classes of transactions, along with any contingencies such as lawsuits, and events that occurred subsequent to the organization's year end. Examples of footnotes[4] are

- description of the organization.
- tax exempt status.
- cash and cash equivalents.
- significant estimates.
- property and equipment (details of land, building, and equipment including depreciation methods and useful lives of assets).
- leases (terms of significant leases).
- debt (loan details including repayment schedule for five years).
- contingencies (such as lawsuits or repayments to funding sources).
- types of restricted net assets (as to purpose or time).

---

4 An organization will only disclose significant items.

- details of investments.
- details of endowments.
- details of split interest agreements.
- concentrations (for example, revenue from a significant funding source).

The level of disclosure is prescribed by GAAP. Footnotes are very helpful in understanding and analyzing the financial position and results of activities.

Voluntary Health and Welfare Organization

A voluntary health and welfare organization is one that derives its support primarily from the public to be used for general or specific purposes connected with health, welfare, or community services. Public support can take the form of

- contributions from individuals (cash and in-kind).
- contributions from corporations (cash and in-kind).
- United Way or other agencies supported by contributions.
- fund-raising events.

Public support does not include fee for service activities or government grants. Services connected with health, welfare, and community services are basically social service in nature and do not include medical services.

When defining a voluntary health and welfare organization, the AICPA Audit and Accounting Guide *Not-for-Profit Entities* is more concerned with the level of contributions than the mission of the organization. Therefore, the definition for health, welfare, or community services is broad enough to encompass not only services to humans but also services to animals or the environment.

Fund Accounting

Nonprofit organizations may use fund accounting internally. Fund accounting separates assets, liabilities, and fund balances (net of assets and liabilities) into separate accounting units that are either associated with *activities*; donor imposed restrictions such as an endowment fund; or objectives such as a property, plant, and equipment fund. Although fund accounting is very useful for internal purposes, it is rarely used for external reporting purposes. Beginning in 1996, accounting literature prescribed that nonprofits present information about their assets, liabilities, and activities in total and by net asset class for external reporting purposes. Examples of funds follow:

- Endowment funds account for endowments or amounts permanently restricted by donors and the activity related to those assets.
- Plant and equipment funds account for plant and equipment and funds designated for those purposes.
- Debt service funds account for debt (such as bonds) and payments on the debt.
- Restricted purpose funds account for funds held for specific purposes designated by donors.

- Agency funds account for funds held for other organizations.
- Split interest funds account for split interest arrangements (discussed more fully subsequently in this chapter).
- Loan funds account for loans made to students, employees or other parties.
- Operating funds account for general operations.

Following is a set of financial statements for a voluntary health and welfare organization. Note that all nonprofits will have the first three statements. The footnotes, although important for analysis, have not been presented here due to space considerations. Readers can find a full set of financial statements on the Nonprofit Board Resource website (nonprofit boardresource.com/).

Community Youth Center Statement of Financial Position June 30, 2010 and 2009		
	2010	2009
Assets		
Cash and cash equivalents	$ 84,426)	$ 311,984)
Pledges receivable less allowance for doubtful accounts	56,933)	36,059)
Grants receivable	287,507)	251,089)
Inventories	20,550)	25,550)
Prepaid expenses	21,365)	20,251)
Investments	385,019)	350,462)
Property and equipment less accumulated depreciation	559,113)	465,972)
Other assets	15,349)	7,999)
Total Assets	**$1,430,262)**	**$1,469,366)**
Liabilities		
Accounts payable	76,465	71,945
Accrued expenses	22,350	25,409
Deferred revenue	54,870	108,529
Mortgages and notes payable	592,517	605,057
Other liabilities	3,202	1,823
Total Liabilities	**$ 749,404**	**$ 812,763**
Net Assets		
Unrestricted	662,658)	601,603)
Temporarily restricted	18,200)	55,000)
Total Net Assets	**$ 680,858)**	**$ 656,603)**
Total Liabilities and Net Assets	**$1,430,262**	**$1,469,366**

Community Youth Center Statements of Activities Years Ended June 30, 2010 and 2009		
	2010	2009
Unrestricted Net Assets		
Unrestricted revenues		
Contributions	$ 471,650)	$ 421,729)
Government grants	550,000)	535,000)
Program revenues	111,148)	96,857)
Investment return	13,135)	(83,973)
Total Unrestricted Revenues	**$1,145,933**	**$ 969,613**
Net assets released from restriction		
Expiration of time restriction—United Way	12,800	10,000
Total Unrestricted Revenues and Other Support	**$1,158,733**	**$ 979,613**

(continued)

(continued)

Community Youth Center Statements of Activities Years Ended June 30, 2010 and 2009		
	2010	2009
Expenses		
Salaries and wages	734,735)	684,734)
Postage and shipping	4,502)	2,689)
Occupancy	48,000)	48,000)
Equipment rental and maintenance	1,952)	1,416)
Printing and publications	3,502)	2,488)
Travel	4,400)	4,470)
Interest	58,632)	56,475)
Depreciation	49,658)	44,000)
Food and supplies	181,949)	167,343)
Utilities	5,309)	5,726)
Marketing and public relations	2,200)	2,997)
Professional fees	15,222)	15,091)
Licenses and fees	4,262)	3,185)
Insurance	7,355)	7,326)
Total Expenses	**$1,121,678)**	**$1,045,940)**
Increase (Decrease) in Unrestricted Net Assets	**$ 37,055**	**$ (–66,327)**
Temporarily Restricted Net Assets		
Net assets released from restrictions	(–12,800)	(–10,000)
Decrease in Temporarily Restricted Net Assets	**(–12,800)**	**(–10,000)**
Increase (Decrease) in Net Assets	**$ 24,255**	**$ (–76,327)**
Net Assets at Beginning of Year	**$ 656,603**	**$ 732,930**
Net Assets at End of Year	**$ 680,858**	**$ 656,603**

Community Youth Center Statements of Cash Flows June 30, 2010 and 2009		
	2010	2009
Cash Flows From Operating Activities		
Change in net assets	$ 24,255)	$ (76,327)
Adjustments to Reconcile Change in Net Assets to Net Cash Provided by Operating Activities		
Realized and unrealized gains and losses on investments	(13,135)	83,973)
Depreciation and amortization	49,658)	44,000)
Changes in Assets and Liabilities		
Pledges receivable	(20,874)	12,759)
Grants receivable	(36,418)	123,475)
Inventory	5,000)	2,000)
Prepaid expenses and other assets	(8,464)	247)
Accounts payable and accrued expenses	1,461)	3,515)
Deferred revenue	(53,659)	(11,203)
Other liabilities	1,379)	1,212)
Net Cash Used in Operating Activities	**$ (50,797)**	**$ 183,651)**
Cash Flows From Investing Activities		
Purchase of equipment	(142,799)	(4,167)
Proceeds from sale of investments	23,000	28,500
Purchase of investments	(44,422)	(335)
Net Cash Used in Investing Activities	**$ (164,221)**	**$ 23,998**
Cash Flows From Financing Activities		
Payment on debt	(12,540)	(12,540)
Net Cash Provided by Financing Activities	**$ (12,540)**	**$ (12,540)**

Community Youth Center Statements of Cash Flows June 30, 2010 and 2009	2010	2009
Net Change in Cash and Cash Equivalents	$ (227,558)	$ 195,109)
Cash and Cash Equivalents-Beginning of Year	$ 311,984)	$ 116,875)
Cash and Cash Equivalents-End of Year	$ 84,426)	$ 311,984)
Supplemental Cash Flow Information		
Cash Paid for Interest	$ 58,632)	$ 56,475)

Community Youth Center Statement of Functional Expenses Year Ended June 30, 2010	Program Services		Supporting Services		
	Youth Program	Preschool Program	Management and General	Fundraising	Total
Salaries and wages	$345,327	$220,420	$132,252	$36,736	$ 734,735
Postage and shipping			2,420	2,082	4,502
Occupancy	24,960	12,000	8,640	2,400	48,000
Equipment rental and maintenance			1,952		1,952
Printing and publications	1,105	550	630	1,217	3,502
Travel			2,450	1,950	4,400
Interest	28,143	17,003	10,554	2,932	58,632
Depreciation	23,836	10,922	12,450	2,450	49,658
Food and supplies	110,988	70,961			181,949
Utilities	2,200	2,109	750	250	5,309
Marketing and public relations			2,200		2,200
Professional fees			15,222		15,222
Licenses and fees	462	400	3,400		4,262
Insurance	3,456	2,207	1,342	350	7,355
Total Expenses	$ 40,477	$336,572	$194,262	$50,367	$1,121,678

Note that the nonprofit would present the statement of functional expenses for two years if comparative statements are presented. The statement of functional expenses for 2009 is not presented here due to space limitations.

Assets

Assets are tangible, intangible, or future benefits to the nonprofit. Many nonprofits classify their assets and liabilities as current and noncurrent. These designations refer to how quickly they are expected to be converted to cash, with current assets having a conversion time-frame of one year or less. Other nonprofits list their assets in order of liquidity, with those that are the easiest to be converted to cash closest to the top.

◼ Example

Leslie, a nonprofit board member, was trying to understand why the assets needed to be in liquidity order. The financial officer told her that it was important for the reader of the financial statement to be able to see how well the entity could pay its bills. For example, if it owed money to employees for salaries, utilities and other expenses that needed to be paid within a year, could it pay those amounts?

Leslie was still unclear as to what was liquid and what was not. The financial officer told her that "Cash is the most liquid because it can be spent immediately. The pledges receivable are fairly liquid because we believe we will collect them in the next few months. The buildings and equipment are not liquid because we would have to sell them to get the money, and we need them to run the business of the organization so they are not liquid. That's why they are noncurrent. Also, if we had some investments that we wanted to hold to buy new equipment we would call them noncurrent if we did not expect to buy the equipment within the year. The liabilities we will be paying out within a year are current but the debt that we will pay in the next several years is not."

Cash and Cash Equivalents

Cash and cash equivalents are combined together in one line item and include currency on hand, deposits held by financial institutions, and highly liquid investments that are readily converted to cash and so near their maturity (original maturities of three months or less) that there is a very slight risk of loss. Examples of cash equivalents are money market funds, commercial paper, or treasury bills.

A nonprofit may have restrictions on its cash. These restrictions could be imposed by donors, by contracts, or by regulatory requirements. When the restrictions require cash to be held for a period longer than one year, it should be segregated on the statement of financial position and, if the statement is classified, shown as a noncurrent asset.

Evaluation Point: Management should evaluate the amount of cash that is deposited in a financial institution. The Federal Deposit Insurance Corporation presently insures amounts up to $250,000. This level of insurance will remain through 2013.

Management should also review the prospectus of money market funds. Certain funds have provisions that make the funds or part of the funds illiquid. For example, the prospectus might state that management of the fund has a right to restrict the rate at which account balances may be withdrawn so that 50 percent may be withdrawn immediately, another 30 percent in 6 months and 20 percent in 2 years.

Revenue, Receivables, and Deferred Revenue

Nonprofit organizations receive revenue from a variety of sources. Some sources may represent contributions, and some represent exchange transactions. With contributions, the donor receives no reciprocal value in exchange for the donation. With exchange transactions, there is value delivered in exchange for the payment.

Donations	Exchange Transactions
Contributions of cash, goods, or services from individuals or corporations	Grants from federal and state agencies
Grants from foundations	Fees charged for services

As described in this chapter, revenue is recognized when earned. For exchange transactions, the earnings process is complete when the goods are delivered or services performed. In the case of government grants, this means when the grant money was spent. When the nonprofit bills for services performed, an account or grant receivable results. When the cash is received, the receivable is removed from the books. If cash is paid in advance, a liability called *deferred revenue* is recorded until the amounts are earned. Exchange transactions are always unrestricted.

Most nonprofits receive contributions from donors. Contributions are gifts that are nonreciprocal in nature. That is, the donors expect nothing of substance from the nonprofit in return for them. As noted, contributions are not really earned the way revenue is earned in commercial entities. They are recorded when the pledge is made or the contribution is received. Accounting for contributions is one of the most complex areas for a nonprofit because there are so many different types of contributions. Contributions can be unrestricted, temporarily restricted, or restricted. But when restricted, it is always the donor who restricted them. Boards cannot restrict; they can only designate. This means that the board can change its mind and decide to "undesignate" the amounts and do something else with the money.

Donors can place temporary restrictions on contributions such as for specific purposes (for example, to be used for a children's program) or for use in a specific period of time (for example, ratably over two years). Contributions can also be permanently restricted. This means that the corpus (original gift amount) of the contribution is restricted in perpetuity. The donor may specify what is to be done with the earnings from the permanently restricted contribution or may be silent. This way the nonprofit has discretion.

> **Evaluation Point:** Management should consider setting a floor on the amount that a donor must give in order for him or her to be able to restrict the donation for a particular purpose. A pledge card that states that all donations that are fewer than $1,000 (or whatever is reasonable for the organization) will be considered unrestricted will limit the number of temporarily restricted donations, enabling the nonprofit to make the decision on how the donation is used and reduce the amount of record keeping involved.

Contributions may take the form of cash, investments, goods, services, right to use space or utilities, or loans at interest rates below market. They can be received at the date of donation or may be in the form of a pledge from a donor for a future contribution. Regardless, they are recorded at the fair value of the item at the date of donation. For cash, this is a simple matter. For goods, services, and the right to use the donor's space or utilities, management will need to do the necessary work to determine the fair value.[5]

Generally, when a donor makes a pledge, the revenue will be recorded as temporarily restricted because of the implied timing restriction. The restriction is implied because technically the money is not available to be spent until received. However, if a donor specifically states that the pledge is to be used to support current operations, then it may be recorded as unrestricted. At the end of a period, management should evaluate the collectability of pledges receivable and record an allowance for uncollectible pledges if necessary. The allowance will reduce the amount of pledges receivable on the balance sheet. It will also be charged to bad debt expense or a loss on the statement of activities depending on whether the contribution was recorded as unrestricted (bad debt) or temporarily restricted (loss). When the pledge is due (this may be before it is received), it should be released from restriction and reclassified as unrestricted unless the donor has also restricted it for a specific purpose. Once this occurs, the money can be spent. If there is also a purpose restriction on the contribution, then it will be released from restriction as soon as the organization spends it for that purpose.

 Example

The Be Kind to Animals Association (BKAA) received the following pledges in 2010:
- $100,000 in unrestricted donations, of which $20,000 was pledged and had not been paid at the nonprofit's year end
- Food and medical supplies with a fair value of $2,000
- $5,000 in donations restricted for the purpose of constructing a new exercise area

---

5 Fair value is the price that a purchaser would pay for the asset or liability in an orderly transaction under current market conditions. For investments that are actively traded, this value would be easy to establish from a source such as *The Wall Street Journal*. For assets and liabilities that are not actively traded, the valuation is much more difficult and often requires a valuation specialist.

- $100,000 endowment with the income and appreciation to be used for placement services for the rescued animals. This donation was received at the end of the year so there was no investment income in 2010.

BKAA recorded the revenue as follows.

Contributions	Unrestricted	Temporarily Restricted	Permanently Restricted	Total
Unrestricted	$80,000	$20,000		$100,000
In kind donations	2,000			2,000
Donations for exercise area		5,000		5,000
Endowment fund			$100,000	100,000
Total contributions	$82,000	$25,000	$100,000	$207,000

The $82,000 was available to be spent (or in the case of the in-kind donations, used) during the period. The $20,000 temporarily restricted contributions were not available to be released from restriction until the date the cash was promised to be paid. The $5,000 temporarily restricted contribution could not be released from restriction until it was used for the exercise yard. The $100,000 endowment will never be released from restriction although the income that will be generated in the next year would be used for the purpose specified by the donor.

Boards of directors cannot restrict the net assets of the nonprofit. However, they can designate net assets to be used for a specific purpose. The distinction between restriction and designation is that the board can always decide to change the designation on net assets but cannot change a restriction made by a donor. Therefore, designated net assets are always unrestricted.

Example

The board of directors decided that that it wanted to designate certain net assets for the purpose of building a new facility. The nonprofit was doing well, and so each year $100,000 was designated for construction to begin in 5 years. That amount was also set aside in an interest earning account. Three years after they started this plan, a major funding source decided to begin giving to another nonprofit. The nonprofit needed money to fund its operating expenses until new funding could be found. The board removed the designation on the net assets so that the accumulated funds could be used for operating expenses.

In-Kind Contributions

In-kind contributions are gifts of goods to the nonprofit. They are frequently given to nonprofits for their use or to sell. Good are valued at the fair value at the date of donation. The donor may have the items appraised in order to determine the amount of their tax deduction and may provide the appraisal to the nonprofit. If it appears reasonable, then the nonprofit may use the information to record the contribution. Nonprofits are not required and are, in fact, encouraged **not** to provide donors with an estimated value for the donor's tax return. If the items are likely to be sold within the fiscal year or are of uncertain value, it may be wiser to wait until they are sold to record the contribution. If the contribution has been recorded and the nonprofit receives either more or less on the sale, the contribution is adjusted on the books to equal the amount received. In-kind contributions may also take the form of donated space, utilities, or interest-free or below-market loans. In those cases, the nonprofit will not only have contribution revenue but will also have an expense because the items are used in the nonprofit's operations. In cases in which the goods are capital items such as land or cars, the nonprofit will have contribution revenue and a capital asset.

 Example

Charles donated his collection of Star Trek memorabilia to a nonprofit. He told the nonprofit that the collection was worth $3,000. Management of the nonprofit intended to sell it along with other items donated in its silent auction, but the auction was not scheduled to be held until the following fiscal year. Because management was uncertain that the collection would sell for anywhere near that amount, they decided to wait until it was sold to record the contribution.

Evaluation Point: Management should be careful when accepting donations. Good hearted donors may believe that they are doing the nonprofit a service by giving items they consider of value to the organization when they do not have cash to spare. However, more than one nonprofit has been saddled with land with hidden environmental liabilities or assets that may be difficult to sell, such as a share of a limited partnership or objects of art. When nonprofits receive goods instead of cash, they should sell them as quickly as possible unless the goods can be used in operations or are intended to be sold for a fund-raising event like a silent auction. This way, there is less likelihood that they could be stolen, damaged, or misplaced.

Donated services can also be an important source of assistance for the nonprofit. However, not all donated services are recorded as contributions. When a donated service enhances or creates a nonfinancial asset, such as a building, a contribution is recorded. When donated services are performed by a person with specialized skills, a contribution is also recorded. However, if a person donates his or her time to raise money or perform services that are not within his or her specialized skill set, then the contribution is not recorded.

Example

Jane is an attorney with a special interest in a charity that serves the homeless. She donates her legal services to help the nonprofit fulfill its mission. She also helps with the annual fundraiser. Her legal services are considered contributions to the nonprofit because they are performed using her specialized skill. But because Jane is not a professional fundraiser, assistance with the fund-raising event is not recorded as a contribution.

Evaluation Point: A nonprofit is not able to record most of the services provided by volunteers, including board members, as contributions. However, these services are very important when it comes to running the nonprofit. Management should consider disclosing the approximate number of hours of service provided by volunteers in the notes to the financial statements. This will demonstrate that the organization receives more by way of support than just cash.

Long Term Contributions

Nonprofits frequently have capital campaigns and ask donors for long term commitments. When the pledges come in, the nonprofit should aggregate and then discount them to their net present value after considering

- time that the pledges are to remain outstanding.
- the nonprofit's collection experience or experience of a similar nonprofit.
- the nonprofit's policies concerning the enforcement of promises to give (pledges are legally enforceable but nonprofits tend not to enforce them for public relations reasons).
- expectations about possible variations in the amount or timing of cash flows.

The net realizable value is recorded as temporarily restricted contributions because of the timing restriction unless the donor specified that the contribution was to be used as current support. There may also be a purpose restriction, for example, to use to build a building or provide scholarships.

As time passes and payments are scheduled to be made, the receivable is relieved, and the contributions are released from restriction so they can be spent. This will not occur until both the timing and any purpose restrictions have been met. The discount is amortized over the life of the pledge into contribution revenue at the same time. For most nonprofits, the discount rate is not revised. Therefore, long term contributions are not marked to fair value on a recurring basis. Although most nonprofits do not elect it, FASB provides an option to record most financial assets and liabilities at fair value on a recurring basis.

FASB provides guidance on the methods that could be used to record the discount. The least complicated way to do this is to use a rate that would be commensurate with the risk of the donor. For example, if the donor was an individual, an unsecured borrowing rate could be used commensurate with the nonprofit's knowledge of its donors. If the donor were a corporation, an unsecured corporate borrowing rate could be used.

Each year, after the pledges have been recorded, management will estimate how much of any pledges outstanding are likely to be uncollectible. If the pledges were unrestricted, then bad debt expense will be charged and an allowance for uncollectible recorded. If pledges were temporarily restricted, then the amounts likely to be uncollectible will be recorded as a loss in the temporarily restricted net asset class.

■ Example

A nonprofit held a capital campaign in order to build a new facility and received pledges of $1,000,000 to be collected ratably (at the same amount each year) over a 4 year period with the first installment due at the beginning of the nonprofit's next fiscal year. The development director maintained records of the amount of pledges that were not collected in previous capital campaigns. The finance director used that information in addition to the prevailing interest rates at the time, the creditworthiness of the donors, and the knowledge that the nonprofit never enforced collections on pledges to determine a discount rate for the pledges receivable. The pledges were discounted using the rate that could be earned on a 4 year U.S. Treasury obligation, which was 4 percent at the time, and then the rate was adjusted for risk so that the resulting rate was 5 percent. The finance director recorded a contribution of $560,185, which approximated the net realizable value of the pledges. The contributions were temporarily restricted due to both timing and purpose. At the beginning of each fiscal year, the finance director released 25 percent of the temporarily restricted contribution from restriction ($140,046) and recorded 25 percent of the discount ($59,954) as unrestricted contribution.*

---

* The interest method should be used to amortize discounts unless another method, such as the straight-line method, would not provide a materially different result. In practice, most nonprofits use the straight-line method (ratably over the period).

Evaluation Point: Management should consider setting up a system to evaluate the collectability of pledges. In times when the economy is uncertain, this is particularly important. Although nonprofits can take legal action against donors who renege on their pledges, they seldom do. In cases in which pledges are for multiple years, a donor's failure to pay is more likely because the gift is based, in part, on the donor's expectation to be able to make good on the pledge at the time the gift was made. Management should follow up on collection of pledges because often a reminder is all it takes to cause the donor to give what he or she can, even if it is not the entire amount. Pledges could also be postponed a year. When this happens, management will want to re-categorize those amounts as noncurrent.

Conditional Promises to Give

Some nonprofits receive bequests from donors. A contribution cannot be recorded until the donor is deceased and the will has been probated because the will can always be changed. Another type of conditional promise is a challenge grant. A contribution cannot be recorded until the terms of the challenge have been met.

 Example

Joe wanted to help establish an endowment to fund a program to provide services to children with autism. He was able to contribute $100,000 but believed the program needed $200,000 to be sustainable. He told the nonprofit that once it raised $100,000 from other sources, he would match the funds. Until the $100,000 was raised, Joe's contribution was conditional.

Conditional contributions can be described in the notes to the financial statements even though they cannot be recorded.

Endowments

Endowment funds are donations that are permanently restricted by the donor. As previously noted, the donor may specify how the interest, dividends, and gains may be spent. If the donor specifies, then the income and appreciation in the fund is temporarily restricted. If the donor does not specify, then the amounts are unrestricted unless the nonprofit is in a state that has enacted a version of the Uniform Prudent Management of Institutional Funds Act (UPMIFA). The act was introduced as a model law; therefore, state legislatures may enact their own version of it. As of December 2010, 48 states had either enacted a version of UPMIFA or were in the process of doing so.[6]

Upon enactment of UPMIFA, all investment income and appreciation should be classified as temporarily restricted until it is appropriated for expenditure by the board of directors. The board should develop a prudent spending policy using the provisions of the state's version of UPMIFA as a guide. Once appropriated, the amounts can be transferred to unrestricted net assets and spent. The objective is to prudently spend the resources generated by the endowment fund to support the nonprofit's programs and services unless the donor has specified where the income or appreciation is to be used.

UPMIFA allows the nonprofit to spend down the original gift in times when there is little appreciation or when the value of the investments in the endowment fund has declined below the original gift amount. This is very different than previous law under which the original gift was not to be spent. Management and its boards should be careful to document all spending policy decisions and actions because this concept will be very new to donors

---

6 The Uniform Prudent Management of Institutional Funds Act (UPMIFA) website, www.upmifa.org, provides the status of states that have either enacted UPMIFA or are considering it.

and because it may not appeal to them. In the future, donors may decide to specify that the original gift is not to be spent.

 Example

A nonprofit in a state that had enacted UPMIFA had an endowment fund of $500,000. The donor made no stipulations on what was to be done with the income from the fund or the appreciation. The state's version of UPMIFA called for the board to implement a prudent spending policy. The board of the nonprofit decided that 4 percent of the average beginning balance of the investment fund over the last 3 years was prudent. Therefore, each year the board appropriated that much for expenditure and released it from restriction. The remainder was retained as temporarily restricted net assets.

Evaluation Point: Boards should be very careful when drafting spending policies to ensure that the spending policy conforms to the state's version of UPMIFA. In some states, there is clear guidance on the maximum prudent percentage an organization can appropriate for expenditure in any one year. Boards have a fiduciary responsibility to maintain the permanently restricted endowment fund and manage it prudently. UPMIFA's provision that the corpus of the fund can be spent when investment return is down is a new concept, and many donors may not welcome the idea that this could happen. The board should consider appointing an investment committee to oversee the activity of endowment funds and thoroughly document its decisions.

Split Interest Agreements

Split interest agreements are arrangements in which the nonprofit and the donor each have an interest in the donated assets. The most popular forms of split interest agreement are charitable remainder trusts, charitable lead trusts, and charitable unitrusts. The trusts may be held by the nonprofit or by an outside trustee. In charitable gift annuity arrangements, the assets and liabilities are held in the general assets and liabilities of the nonprofit.

Perpetual trusts are also very common. The trust is held in perpetuity by an outside trustee and is valued at the fair value of the investments. In these trusts, the nonprofit generally receives the income from the trust and records it as investment return (investment income and appreciation). The value of the trust is not adjusted because the return is distributed to the nonprofit. However, these arrangements can also take other forms. For example, there are some trustees that distribute the interest and dividends, and the appreciation or depreciation is retained in the trust. The nonprofit receives a statement so that it is able to adjust its beneficial interest in the trust, and any adjustment is also made to permanently restricted net assets because the trust is a perpetual trust.

In a charitable remainder trust in which there is an outside trustee, the trustee invests the assets and makes distributions to the donor according to the agreement until he or she dies. When the donor dies, the remaining investments are a contribution to the nonprofit. In a charitable lead trust, the periodic payments are made to the nonprofit, and the remainder goes to the donor's heirs at the donor's death. When the trustee is an outside party, the nonprofit receives the information relative to its beneficial interest in the trust. The beneficial interest is initially recorded at fair value and adjusted to fair value on a recurring basis.

When the nonprofit is the trustee, management will estimate the present value of the payments to the donor and contribution to the nonprofit at inception. Management should calculate the amount of the total payments it expects to make to the donor in a remainder trust or the amounts it expects to receive in a lead trust. Management then will discount those benefits using the expected return on the investments at the time of donation. In the present value calculation, management will need to estimate the life expectancy of the donor.

Although it may be tempting to use IRS guidelines and mortality tables in determining the donor's life expectancy, this is not appropriate. The AICPA[7] cautions that these tables can be up to 10 years old. According to its white paper "FASB Accounting Standards Codification Section 820, Fair Value Measurements and Disclosures, for Certain Issues Pertaining to Not-for-Profit Entities," the tables that were issued in May 2009 were based on a census taken in 2000. They are not expected to be replaced until 2019. The AICPA also points out that the tables are based on the life expectancy of the average population and notes that people who are likely to enter into split-interest agreements generally have a longer life expectancy. The AICPA suggests using statistics from the National Center for Health Statistics instead because of its more current information.

The amount recorded as a contribution is the difference between the value of the investments and the present value of the amounts expected to be paid to the donor. Once calculated, the discount rate is not revised unless the nonprofit elects the fair value option under professional literature. This rarely happens. Adjustments are subsequently made to the arrangement if it appears that the life expectancy of the donor has changed.

In recent years, life expectancies have gotten longer. Nonprofits with older split interest agreements may find that the amounts they are distributing to the donors under charitable remainder trusts are leaving very little, if any, remainder for them. And donors with charitable lead trusts are seeing that there is little left for their heirs. Because these agreements are irrevocable, there is little that can be done about it once the arrangement has been made. However, new agreements can be written in such a way that there is less risk.

Unitrusts are arrangements in which the periodic payment is not based on a preforecasted annuity but on the value of the investments in the trust. In addition, some split interest agreements are being written to terminate after a period of years if the donor has not died. In circumstances in which the payment is not solely based on the donor's life expectancy and the payment is based on the value of investments, the instrument will contain a derivative that needs to be valued at fair value each year. The simplest way to do this is to revalue the agreement using a current market rate of interest.

---

7 "FASB Accounting Standards Codification Section 820, Fair Value Measurements and Disclosures, for Certain Issues Pertaining to Not-for-Profit Entities," (AICPA, Financial Reporting Executive Committee, January 2010).

Example

When she was 50 years old, Nancy made a contribution of $50,000 to her college in the form of a charitable remainder trust. According to the agreement, she would receive payments once a year, and when she died, the nonprofit would receive the remainder. At the time the gift was made, the development director estimated that Nancy would live to be 75 years old. The payments to Nancy were set at a specific amount per year so that the nonprofit would receive approximately $30,000 when she died. This was based on the 25 years the college expected to pay Nancy and an average rate of return on investments of 8 percent a year. Nancy lived to be 104, and in the 2 years just prior to her death, the average return on the investments was only 1 percent due to a severe market decline. The nonprofit's remainder was only a fraction of what it was expecting when it entered into the arrangement.

Evaluation Point: Management should carefully evaluate all split interest agreements to ensure that they meet the needs of the nonprofit and justify the cost of the recordkeeping involved. It may be wise to either set a cap on the split interest payment period or base the payments made to donors on the value of the investment account instead of providing donors with a fixed annuity. It is also very important to explain this to the donors so that they will not be expecting payments at a certain level and then be disappointed.

Agency Transactions

Some nonprofits enter into transactions in which they perform certain functions for others. They may

- serve as a conduit for cash or noncash donations to be passed through to another organization.
- solicit funds for another nonprofit organization.
- hold and manage investments for another nonprofit organization.

The two parties may be related or unrelated. The parties to the transaction are as follows:

- **Donor.** One who gives a donation.
- **Resource provider.** One who transfers resources but is not giving a donation.
- **Recipient.** One who receives the resources on behalf of another and serves as a conduit.
- **Beneficiary.** The party that ultimately benefits from the transaction.

Nonprofit Serves as a Conduit for Cash or Noncash Donations

Organizations such as United Way raise contributions that are intended to benefit a wide variety of nonprofits. Donors are given the ability to give to United Way permitting the United Way to allocate the funds in accordance with its policies. Donors can also designate specified beneficiaries. In the latter case, United Way serves as a conduit. When serving as a conduit, the recipient of the funds (in this case United Way) records an asset and a liability rather than revenue. The recipient must notify the designated nonprofit beneficiary of the funds received, and the beneficiary records the revenue. The recipient will generally keep a portion of the money as an administrative fee. The beneficiary records the entire amount as contribution revenue and the administrative fee as fund-raising expense.

Organizations such as United Way do not benefit as much when the donor gives to a designated beneficiary because it is not able to record contribution revenue. However, it still has fund-raising expenses. It would much prefer to receive the donation and then allocate it among the various nonprofit agencies it serves. Donors like to designate where their money goes because of their own personal preferences to support or even **not** support various types of nonprofits. To assist donors and still have the ability to record contribution revenue, United Way initiated a method of donation by which a donor could give to a "cause" instead of a designated beneficiary. This appears to be a win–win situation for both: United Way is able to record revenue, and the donors are able to target their favorite causes.

When it comes to being a conduit for noncash donations, the recipient has a choice. It can either record an asset and a liability to the designated beneficiary, or it can just maintain records off line. The designated beneficiary records a contribution.

Nonprofit Solicits Funds for Another Nonprofit Organization (Unrelated)

When an organization such as a community foundation (CF) solicits funds for or in the name of another organization, it should ensure that the pledge materials state that it has the ultimate discretion over the disposition of the funds if it wants to record revenue. This is called *variance power*. Another way to look at variance power is the ability to vary the donor's instructions. Without variance power, the organization would record an asset and a liability.

> ### 🔲 Example
>
> A nonprofit organization established a fund at the local CF. The CF agreed to solicit contributions in the name of the nonprofit but stated in the pledge materials that if the nonprofit was no longer viable, was not fulfilling a purpose that was in line with that of the CF, or no longer needed the money, the CF had the right to distribute the return on the investments to another organization. When the CF has this variance power, it has the ability to record the donations as revenue even if they were originally intended for a specific organization. The nonprofit does not have revenue until the CF makes the decision to provide the other organization with the resources.

Nonprofit Holds Funds for Another Nonprofit Organization (Unrelated)

Unrelated organizations such as CFs also manage investments for nonprofit organizations. This is very helpful for the nonprofit because the amount of investments held at such an organization are much larger than those that would typically be held by most nonprofits, which aids in diversification. In addition, these organizations typically have greater expertise in money management than an individual organization might possess. Nonprofits might choose to put their funds at a CF because it establishes a relationship with the CF, which enables the nonprofit to apply for grant funds or even ask to have its debt guaranteed by the CF, resulting in a lower interest rate for the nonprofit.

When a nonprofit transfers resources to the CF or another unrelated organization (recipient), the recipient records a liability to the nonprofit because those resources do not belong to it. The nonprofit that transfers the resources will record an interest in the assets it transferred to the recipient and will adjust its interest up and down depending on the value of the assets. Because the assets typically become a part of a larger pool, the term *interest in net assets* is used, meaning the pro-rata share of the larger pool that is owned by the nonprofit.

 Example

A nonprofit charity (NPC) received a large bequest from a donor. Management decided that it did not have the expertise in house to manage the investments and transferred them to the Any City Community Foundation (ACCF). The NPC removed the investments from its books and recorded an interest in the net assets of the ACCF. Each year, the NPC received a statement that documented its share of the increase or decrease in market value of the entire fund managed by ACCF as well as its share of the interest and dividends earned on the fund. The NPC was given the ability to draw down a certain amount of the fund each year to use as the donor intended. The statement provided by the ACCF helped the NPC to adjust its interest in the net assets of the ACCF.

Nonprofit Enters Into Transactions With Related Foundations

Nonprofits may also participate in transactions with foundations that are financially interrelated. A foundation is financially interrelated if the organizations are affiliates, if one entity has considerable representation on the governing board of the other, or if the charter or bylaws state that one organization's activities are limited to those that benefit the other. In some cases, there could also be an agreement between the two that allows one to actively participate in the policy making process of the other. When any of these situations occur, one organization will have an ongoing economic interest in the other.

Example

A nonprofit hospital system (NPHS) was affiliated with a foundation (NPHS-F) that was created to solicit contributions specifically for it and then manage the resulting investments. The two were financially interrelated because the NPHS-F's activities were limited to those that benefitted the NPHS. When the NPHS-F received contributions, it recorded contribution revenue on its books. The NPHS recorded an interest in the net assets held by the NPHS-F as described in the unrelated foundation example mentioned previously.

When a nonprofit sets up a foundation and transfers assets to it to manage, management must determine whether the transaction is an equity transaction. The transfer will be considered an equity transaction if the nonprofit specifies itself or an affiliate as the beneficiary of the return on the investments but does not expect the foundation to return the investments. In addition, to be an equity transaction, the two organizations must be financially interrelated. When an equity transaction occurs, the nonprofit will record an interest in the net assets of the foundation on its books and adjust it as described in earlier examples. The foundation will record the receipt of the investments and an equity transaction. The equity transaction will be displayed as a separate line item on the statement of activities because the transfer to the assets was not a contribution to the foundation.

Inventories

Most nonprofits do not have significant amounts of inventory. However, when large amounts of books, supplies, goods to be sold in gift shops, commodities such as food or medical supplies (whether they are used in programs or resold), or donated items to be sold later at a fund-raising event are on hand at the end of the period, those items should be valued at the lower of cost, if purchased, or fair value, if donated. If the items are to be sold later, the nonprofit will want to be sure that the ending inventory is adjusted to market or the price it would expect to receive for them when sold if it is lower than cost. If the items are donated, revenue is reduced when sold if cash is less than the amount recorded or increased if the cash is more than the amount recorded.

 Example

A nonprofit organization solicited items for its silent auction. The silent auction was not scheduled to be held until the following fiscal year. As the pledges came in, the nonprofit recorded them at their fair value, if it could easily be determined. Management knew that certain items such as the use of a member's vacation home for a week generally brought in $2,000 and use of another member's season football tickets generally brought in $75

(continued)

(continued)

per ticket for the 6 tickets. These items were recorded as inventory and contribution revenue at the date of donation. However, the 15 art objects and other collectibles that were donated were not recorded at the time of donation because the organization had little confidence in the amount it would receive for these items. When the silent auction was held the following year, the nonprofit received $2,800 for the use of the time share and $50 for each of the 6 football tickets. Revenue was increased $800 for the time share and reduced $300 for the tickets. The art objects sold for $350 in total. Management recorded the contribution revenue when they were sold.

Prepaid Expenses and Investments

Prepaid expenses are items that are paid in advance, such as amounts for insurance policies and rent. Prepaid expenses are recorded at the amount of value of the future benefits.

Nonprofits generally invest in securities that have fair values that are readily determinable. The return on the investments comes in the form of interest, dividends, and appreciation or depreciation in the fair value. The investments are adjusted up or down to their fair values, which gives rise to the appreciation or depreciation. Dividends and interest and the appreciation or depreciation are recorded as investment income. The fair value of these investments is generally provided by the custodian of the investments.

Evaluation Point: Management is responsible for the amounts presented in the financial statements. Management and the board have the responsibility to create an investment policy, monitor compliance with the investment policy, and analytically review the results of the investment account. Simply trusting that the custodian or investment advisor, where there is one, will do this is not appropriate. The nonprofit has the responsibility to the community and to the donors to ensure that all third parties handle the organization's assets in a responsible manner according to the nonprofit's investment policy.

Nonprofits only need to look at the devastation caused by Bernie Madoff to understand why this is important. Trust is only wise when it is warranted.

Alternative Investments

Some investments are considered alternative investments because their fair values are not readily determinable. Examples of alternative investments are an interest in a limited partnership, funds that are not traded on a stock exchange, real estate, or even a share of a race horse. These investments bear more risk and are considered illiquid because there is no active market for them and because they cannot easily be sold. Sometimes nonprofits received these investments as donations.

Voluntary health and welfare organizations and educational institutions are permitted to maintain these investments in their records at cost, unless their fair value is less (in which case the investments should be written down to fair value. Other types of nonprofits should adjust these investments to fair value each year.

Investing in alternative investments requires due diligence on the part of the investment committee to ensure that the investment is appropriate for the organization and monitoring to ensure that the investment is sold if it becomes too risky. A specialist may be necessary to determine the investment value. Nonprofits should also consider any liabilities that may be associated with donated investments such as land that has environmental issues that need to be addressed.

> **Evaluation Point:** The investment committee of the board should be involved whenever a decision is made to invest in alternative investments no matter how reliable the person or organization recommending the investment appears to be. The desire to obtain a higher rate of return is certainly commendable, but with a higher rate also comes higher risk. Nonprofits need to remember that balancing risk and return is very important and that if it sounds too good to be true, it probably is.

Property and Equipment

Property and equipment consists of land, buildings, equipment, vehicles, and other similar assets. Buildings, equipment, and vehicles are depreciated. Land is not. When assets are depreciated, management divides the dollar value of the asset by its estimated useful life and charges that amount to expense for the number of months in the period. Although there are methods other than the straight-line method just described, it is the most widely used by nonprofits. Depreciation attempts to match the productivity of the asset in the provision of the services provided by the organization. Property is recorded at cost less accumulated depreciation.

Liabilities

Accounts Payable and Accrued Expenses

Nonprofits, like commercial entities, incur liabilities. Some may be in the form of accounts payable in which the entity owes specific amounts that are billed by vendors, utility companies, and others. They also generally have accrued expenses that are not supported by an invoice but represent management's estimate of amounts owed. Accounts payable and accrued expenses are generally expected to be paid within 30 days to 2 months.

Example

A nonprofit paid its employees every 2 weeks by direct deposit. The deposit was made on the Tuesday following the end of the biweekly pay period. At June 30, 2009 (the company's year end), the biweekly pay period had ended on Friday June 26. This left two days (June 29 and 30) for which the employees had not been paid but were part of that year end's expenses. Management made an estimate of the pay owed to employees for those 2 days (weekly pay divided by 10 days multiplied by 2 days) and recorded it as an accrued expense.

Mortgages and Notes Payable

Mortgages and notes payable are long term obligations. The mortgage or note amount is recorded when originated. Mortgage payments represent principal and interest. The interest is recorded as expense, and the principal is recorded as a reduction of the outstanding mortgage balance.

Evaluation Point: Management should evaluate any debt covenants on at least a quarterly basis to ensure that the organization is in compliance. Debt covenants can range from meeting certain ratios such as the current ratio (current assets divided by current liabilities) to, for example, restrictions on what can be done without the bank's permission (such as additional purchases of plant and equipment). The organization may also need to meet certain compensating balance requirements. This is important particularly in bad economies when banks are likely to not renew lines of credit or to raise interest rates on variable debt. A good relationship with the lending institution is of critical importance.

Net Assets

Unrestricted net assets represent the excess of revenues and other support over expenses (or excess of expenses over revenues) since the inception of the organization. Temporarily restricted net assets represent amounts of net assets that have not been spent in accordance with donor instructions or, in the case of endowment funds in states that have adopted a version of UPMIFA, have not been appropriated for expenditure by the board. Permanently restricted net assets represent those that have been restricted in perpetuity by the donor.

Revenues and Expenses

Revenues were described in this chapter along with receivables. One distinguishing feature of the statement of activities is the line titled "release from restrictions." As can be noted in the sample statement of activities, the temporarily restricted net assets are reduced at the bottom of the statement and added back in at the top of the statement as net assets released from restrictions.

Nonprofits incur the same sorts of expenses as other organizations. The statement of activities illustrated shows the expenses by natural classification. A natural classification shows the expense detail with captions such as salaries and wages, rent, depreciation, supplies, and utilities. There is no GAAP requirement for specific captions or how much detail needs to be shown. The statement of functional expenses shows the expenses by natural classification and also by functional classification to provide information on the amounts spent for program, management, and general and fund-raising purposes. The nonprofit is not required to list a specific number of programs, only the number that makes sense for the nonprofit's board and constituents.

If the financial statements were not those of a voluntary health and welfare organization, it is likely that there would be a caption for program expenses, management, and general expenses and fund-raising expenses on the statement of activities instead of all the detail of a natural classification.

Evaluation Point: Management and the board will want to make comparisons between the budget for revenue and expenses and the actual revenue and expenses on a monthly basis. Comparisons should also be made between the prior year to date and the current year to date. Significant variances should be examined. Other financial statement analysis points will be discussed in chapter 7. Because donors and funding sources are very interested in the percentage of the expenses that are devoted to fund-raising and management and general expenses, management and the board should examine this area critically. It is important to be transparent and disclose the actual expense for these areas. Funding sources typically like to see at least 75 to 80 percent of resources devoted to programs. The board should evaluate the situation and spend as much on administration and fund-raising as they believe will be necessary to have accurate and transparent reporting, compliance with laws and regulations, and responsible fund-raising.

Conclusion

The ability to read and understand the nonprofit's financial statements is important to anyone who wants to really understand the organization. Nonprofit board members, executives, and those people involved in the financial management of the organization who have not been previously trained in nonprofit accounting can use this chapter as a reference when encountering unfamiliar concepts and situations.

Board members and executives, other than the financial officer, do not need to have the same depth of knowledge as those who work in the accounting function. However, they do need enough knowledge of the financial statement contents to perform their duties related to financial oversight.

Chapter 6

Risk Management

Jamie, the executive director of the Humanity Project, sat at her desk and wondered, "How could this catastrophe happen to us?" The gala event was well planned and was supposed to be the largest fundraiser of the year. Many of the city's wealthiest people were scheduled to attend, and the board was expecting the fundraiser to set the organization up to expand its work into additional developing countries where the need was great.

Jamie couldn't stop thinking about what happened. In her mind's eye, she could see the well-dressed donors and friends of Humanity Project sitting at their tables enjoying the entertainment on stage. One of the board members chaired the entertainment committee and invited a circus troupe complete with acrobats and a magician to entertain. The committee was proud of the fact that they found entertainment that would only cost the organization $500 for the night, making the fundraiser even more profitable.

One of the acts involved two acrobats, a juggler, and a circle of fire. During the middle of that act, one of the performers slipped, causing the juggler to fall off the stage. The ring of fire then hit the closest table, and the table cloth caught fire. Fortunately the overhead sprinklers came on, and no one was seriously hurt. But the patrons in their finery were drenched and so were the furnishings in the banquet hall.

Jamie shook her head. By morning, the event was all over the newspapers, television, and the internet, causing embarrassment to Jamie and the board. And to add to the pain, the organization had gone into debt to put on the fundraiser. The rent for the venue and the food, beverage, and entertainment charges amounted to $50,000. And the only donations received were the ones that the Humanity Project received before the event, approximately $20,000. Jamie didn't expect any more based on the feedback she received from the attendees.

But that wasn't the worst part. Earlier that morning, Jamie received a call from the owner of the Palisades, the venue where the fundraiser was held. He wanted to know how the Humanity Project was going to settle its bill for the damages to the banquet hall amounting to $75,000. Immediately Jamie called the board member who was responsible for the event and learned that the entertainment committee neglected to purchase event insurance and that the circus troupe was not insured. She should have followed up to make sure that all the contingencies were covered, but she thought that the board member and volunteer committee had it under control.

Some Risk Can't Be Mitigated With Insurance

Jamie might have been able to mitigate the damage to the Humanity Project if she had followed up with the board member to ensure that event insurance had been purchased. The organization might have further mitigated the damage if it had a system to respond quickly to repair the injury to its reputation arising from a negative event.

In March 2009, Milton, a board member of Preservation Green (a small nonprofit that addresses ecological and other environmental issues), got a call from Jim, the chair of the board, asking Milton to attend an emergency meeting the following Wednesday. Milton was still reeling from the effect that the downturn in the market had on his personal financial situation, but he responded affirmatively. At the meeting, the chair of the board informed the other board members that Preservation Green was all but bankrupt. The organization's endowment was down 40 percent since October 2008. Preservation Green counted on investment return to pay for many of its program expenses. Its only other sources of funding were a government grant and about 20 faithful donors. The decline in the portfolio was perhaps even worse than for other nonprofits because management had pursued a very aggressive investment strategy in an effort to generate income with which to subsidize operations. The state of Idaho, which in the past could be counted on for at least a $100,000 grant, was also severely affected by the economy and informed the executive director that Preservation Green could only expect $25,000 for its fiscal year 2010, which would begin in July. Milton was also concerned about the donors and their ability to live up to their pledge commitments. He had never considered these risk.

All entities face risk because all entities exist in a world of uncertainty. Merriam Webster defines *risk* as the possibility of loss or injury.[1] In the business context, risk is the possibility that an event will occur that will affect the entity negatively in some way. **Risk is a pervasive aspect of business, even in a nonprofit, and the world has become increasingly complex.** Nonprofits have not yet recovered from the 2008 financial crisis that hit not only the domestic but also the international economy. Many will never recover. Is this something that could have been anticipated and minimized with a better risk management strategy? If had boards put more emphasis on analyzing and overseeing their exposure to risk, would they be struggling today? Boards should be asking these questions.

There is more scrutiny on risk management following the 2008 financial crisis. The New York Stock Exchange's corporate governance rules require audit committees of listed entities to discuss risk assessment and management policies. In addition, Standard and Poor's and other rating agencies are including an evaluation of an entity's risk management process as part of its ratings process. Mary Shapiro, the Chairperson of the Securities and Exchange Commission (SEC), noted that the SEC would be considering additional disclosure about how a company and its board manage risks. The U.S. Treasury Department is considering

---

1 Retrieved from www.merriam-webster.com/dictionary/risk on April 16, 2011.

ways to align compensation of executives with risk management policies.[2] Although it is true that nonprofits do not answer to the SEC, they have seen the trickle down from legislation such as the Sarbanes Oxley Act of 2002. **And some larger nonprofits issue tax exempt debt, bringing them into the focus of regulatory bodies, rating agencies, and the public.**

Most large commercial enterprises have risk management systems in place to identify and deal with uncertainty. Unfortunately, smaller entities, which include many nonprofit organizations, do not. But even the larger entities are not all satisfied with their boards' risk oversight processes. According to a study commissioned by the Committee of Sponsoring Organizations of the Treadway Commission (COSO),[3] which was published in December 2010, approximately half of 200 participating boards believe they are performing their risk oversight responsibilities in an effective manner. Others indicated their boards are not sufficiently proactive in their oversight process. Seventeen percent of the study participants were boards of nonprofit organizations.

Traditional risk management approaches generally focus on asset protection and compliance with laws, regulations, and contractual arrangements. Consequently, the risk response generally applied is the purchase of insurance. This may take the form of insurance on property, buildings, and equipment or liability insurance against actions of employees and mishaps on the part of others. Although these things are important, they may not be enough. A nonprofit has significant sources of value that need to be protected, which may include physical assets and liability to others at special events and can include much more.

In their book *Cracking the Value Code: See What Matters, Invest in What Matters and Manage What Matters in the New Economy*, Richard Boulton, Barry Libert, and Steve Samek mention five broad categories of assets that represent sources of value.[4] These categories expand the notion of risk management to cover a broader spectrum and address areas that are not always considered. The categories are illustrated in figure 6-1.

This chapter discusses the types of risk nonprofits face and the methods used to identify and implement an appropriate response.

A Nonprofit's Most Important Resource

Nonprofit boards and management need to consider risk and uncertainty in the light of their unique characteristics:
- A nonprofit's products are its programs.
- A nonprofit's main value is its reputation.
- Nonprofits have employees, but they also deal with unpaid personnel in the form of volunteers over whom they are not able to exercise the same level of control. However, they are deeply affected when volunteers exhibit inappropriate or fraudulent behavior.

---

2 "Effective Enterprise Risk Oversight, The Role of the Board of Directors," Committee of Sponsoring Organizations of the Treadway Commission (COSO), 2009.

3 "Board Risk Oversight, A Progress Report," COSO and Protiviti, December 2010.

4 Richard E. S. Boulton, Barry D. Libert, and Steve M. Samek, *Cracking the Value Code: See What Matters, Invest in What Matters and Manage What Matters in the New Economy* (New York: HarperCollins Publishers, 2000).

Figure 6-1: *Sources of Value in a Nonprofit Organization*

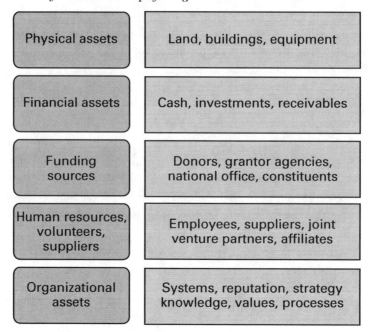

Physical assets	Land, buildings, equipment
Financial assets	Cash, investments, receivables
Funding sources	Donors, grantor agencies, national office, constituents
Human resources, volunteers, suppliers	Employees, suppliers, joint venture partners, affiliates
Organizational assets	Systems, reputation, strategy knowledge, values, processes

The reputation of the nonprofit is its foundation. Donors and other funding sources consider the standing of the organization in the community as well as what they know of management and the board's integrity when determining whether to donate or to provide funding. This point cannot be overemphasized. But fraud and other adverse circumstances happen to many organizations. Some survive with the help of risk management strategies, but some do not. Consider the following.

In 1982 and then again in 1986, Johnson and Johnson (J&J) faced negative events of monumental proportions. Seven people died in 1982 when Tylenol, a leading analgesic, was laced with cyanide. The company could have tried to wait out the scandal but instead re-called 31 million bottles of the product. James Burke, the CEO, was the calm in the storm, appearing on television and meeting the situation head on. In 1986, Tylenol capsules were poisoned again. This time, in addition to recalling the product, the company introduced "tamper-proof" packaging and stopped making capsules. These actions cost the company approximately $200 million. The cost was high for J&J, but the brand survived. The way that J&J handled the situation is taught in Harvard Business School today. The Tylenol scandal is a good example of corporate ethics at the forefront of a risk management program. The company's mission stresses its responsibilities to the consumers and medical profession-als using its products, employees, the communities where its people work and live, as well as its stockholders. Clearly, the risk management plan was deployed in an effective manner.[5]

Other entities have not been as successful, resulting in loss of not only their reputation but also the company itself. A good case in point is Arthur Andersen, which was one of the

---

5 Jia Lynn Yang, "Getting a handle on a scandal," *Fortune* (May 22 2007). Retrieved from money.cnn.com/magazines/fortune/fortune_ archive/2007/05/28/100033741/index.htm.

"Big 5" accounting firms. It, like other professional service firms, had the equivalent of malpractice insurance that insured against lawsuits filed against them due to failed audits. In 2002, it faced one of those failures, but its risk management plan was not up to the challenge. Due to the actions of a few partners and other professionals in the firm who interfered with the investigation and tried to cover up their actions, and due to the inability of the firm to manage the negative publicity, clients started leaving the firm. Once the clients expressed lack of confidence, it was all over for the firm, even though Arthur Andersen was exonerated in 2005 of its obstruction of justice conviction.

To protect the assets of the organization, nonprofits should adopt a risk management system. The system must be the right size to fit the needs of the organization. Boards should remember that they have a responsibility to the organization and to its constituents to monitor risk.

Risk Management Approach

Risk management systems can be broadly divided into four important phases:
1. Identify the possibilities of risk to the organization.
2. Understand the likelihood that this risk could occur and the magnitude of the ramifications to the organization if it did occur.
3. Plan for a response before, not after, the fact.
4. Put mechanisms in place to mitigate the risk.

Enterprise Risk Management

Enterprise Risk Management (ERM) is a concept that was popularized by COSO in 2004 when it issued its *Enterprise Risk Management—Integrated Framework* (COSO framework). The COSO framework was designed to provide the board and management with a comprehensive system of risk identification, prioritization, and implementation. ERM can be implemented by both large and small organizations. ERM is a more structured approach of understanding both the external and the internal environments and proactively identifying the risk of loss to all sources of value to the organization that are inherent in its business model. COSO's *Internal Control—Integrated Framework*, which is discussed in chapter 7, is designed to be incorporated within the COSO framework.[6]

ERM has seven important components, as described in the following paragraphs.[7]

ERM Component One

ERM is a process. This means that it is not performed one time but is an ongoing activity that is regularly evaluated, modified with changes in circumstances and improved. Most organizations that have been in existence over time have modified their programs and methods of conducting business. With changes in the business model come additional risks.

---

6 *Enterprise Risk Management—Integrated Framework*, COSO, 2004.

7 Adapted from the definition of *enterprise risk management* in *Enterprise Risk Management—Integrated Framework*.

The Alzheimer's Project was founded in 1985 to provide counseling and respite to Alzheimer's patients and their families. Up until 2007, fund-raising was primarily conducted by direct mail campaigns and various fund-raising events. In 2007, concerned about the cost of postage and wanting to expand the donor base, the Alzheimer's Project hired a professional to update its website so that it was more interactive. The website would collect the names and addresses of interested people, and fund-raising appeals could be sent out to the entire database by use of its automatic response generator with the touch of a button. The messages could be written in advance and set up to be sent out at predefined intervals, saving time and postage. People who cared about the disease could post content to the site that they believed would be helpful to other interested parties. With the new website, donors could give online.

Management considered the benefits but did not consider the controls that would be needed when taking donations online, including controls over access to the associated bank accounts and the possibility of inaccurate communication related to donor restrictions. In addition, management failed to consider law and regulations related to spam* as well as the risks involved in permitting content on its website that had not been vetted by the organization.

* Detailed information on spam requirements can be found in the Federal Trade Commission publication "The CAN-SPAM Act: A Compliance Guide for Business" at business.ftc.gov/documents/bus61-can-spam-act-compliance-guide-business.

ERM Component Two

ERM is designed and implemented by people at all levels of the organization. This is significant because if every employee, board member, and volunteer took responsibility for risk, fewer incidents would occur. Additionally, people from different backgrounds may bring new ideas for improvement to the process.

Windward Shelter had many volunteers, including board members, who would assist in preparing and serving meals and performing other tasks associated with the shelter. Preparing and serving food requires diligence from a public health standpoint, and dealing with numbers of people who may be impaired either mentally or through the use of alcohol and drugs increases the risk of incidents happening at the shelter. All volunteers and staff were screened and then trained before they were given responsibilities working with people served by the shelter. Part of their training included watching out for spills or other hazards that could cause falls, maintaining appropriate sanitation standards, and dealing with people seeking assistance at the shelter. Volunteers were instructed how to handle a variety of common incidents that might occur and were told to contact supervisory personnel immediately whenever an incident did occur. In this way, risk was mitigated.

ERM Component Three

ERM is utilized in strategy-setting. When risk management becomes part of the ongoing strategic management process, strategic decisions are made while risk to the organization is fully considered. Decisions made without proper consideration of risk often result in unexpected costs in excess of expected benefit. And often, once choices are made, it is extremely difficult to undo them.

Yeshiva Academy, a large private school with religious affiliation, was considering the economic downturn and how it had impacted the donations that were necessary to keep tuition affordable. The board believed that, to the extent possible, tuition should be subsidized. One of the board members had an idea for raising additional funds. The school was located in an advantageous location, and there was ample room to expand the parking lot. The board voted to expand the bookstore and sell more than just text books and uniforms. The bookstore would sell popular fiction and nonfiction as well as gift items including items of religious significance. There was talk of a kosher coffee shop and café. Market research was performed and construction commenced. The idea was sound, but the risk to the organization from this new venture was not adequately assessed. Consideration of the venture's impact on unrelated business income and tax exempt status never crossed the board's mind. Understanding the impact of these issues on the organization is important. If the board goes ahead with its plans, the processes, controls, and insurance that would mitigate the risk should be implemented before and not after the new venture begins.

ERM Component Four

ERM is applied to every part of the organization; each part is taken into consideration as part of a portfolio, and risk is evaluated accordingly. In larger organizations, this may mean the organization's separate business units or affiliates. In smaller organizations, this may mean specific programs or grantors and funding sources.

Portfolio Approach to Assessment of Risk

ERM Component Five

ERM takes into consideration the entity's "appetite" for risk. This means how much risk the entity is willing to bear. The possible adverse events are evaluated against this risk appetite. Although all nonprofits tend to be conservative, some are more so than others. ERM provides guidelines for a process to identify potential events that would affect the organization so that the entity can manage risk within its risk parameters.

> West Sky Foundation has a very large endowment. Because the purpose of the endowment is to provide funding for West Sky School scholarships, the board took several factors into consideration when assessing the risk that the foundation would be willing to bear:
> - The amount needed to fund a certain number of scholarships per year (spending policy)
> - Other available funding
> - Market factors
> - Time horizon for investment, which for West Sky was 5 years
> - Tolerable loss, which for West Sky was 30 percent (before the market decline)
>
> West Sky had an investment committee that assessed risk and followed a practice of frequent evaluation of its investment policy, diversification, benchmarking, and rebalancing. This practice was performed at least once a year in times when there was less risk in the financial markets. However, when triggering events such as those that caused the 2008–2009 market decline occurred, the risk evaluation was made more frequently.
>
> In light of the market decline, the committee reset its risk tolerance to 20 percent instead of 30 percent and evaluated the amount that would be held in equities, fixed income, and cash. West Sky's risk appetite was sufficiently conservative in that it only permitted 5 percent of its portfolio to be held in alternative investments. Because these were illiquid, nothing could be done to alter that percentage. After evaluating the risk, the committee set the new asset allocation percentages:
> - 5 percent alternative investments
> - 20 percent equities
> - 30 percent fixed income (corporate)
> - 30 percent treasury securities
> - 15 percent cash[

ERM Component Six

ERM provides the board and management with reasonable, but not absolute, assurance that the organization is bearing risk within the parameters set by the board and that there is a plan for mitigating risk. By implementing ERM, the board and management have an enhanced ability to identify potential events, establish responses, and reduce surprises, thereby reducing loss to the organization. The information in table 6-1 illustrates an application of the ERM principles to Big SIS Little SIS, an organization that works with "at risk" children. Big SIS Little SIS relies heavily on volunteers to work with its programs.[8]

---

8 *Enterprise Risk Management—Integrated Framework*, COSO, 2004.

Table 6-1: *ERM Approach for Nonprofits—Example*

ERM Component	Volunteer Services—Big Sis, Little Sis
Internal Environment: Sets a basis for how risk is viewed and addressed by the organization including the risk appetite, integrity, and ethical values.	The organization views volunteers as part of the organization. They are screened and trained in the same way as employees to try to ensure that incidents do not occur and, if they do, that the volunteers are able to handle them.
Objective Setting: Management has a process in place to set objectives that support the organization's mission and are consistent with the risk appetite.	The organization maintains adequate insurance to cover liabilities that could rise due to the action of volunteers. Those that handle cash are bonded.
Event Identification: A process is in place to identify both internal and external events that would affect how objectives are achieved.	Volunteers are provided with training on the risks related to working with at-risk children and are given explicit instructions on how to handle themselves in crisis situations. A licensed social worker on staff is always on call to field questions and intervene, if necessary.
Risk Assessment: Management analyzes risks to determine how they should be managed. When considering risk, the likelihoods of occurrence and impact are assessed.	Management screens and evaluates the background and capabilities of individuals prior to permitting them to work with children. Licensed social workers evaluate the children in the program and match them to volunteers. Monthly meetings are held to proactively assess risk related to the program and discuss any issues that have occurred. More frequent meetings are held, if necessary. Risks are analyzed regarding the likelihood of occurrence and impact.
Risk Response: Management identifies the appropriate response for each risk. This could include avoiding, accepting, reducing, or sharing the risk.	Management purchases adequate coverage not only related to liability of volunteer actions but also for special events. Parents of children in the program are required to sign release documents.
Control Activities: Policies and procedures that enable the organization to implement the risk response effectively.	Volunteers must attend training and sign a code of ethics each year. A list of permissible activities is provided. They fill out activity sheets each time they work with a child. A supervisor approves the activities. A report is also made after the activity.
Information and Communication: Mechanism to disseminate relevant information to those who need it so that people can fulfill their responsibilities.	All instructions are in writing and available on an intranet as well as in written form. Channels of communication are open, and quarterly volunteer meetings are led by program staff.
Monitoring: Mechanism to determine whether processes, or the activities that confirm that actions have occurred, are effective.	The program director monitors the control activities weekly. She evaluates the information on the activity sheets to determine if any changes need to be made. Monthly reports are made to the board.

The risk response mechanism is created with the organization's risk appetite in mind. There are many ways to respond to risk:

- **Avoid risk.** After assessing risk of its various programs (whether it is an initial or ongoing assessment), an organization may decide that it does not want to offer that service or will discontinue offering that service. For example, if an organization cannot obtain sufficient qualified personnel or volunteers for one of its programs, then it may decide to discontinue it.
- **Share the risk.** An organization may decide that it prefers to purchase sufficient insurance coverage from an outside party. Another way to share risk is to involve other organizations in the project.
- **Modify risk.** Risk can be modified by changing the way that a certain activity is performed. In the investment example, the risk was assessed and parameters set initially. Once a triggering event occurred, risk was modified by changing the parameter so less harm was likely to occur.

• **Retain risk.** An organization may evaluate the risk of an activity, such as workers compensation insurance for its employees, and decide that it will be less expensive to partially self-fund the risk by entering into a risk pool with similar organizations so that part of the risk is borne by the organization. This decision could be made with consideration given to the organization's risk with employees to date and to the reduction in cost related to this option.

 Example

Golden Years, a nonprofit that provides social services to elder citizens, was approached by the county to perform certain services under a state grant. The state received the funds from the federal government's American Recovery and Reinvestment Act of 2009 (ARRA). The management and the board of Golden Years believed that the project was one that was needed in the community, and, although their administrative resources were stretched to the limit, they accepted the grant. The program was conducted very well, and the state was happy with the results. However, when the federal agency came in and conducted an audit, it found that the funding was not tracked and reported exactly as required by the program. The nonprofit simply did not have the resources to perform the administrative duties on a timely basis. The federal agency wrote a finding. A newspaper was performing investigations into misspent money from the ARRA program, and Golden Years was one of the nonprofits mentioned in the article that did not comply with the program requirements. Management and board members were embarrassed and wished that they had assessed the risk of taking on a high profile program when they had insufficient capacity. Risk avoidance might have been a better approach to deal with this new program.

 Example

During the planning meeting for the upcoming year's programs, Jane, one of the board members of a church, suggested that Morty Hamm, a high profile religious motivational speaker, be invited to speak to the members on a Friday night because he was going to be speaking in a neighboring city the next day. The members agreed that Morty's message was congruent with the church's beliefs, but Morty was not an inexpensive speaker. Other board members were concerned that the offerings taken up at the event might not be enough to cover expenses because the church wasn't very large; the financial risk was too high. Jane had another idea and asked the board if they thought that a joint venture with other churches might bring in sufficient people to not only cover the expenses but provide additional funding that could be shared and used for other programs. The board commended Jane for her creative idea and made a motion to ask other churches if they would be willing to participate in the project. Sharing the risk with others was the right approach.

Example

Briarcreek Animal Clinic is a nonprofit clinic that provides low cost services to animal shelters and the animals of people who either adopt them or provide foster care. After serving the immediate community for 10 years, management and the board decided to extend the clinic's reach by building another center 15 miles away. To do this, they needed to solicit donations. Most of their current donors' contributions were unrestricted.

It was not very difficult to raise some money from the current donors because the organization's donors appreciated the work Briarcreek did in the community. But it would take more funds than current donors could provide to undertake the expansion project. Briarcreek found that new donors wanted to restrict their gifts, not just to the construction but to specific furnishings and other purposes. Unfortunately, these donors did not understand that by restricting donations to a particular purpose they were placing a large administrative burden on Briarcreek. Management also observed that grants came with specific compliance requirements. Briarcreek had never sought out grant funding before this project. Management and the board discussed this situation before accepting the restricted donations and grants. They decided that the best way to minimize the risk of noncompliance with the donor's restricted purposes and to ensure grant compliance was to modify their internal control and operating procedures to include
- analysis of the donor and grant requirements.
- periodic monitoring for compliance.
- communication with the donors, not only by acknowledgement of gift acceptance but also through ongoing progress updates in the form of newsletters.
- evaluation of the restricted donations and grants to ensure that if funds were not able to be spent in accordance with donor or grantor requirements, the individual or entity was contacted to see if modifications would be possible

ERM Component Seven

ERM's goal is to help the board and management achieve organizational goals. These goals are as follows:
- **Strategic.** Promote broad, high level goals that support the mission, vision and values of the organization
- **Operational.** Promote the effective and efficient use of its human and financial resources
- **Financial reporting.** Promote the transparency and reliability of financial reporting
- **Compliance.** Promote compliance with applicable laws, regulations, contract, grant agreements, and donor restrictions

All of these areas are important. However, a challenge that even large organizations face is that it is difficult to implement ERM on all of these goals initially. One key purpose of

ERM is to tie risk management into strategy in order to provide additional value to the organization. As will be discussed in this chapter, organizations face many constraints when trying to do this. And, even though the ERM framework is designed to be comprehensive, individual components can be used to an organization's advantage without implementing them all.

Example Application of a Risk Management System to a Nonprofit Organization

Guiding Light Counseling Center (introduced in the beginning of this chapter) is a non-profit organization with $2,500,000 in revenue. It has several programs and enjoys a large volunteer base. Its volunteers are people with a passion for the mission, and about 40 percent of them are licensed professionals such as social workers, counselors, registered dieticians, and yoga instructors. Other volunteers are kind hearted people that have few relevant skills but want to contribute. Guiding Light has a large endowment from a donor who provided for the organization in his estate. The organization relies on the income from the endowment to support its programs.

At the end of every fiscal year, management and the board attend a retreat and spend time assessing risk. This year, one of its board members suggested that the organization use a technique that he saw used effectively in his company. For step one, prior to the retreat, the members of the board and middle and executive management were asked to identify what they believed were the most significant risks to the entity. They were asked to identify the things that "kept them up at night" and also to review the five categories in which risk could be present. Often there are risks present that board members never even realized were risks. The following list was compiled from the results of that request.

Area	Identified Risks
Physical assets	• Loss of data in its computerized information systems through fire or other destruction of equipment.
Financial assets	• Decline of investment so that income is not available to fund programs. • Lack of segregation of duties in the accounting department could result in error or fraud. • Diversion of funds in evening programs when cash is collected and volunteers are used as counselors.
Funding sources	• Lack of diversity of funding sources, reliance on fee for service income, several large donors, and few small donors.
Human resources, volunteers, suppliers	• Loss of employees due to the lower salaries that are paid compared to commercial enterprises. • Lack of skilled volunteers. • Volunteers who fail to show up for duty.
Organizational elements	• Litigation for malpractice. • Unauthorized entry into the information system causing concerns over confidentiality of information.

For step two, the participants in the session discussed the risks and then assessed each one as to the likelihood that it could occur and the impact (financial and reputational) that it would have on the organization if it did. A scale of 1 to 5 was used, with 5 being the highest. To simplify the tabulation of the results, each participant brought a laptop, and the organization's wireless network facilitated the use of a program called Survey Monkey on the internet (www.surveymonkey.com).

The results follow.

Prioritizing Risks

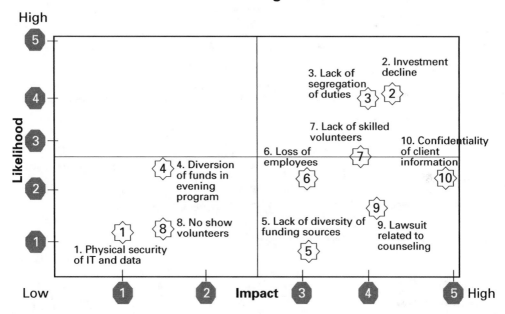

For step three, once the risks had been evaluated as to the likelihood that they would occur and the impact to the organization if they did, the board voted to put its priority on the risks in the upper right quadrant. In this case, because risks numbered 6, 7, and 10 were close to the upper quadrant, they were included in the initial focus. The remaining risks would be addressed, but, because they were either less likely to occur because of programs already in place or would not have a significant impact, they would be addressed as time permitted. The action plan to initially address the most important risks follows.

Risk	Risk Appetite	Response
Possible decline of investment so that income is not available to fund programs	**Low:** Decline of more than 15 percent is unacceptable.	Create investment strategy to respond to risk and monitor quarterly. Committee will be responsible for watching economic conditions to identify any triggering events that would make more frequent evaluation necessary. Consult investment professional for advice.
Lack of segregation of duties in the accounting department that could result in error or fraud	**Moderate:** The organization should be above approach, but employees are expensive. The audit committee can assist with closer monitoring.	Ask external auditor for advice on segregation of duties with present staff. Evaluate bank products, such as positive pay, direct deposit, and lockbox. Implement where benefits justify the cost. CFO will monitor cash controls more frequently. Audit committee will provide monitoring support.
Unauthorized entry into the information system causing concerns over confidentiality of information	**Low:** Any entrance into the IT system would be unacceptable.	Consult IT professionals to determine vulnerability and ways to improve this area immediately.
Lack of skilled volunteers	**Low or Moderate:** Based on the type of volunteer. Volunteers in the programs should be skilled; those volunteering in administrative functions less so. Without sufficient program volunteers, the programs could serve fewer people.	Seek out best practices in volunteer recruiting. Seek out associations where potential volunteers go. Use social networking to increase visibility of organization and volunteer roles. Affiliate with the local university for internship placements.
Potential loss of employees due to the lower salaries that are paid compared to commercial enterprises	**Moderate:** Due to the economy, fewer people are leaving their jobs.	Evaluate employee satisfaction and seek out programs that may be desired by employees (paid time off) but are still inexpensive. Conduct interviews at exit and 1-year postexit to identify practices in need of improvement.

Once the action plan was in place, the board requested that an evaluation be performed and a report prepared monthly for their review on the progress made on each of the goals. In addition, they voted to reassess risk (1) before new programs were launched, (2) when indicators in the economy or market or changes in the nonprofit warranted it, and (3) toward the end of each fiscal year before the preparation of the coming year's budget.

ERM in Smaller Nonprofit Organizations

The ERM framework was written to support the strategic objectives of the entities that use it. In many cases, it may be a goal that is difficult to achieve in its entirety because it was designed to encompass all of the activities of the entity and address strategic, operational, financial reporting, and compliance risks. This may be too much for a smaller nonprofit or its board to tackle. According to "Board Risk Oversight, A Progress Report," commissioned by COSO, almost 75 percent of the respondents to the survey identified at least 3 obstacles to the risk oversight process, including more pressing needs, failure to see the value of ERM, lack of understanding of what it does or can accomplish, and lack of resources to implement it. Some believed it was really more of a compliance activity than a strategic activity.[9]

Smaller organizations can still benefit from using the process in a more abbreviated way, as illustrated in the preceding examples. After an overall risk assessment, more priority could be placed on the areas that management and the board feel are more valuable. Additionally, a more detailed risk assessment for certain activities could be delegated to committees:

- **Audit committee.** Focuses on financial reporting risk and compliance risk related to tax exempt status and compliance with donor requirements and grant agreements.
- **Investment committee.** Focuses on investment risk.
- **Compensation committee.** Focuses on risk related to inappropriate or inadequate compensation or compensation that may be supportable but hard to defend to the public.
- **Program committee.** Focuses on risk related to programs and volunteers.
- **Development committee.** Focuses on risk related to funding sources, primarily raising funds and qualifications of donors.
- **Risk management committee.** Oversees the risk assessment process, helps to guide others in assessing the organization's risk appetite, and prioritizes how risk is addressed with the organization's resources. This is very important when the organization's resources are limited.

Risk Management Committee

Even if the nonprofit is small, a risk management committee of the board may be a good investment of time and effort. This committee would perform the following duties:

- Develop a risk management policy that includes elements of crisis management. This policy would set the overall philosophy of the organization related to risk management and contain a broad statement of the organization's willingness to accept risk (risk appetite). The policy would be presented to the board for approval. This policy would be reviewed each year and modified if necessary.
- Solicit feedback from management and the board as to where the risks lie in the organization related to
  — physical assets;
  — financial assets;
  — compliance with contracts, grant agreements, and donor restrictions;
  — employee behavior;
  — volunteers;
  — information technology; and
  — dealings over the internet and social media programs reputational risks.
- Solicit input as to the likelihood that the risk would occur and the magnitude if it did.
- Suggest risk responses.

---

9 "Board Risk Oversight, A Progress Report," COSO and Protiviti, December 2010.

The board would be briefed on the activities of the risk management committee at least once a quarter and more frequently if necessary.

Crisis Management

The term *crisis* is defined by Merriam Webster Online Dictionary as "an unstable or crucial time or state of affairs in which a decisive change is impending, *especially* one with the distinct possibility of a highly undesirable outcome" or "a situation that has reached a critical phase."[10] Examples of crises a nonprofit could face are

- major funding source decides not to renew a grant or make a donation.
- lack of cash to make payroll or pay other expenses.
- fraud on the part of management or fraud that is more than inconsequential either quantitatively or qualitatively.
- flood, fire, or other peril.
- operational mishap such as an accident (for example, bus accident transporting children or volunteer accused of sexual misconduct with a child in a program).
- disruption of special event (for example, unanticipated snow in the south on the day of a planned event).
- unfavorable publicity, whether warranted or not.
- intense scrutiny from the media or regulatory body.

The best position from which to manage crisis is a position of preparedness. Nonprofits should consider

- establishing favorable ongoing relationships with the media.
- creating a crisis management manual.
- instituting a disaster recovery program for information technology.
- conducting preparedness training for staff and volunteers.
- reviewing existing insurance coverage on a periodic basis to determine if needs are adequate.
- purchasing insurance for special events consistent with the organization's risk appetite (for example, event cancellation insurance).
- formulating strategies to deal with the media when an unfortunate event occurs.
- engaging in business continuity planning for critical programs that are important for the community or the nonprofit's survival.

The committee should create a communications plan in the event of an emergency. According to Melanie Lockwood Herman, from the Nonprofit Risk Management Center, there is evidence to support that many emergencies are predictable and that signs are often evident if someone is looking for them. This could range from watching the weather forecast when tornados, hurricanes, or snowstorms are imminent; to utilizing environmental scanning to be aware of sector trends; to identifying fraud in the organization. She shares several important tips for dealing with stakeholders:[11]

---

10 "Crisis," *Merriam Webster Online Dictionary:* (Merriam-Webster, Inc., 2011). Retrieved from www.merriam-webster.com/dictionary/crisis on April 16, 2011.

11 Melanie L. Herman, *Ready... or Not: A Risk Management Guide for Nonprofit Executives* (Nonprofit Risk Management Center, 2009).

- A person in authority should be the one to discuss the situation and the course of action to be taken.
- Candor is important.
- The spokesperson needs to have the facts. For example, if there were a fire in a nonprofit preschool, the number of people hurt or taken to the hospital would be of crucial importance. Speculation can cause damage.
- Sincerity and compassion are important. The spokesperson should be friendly, compassionate, concerned, and professional.

Stakeholder perceptions are very important. If they can be addressed in communications, a great deal of adverse publicity and bad feelings can be averted.

A crisis management plan needs to consider all the stakeholders of the organization. Some may be quite obvious, such as the staff and their families, clients (or constituents) and their families, volunteers, and members of the board. But others also need to be considered, such as donors, local government officials, grantors, and related organizations. In addition, it is important to communicate with the professional advisors such as accountants, financial advisors, and, of course, insurance professionals.

Revisiting Uncertainty

Nonprofits that employ risk management are more likely to be to be successful in the long run. The nonprofit world has become extremely complex. A nonprofit board should realize that although its organization is designed to be mission-driven, with a primary focus on programs, it can all be derailed when unanticipated events occur. This causes suffering not only for the nonprofit but also for its stakeholders and clientele. Boards need to understand that bad news travels quickly and that nonprofits can be harmed by public perception, even though it may not be entirely accurate. Also, nonprofits are heavily scrutinized by regulators and watchdog agencies, not to mention the media. A risk management system is a business imperative for nonprofits and should be considered in a form that suits the size and complexity of the organization. Boards are ultimately responsible, and a risk management system can provide protection and peace of mind.

Conclusion

All entities face risk because all entities exist in a world of uncertainty. The nonprofit world is becoming progressively more complex and faces ever-changing and frequently brand new risks. In this environment, every nonprofit should have a risk management system that takes into consideration its size and complexity. After reading this chapter, board members and executives should be able to identify the types of risk nonprofits face, methods to identify and implement an appropriate response, and a method for prioritizing risks so that available effort can be focused where it is most needed. A prompt, honest, and proactive response to a crisis is best. Any attempt to cover up is likely to only make the situation worse.

Organizations often give too low a priority to risk management because it is not perceived as urgent. What is likely, however, is that over the course of an organization's existence, one or more of these risks will develop into a crisis. At that point, it is too late to plan ahead; having a response plan ready may make the difference between failure and survival. The old saying is still very true: an ounce of prevention is worth a pound of cure. It is also important to keep in mind that risk management is an ongoing activity and not something that can be done once and put on the shelf. Perhaps the ultimate incentive to give due attention to risk is simply that nonprofits that employ risk management are more likely to be to be successful in the long run.

Appendix A
Risk Management Checklist

This checklist is not meant to be comprehensive but serves as a good starting point for a nonprofit to tailor to its needs.

Risk	Questions/Items Needed	Responsibility	Have? Yes or No
Legal risks: retain important documents and ensure that they are secured in the event of fire or other destruction	• IRS filings, including Forms 1023 and 990 (maintain all years filed) • Charitable solicitation filings • Bylaws • Resolutions • Incorporation documents • Committee charters • Leases • Deeds • Mortgages • Loans • Licenses • Patents, trademarks, and so forth. • Insurance records		
Compliance risk	• Does the mission of the organization still agree with the mission as stated on the Form 1023 and current Form 990? • Does the organization retain the minutes of its meetings of governing boards and committees? • Does the organization retain document of its compensation evaluations and decisions? • Does the organization evaluate its compliance with health and safety regulations? • Does the organization evaluate its compliance with other regulations that are specific to its operations? • Does the nonprofit meet all of the tests for its tax exempt status? • Does the organization comply with IRS rules regarding donor acknowledgement?		
Insurance	• Has risk been evaluated and insurance purchased where needed? — Directors' and officers' liability — General liability — Event insurance — Bonds for employees — Business continuity — Liability for certain circumstances related to operations, such as malpractice or professional liability — Workers compensation — Health insurance		

(continued)

(continued)

Risk	Questions/Items Needed	Responsibility	Have? Yes or No
Board liability	• Is the board performing the appropriate level of monitoring and oversight? • Does the board have the right number of committees to provide expertise in key areas (audit, compensation, risk management, investment)? • Does the organization employ professionals when the expertise is not in house (auditors, investment managers, attorneys, actuaries, valuation specialists, and so forth)? • Are there antifraud controls in place? (See chapter 7 for more description.) • Does the board regularly evaluate key executives, in part, on risk management? • Does the board receive the appropriate amount of training?		
Third party use of the organization's property	• Does the organization carefully evaluate any requests for use of the facilities by a third party to assess the risk involved? • Does the organization require third parties to provide proof of liability coverage prior to allowing them to use the facility? • Does the organization carefully evaluate the activities of third parties to ensure that they do not affect the organization from a reputational standpoint? • Does the organization ensure that the fees charged are appropriate and that the possibility of unrelated business income is evaluated?		
Property issues	• Does the organization comply with zoning requirements? • Did the organization evaluate any issues related to environmental hazards? • Has there been an evaluation of occupational health and safety?		

Risk	Questions/Items Needed	Responsibility	Have? Yes or No
Employment and volunteers	• Does the nonprofit conduct adequate background and reference checks, including whether or not legal actions have been brought against the applicant? Charges of abuse against children (if applicable)? Sexual harassment charges? • Are volunteers screened in the same manner as employees? • Are board members screened in the same manner as employees? • Are laws governing nondiscrimination followed? • Is there a code of ethics and conflict of interest policy? • Has the code of ethics and conflict of interest policy been signed by those deemed necessary by the organization? • Is there a disciplinary process for infractions of the code of ethics or conflict of interest policy, or both? • Is there a whistleblower policy and a way for employees and volunteers to report incidents that make them uncomfortable without reprisal?		

Gift acceptance	• Is there a gift acceptance policy?
	• Are there guidelines on when to consult legal counsel before accepting gifts?
	• Does the policy state
	  — what types of gifts the organization accepts, and what it does not accept?
	  — under what circumstances gifts will be accepted?
	  — how gifts will be recognized and tracked?
	  — how major gifts, such as real estate, life insurance policies, and stock, will be handled?
	• If the organization uses some of its restricted gifts for operations, do the campaign and pledge materials state that some of the restricted gift is withheld and deemed unrestricted in order to administer the contribution?
	• Does the organization have a policy related to the types of planned gifts that will be accepted?
	• Does the organization review its gift acceptance policy at least annually?		

(continued)

113

(continued)

Risk	Questions/Items Needed	Responsibility	Have? Yes or No
Crisis management	Has the organization addressed how it will address crises, including the following: • Spokesperson • Media contact • Contact with stakeholders • Other pertinent issues		
Financial	• Does the organization have adequate segregation of duties? Are all regulatory filings (for example, payroll, IRS annual forms, benefits return or report [that is, Form 5500]) made on a timely basis? • Are internal controls evaluated for adequacy to prevent or detect and correct errors or fraud, or both? • Is there an audit committee in place? • Does the board review the financial statements monthly? • Are audited financial statements reviewed by the board? • Is Form 990 reviewed by the board? • Does the organization only spend restricted funds for restricted purposes? • Are accounts reconciled to the general ledger?		

Chapter 7

Internal Controls: What Every Executive and Board Member Needs to Know

Carl sat at the head of the boardroom table looking somber. He had just left a meeting with the CFO of his nonprofit, Cheerful Giver, an organization that raised money to fund social service organizations. He knew he had to tell the board that giving was at an all-time low. In fact, contributions to the organization declined from $25 million in 2009 to $7.5 million in 2010. Sure, the economy was at fault, but the root cause of the decline was due to a fraud that was brought to light by one of the organization's accountants early in the year. It had been going on for 5 years. Once the fraud was exposed in the news media, word crept like a virus across the internet, and longtime donors started calling to try to understand what happened. To make matters worse, once the new fund-raising campaign started, donors stopped returning phone calls. It was evident that they didn't want to give money to an organization that would let a fraud go on for so long.

Who would have believed that the CEO, a person in a position of trust, could have stolen money from his own organization? Who would have believed that the board could have let this happen? The words of the external auditor came back to him. "Management and those charged with governance (the board) are responsible for implementing and maintaining internal control over financial reporting and compliance with laws and regulations and provisions of contract and grant agreements." The CEO always said that implementing internal controls was disruptive and cost too much money, money that should be spent on the organization's programs. To be honest, Carl knew he couldn't even identify what internal controls could have prevented this fiasco. He thought that management would handle it. But how do you explain that to donors?

Characteristics of Nonprofits

The preceding story was based on a very high profile case of fraud that gained national attention in 2004. The sad thing about it is that even as recently as 2008 donations had never recovered. And this is not an isolated incident. Nonprofit boards and executives often have a belief that it could never happen to them. Gerard Zack calls this the NIMO (not in my organization) complex.[1] In 2010, the Association of Certified Fraud Examiners (ACFE)[2] reported that incidents of fraud account for a loss of 5 percent of total revenue.[3] At 5 percent, this equals approximately $95 billion annually.[4] But for nonprofits, it isn't just the money. It's the lack of trust that develops on the part of the donors, funding sources, and people who work for these organizations. There are several characteristics that make nonprofits vulnerable to fraud:

- Control by a chief executive; employees believe that there is no one to whom they can report unusual actions or requests.
- Existence of transactions, such as contributions, that are very easy to steal.
- Environment of trust, especially in financial personnel. The ACFE report states that accounting people are more likely to steal than anyone else in the organization.
- Focus on the mission to the exclusion of administrative systems of controls and risk management.
- Failure to devote sufficient resources to financial management.
- Failure to include people with financial oversight expertise on the board.
- Failure of the board to challenge the chief executive for fear of losing him or her.
- Fear that the cost of implementing controls will outweigh the benefit and spend money that, in their view, would be better spent on programs.

This chapter addresses the nonprofit's need to design a system of internal controls to prevent or detect and correct both error and incidents of fraud. The five levels of internal control that are generally used in most organizations are defined. In addition, this chapter discusses the major fraud schemes that are perpetrated against nonprofits along with controls that might have prevented them or detected them sooner.

Internal Control Defined

Internal control is the process put in place by an entity's board of directors, management, and other personnel, that is designed to provide reasonable assurance that

- the entity has accurate and reliable financial reporting;
- the entity complies with applicable laws and regulations, contracts, and grant agreements; and
- management's objectives are met regarding the effectiveness and efficiency of operations.

This definition comes from a framework that was developed by the Committee of Sponsoring Organizations of the Treadway Commission (COSO) in response to the Foreign Corrupt Practices Act of 1977. Financial statement auditors have used this definition since the mid-1980s when it became part of their professional literature.

---

1 Gerard Zack, *Fraud and Abuse in Nonprofit Organizations: A Guide to Prevention and Detection* (Hoboken: John Wiley & Sons, Inc., 2003).

2 Association of Certified Fraud Examiners, *2010 Report to the Nations on Occupational Fraud and Abuse*, www.acfe.org.

3 The entities represented in this survey encompassed various industries and were in many different countries. To view the breakdown, see the *2010 Report to the Nations on Occupational Fraud and Abuse* at www.acfe.org.

4 *Public Charities, Giving and Volunteering*, 2009. Retrieved from www.urban.org/publications/412085.html on April 16, 2011.

Management, the board, donors, other funding sources, regulatory authorities like the IRS, and creditors need to be able to rely on the financial statement amounts and footnote disclosures in the financial statements. Therefore, internal controls should be designed and implemented in order to prevent or detect and correct both errors and fraud that might be in the financial statements.

The nonprofit organization should also have internal controls to prevent or detect noncompliance with laws and regulations and provisions of contracts and grant agreements. Compliance is very important to the nonprofit because noncompliance could cause the organization to lose funding and even its tax exempt status. Internal control over compliance will be briefly discussed in this chapter. Although it is also important for the nonprofit to meet its objectives relating to effectiveness and efficiency of operations, these controls will not be addressed because they are beyond the scope of this book.

Another way of defining internal control might be actions that management and employees take in the course of their assigned functions to prevent or detect and correct fraud and error. The board is responsible for seeing that these actions are carried out and should delegate the design and implementation of the controls to management. However, the board is still responsible for ensuring that the organization maintains adequate internal control.

Distinguishing Error From Fraud

Internal controls are designed to address improper transaction processing, whether due to error or fraud. In this chapter, the most of the examples are related to fraud and are designed to increase the reader's awareness of how fraud can occur. But preventing, detecting, and correcting error is also an important function of internal controls. By implementing controls that are designed to accomplish those objectives and by adding in certain controls to address the risk of fraud, management and the board will help to ensure that their goals of complete and accurate processing are achieved.

Sometimes it is difficult to tell the difference between error and fraud. Fraud is an intentional act to misappropriate assets or improperly report account balances, transactions, and disclosures in the financial statements or to violate contracts and grant agreements. But if the nonprofit's personnel are not properly trained, a transaction that might be fraudulent in other circumstances could be an error.

 Example

Sue was an accountant at a private school. She was responsible for recording donations as they were received. Sue did not fully understand the difference between unrestricted and temporarily restricted donations and recorded them all as unrestricted. This was an error because Sue was not properly trained.

((continued)))

(continued)

Jackie was in charge of donor development at a charity. The organization was very small, so Jackie also opened the mail and coded the donations received as unrestricted, temporarily restricted, or permanently restricted. She also wrote the acknowledgement letters to the donors. In 2010, she was able to secure a $100,000 challenge grant. In order to get the $100,000, the organization had to raise $50,000 from donors. These donations needed to be unrestricted in order to count toward the challenge grant. Jackie wanted to get this grant so she knowingly misrepresented $25,000 in pledges to the organization as unrestricted when they were really temporarily restricted for a specific purpose. Jackie's acted with the intention to defraud or misrepresent a situation to a funding source.

Both situations resulted in inaccurate financial statements. Internal controls are designed to prevent or detect and correct misstatements whether due to fraud or error, but in both of these cases, controls were lacking. In the case of Sue, she needed training (a control environment control) and supervision (a monitoring control) to help her understand appropriate accounting. In the case of Jackie, she knew she was in the wrong. Segregation of duties between the person who has custody of the assets (opening the mail) and the person who processes the assets (recording the transactions) should be maintained.

It is important to note that even the best, most comprehensive set of controls can only provide reasonable assurance that fraud or errors will be either prevented or detected and corrected. This is because there is always the possibility of human error, malfunctions in technology, or collusion. And because internal controls cost time and money to implement and maintain, it is important to weigh their benefits versus their cost and choose them wisely.

Controls for Smaller Organizations

When considering internal controls, it is important to keep in mind the size of the entity as well as its degree of complexity. Size is determined by the size of the budget, the amount of endowment funds, the amount of transactions processed for others (agency transactions), and other factors. Complexity is determined by a number of factors: the degree to which the entity is regulated, its use of sophisticated information technology, its number of locations, and other factors.

 Example

A charity, which is a local affiliate of a national organization, has contribution revenue of $500,000 a year. It has approximately $150,000 in grant revenue and a small amount of interest income. It operates from one location and uses QuickBooks to process and record its transactions. Its investments are held at the local community foundation. It has no endowment.

An arts organization has total revenue of approximately $100 million. Its revenue comes from several sources. A significant amount comes from contributions, many of which are restricted. It also has membership income, sells items in its gift stores and through the internet, and has significant investment income coming from its endowments. It processes many of its transactions online and uses a check scanner to deposit the contributions it receives. It operates two stores that sell merchandise, and many of its customers use credit cards. The organization also runs an art school and has tuition revenue. It uses PeopleSoft, an enterprise application, that has been customized to fit its needs.

The arts organization would be considered a large complex organization due to its size, use of technology, number of locations, and numerous sources of revenue. The charity would be considered a small, noncomplex organization. Both need to implement and maintain adequate internal controls, but the number and types of controls will be different.

COSO's *Internal Control—Integrated Framework* (the COSO framework), published in 1992, identifies five broad interrelated categories of internal control over financial reporting. In 2006, the original COSO framework was modified for smaller companies that were trying to prepare for reporting under the Sarbanes-Oxley Act of 2002. Management of these companies criticized the original COSO framework saying that it did not reflect their needs and financial constraints. COSO responded to the challenge and issued its *Internal Control over Financial Reporting—Guidance for Smaller Public Companies*.[5] This guidance was not intended to replace the COSO framework. Instead it provides examples of internal controls that are relevant to smaller and midsize entities.

Smaller companies were not defined by the size of their assets or revenue. Instead, COSO provided several characteristics common to a smaller company:[6]
- Fewer lines of business or products
- Larger span of control for management
- Leadership by management with significant ownership or rights
- Less complex information technology
- Fewer employees who often have diverse duties

These characteristics are common too small to mid-size nonprofits.

One of the most important lessons learned from the *Internal Control over Financial Reporting—Guidance for Smaller Public Companies* is that larger organizations have a higher proportion of controls in the category of control activities. This is because they have more people among which to segregate the duties. In addition, their information technology is more robust, and there are more automated control activities. The guidance also points out that smaller organizations will have a very different distribution of internal controls in that the

---

5 *Internal Control over Financial Reporting—Guidance for Smaller Public Companies*, Committee of Sponsoring Organizations of the Treadway Commission (COSO), 2006, www.coso.org. It can be purchased from the AICPA CPA2Biz website, www.cpa2biz.com/index.jsp.

6 *Internal Control over Financial Reporting—Guidance for Smaller Public Companies*, COSO, 2006, www.coso.org. It can be purchased from the AICPA CPA2Biz website, www.cpa2biz.com/index.jsp.

majority of the controls will be in the categories of the control environment and monitoring. With a strong tone set by management and the board and a high degree of monitoring, the lack of segregation of duties is mitigated somewhat. This puts even more significance in the board's and management's roles and responsibilities in setting the tone for integrity and ethical values and monitoring.

Categories of Internal Control

The five categories in the COSO framework can be viewed as a portfolio of integrated controls. These are used in combination to help the organization meet its need for accurate financial reporting and for compliance with laws and regulations, contracts, and grant agreements. Some of the controls serve to lay a good foundation for the entire organization, and others support the processing of transactions. Together they make up the internal control structure.

Figure 7-1: *Internal Control Structure*

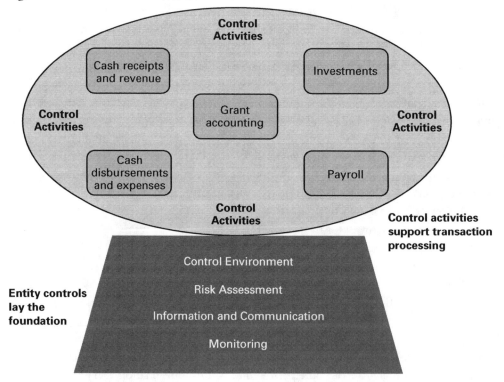

As illustrated in figure 7-1, the entity controls are those that lay the foundation for effective internal control. With a good foundation, the organization can have better assurance that transactions are accurately authorized, processed, recorded, and reported. The controls that support transaction processing are the control activities. The purpose of these controls, along with examples, is discussed in this section.

There are five categories of entity controls.

- **Control environment.** Sets the tone from the top of the organization. This category of controls includes integrity and ethical values, commitment to competence, attention and direction provided by the board of directors or audit committee, management's philosophy and operating style, organizational structure and the manner of assigning authority and responsibility, and human resource policies and procedures. Many of these controls were discussed in the 33 good governance principles in chapter 2. As noted in that chapter, a strong control environment is the best deterrent to fraud.

- **Risk assessment process.** Refers to the process the organization goes through to identify the risks that would prevent it from meeting its objectives. These could be internal factors such as lack of diversity of funding sources, turnover in key positions, implementation of a new IT system, entering into new programs, and significant, rapid growth with insufficient infrastructure to support it. Risk can also be present from external factors such as deterioration of the economy affecting its funding sources or changes in accounting principles and reporting requirements. Risk assessment is more fully discussed in chapter 6.

- **Information controls.** The technology and processes necessary to initiate, authorize, process, record, and report transactions and events in the financial statements and to communicate the results to management and employees who have a need for the information. Information controls are considered to be entity controls in that there are controls over information technology that set the foundation for the system as a whole. There are also control activities at the point of processing transactions. A comprehensive discussion of controls over information technology is beyond the scope of this book.

- Organizations that have complex and sophisticated information technology systems should be aware of the framework created in 1998 by the IT Governance Institute called *Control Objectives for Information and related Technology* (COBIT). The COBIT framework is designed to instill good practices into the organization to ensure that the organization's information technology supports its business objectives. Use of this framework should also result in greater efficiency and optimum use of the information produced by the organization. It can be obtained from the website of the Information Systems Audit and Control Association at www.isaca.org/Knowledge-Center/cobit/Documents/CobiT_4.1.pdf.

  The *Internal Control over Financial Reporting—Guidance for Smaller Public Companies* contains a very good description of those controls for smaller organizations using packaged software that cannot be significantly customized.

- **Communication controls.** Involves the quality of communications between the board and management; the board and the external auditors and internal auditors, if any; staff and management; and management and donors, funding sources, and vendors. Two-way communication is very important to ensure transparency, accountability, and the dissemination of knowledge employees need to perform their assigned duties and to enable issues to be identified at the ground level for prompt management consideration and action.

- **Monitoring.** Monitoring is a very important control function. It occurs when management follows up to determine whether the nonprofit's staff members are performing their duties as expected. It also occurs when the board follows up to determine that its objectives are being met. Monitoring is such an important part of the COSO framework that in 2009 COSO published a book, *Guidance on Monitoring Internal Control Systems*. This is not intended to replace either the COSO framework or *Internal Control over Financial Reporting—Guidance for Smaller Public Companies*; it is designed to highlight and expand the basic principles in both documents. Monitoring controls can be performed at the overall entity level and also at the transactional level.

Control Activities

Control activities are performed at the transaction level. These controls are designed to prevent or detect and correct misstatement. Whereas the entity level controls set the foundation and affect all of the financial processes, the control activities are specific to a particular transaction cycle such as revenue and cash receipts, expenses and cash disbursement, payroll, investments, or grant accounting. When management prepares financial statements, it is making assertions that transactions and events

- exist (assets and liabilities) and actually occurred (revenues and expenses).
- are complete. In other words, all of the transactions and events are recorded.
- are appropriately valued.
- represent the rights to assets and obligations of the organization. For example, if the organization receives and holds assets for another organization, these are appropriately reflected as amounts due to that organization.
- are recorded accurately and in the proper period.
- are disclosed in the right net asset classification. For example, the donations to the endowment that are restricted in perpetuity are recorded as permanently restricted.
- are disclosed in the financial statements in such a way that they are understandable.

Control activities support management's assertions.

 Example

Roger perpetrated a fraud against a small nonprofit that nearly bankrupted the organization. He was the sole accountant, responsible only to the board of directors. He collected the receipts from donors, grantors, and clients and was also responsible for recording them in the general ledger. Many did not get recorded because he deposited the checks in his own checking account. He was also responsible for paying the bills. He received the invoices and wrote, signed, and mailed the checks. Because he had custody of the assets (cash), he wrote checks to himself, to vendors to pay his own bills, and to a fictitious vendor he created. Those checks he deposited in a bank account he set up for himself under that name. Because no one approved the invoices for payment, no one identified the fictitious vendor. To the organization's credit, they terminated Roger and prosecuted him for fraud. If the organization had performed a background check on him before he was hired, they would have seen that he had previously been prosecuted for fraud against another nonprofit.

One of the most important control activities is the segregation of duties. Duties should be segregated so that no one person has the ability to initiate and approve transactions while also being able to have access to the technology to record those transactions or have custody of the assets.

In this example, the lack of segregation of duties was not mitigated by any other controls, such as monitoring by an executive director (ED) or the board of directors. Smaller organizations are at a disadvantage when it comes to segregation of duties. However, the consequences of having too much control vested in one or two people are so calamitous that it is wise to make an effort to segregate them as much as possible. Even in cases in which there are very few employees, the board can be enlisted to perform analytical reviews of revenues and expenses to see if the amounts are reasonable. Figure 7-2 illustrates a way that segregation of duties might be accomplished by two with additional support from the board of directors.

Figure 7-2: *Example of Segregation of Duties with Two Employees*

Chief Executive	Employee
• Write acknowledgement letters to donors and review donor correspondence • Sign checks • Review bank reconciliation • Approve payroll and make compensation adjustments • Authorize purchases • Authorize invoices for payment • Authorize positive pay based on checks approved for payment • Perform analytical procedures for review by the board	• Process cash receipts, disbursements, and payroll transactions • Write checks • Perform bank reconciliation • Mail checks • Make deposits

Small organizations often suffer from lack of segregation of duties. A strong control environment, coupled with monitoring by the board of directors, can help to mitigate the lack of segregation of duties. A receptionist, other administrative employee, or program employee could mail checks and make deposits to further segregate duties.

Designing a System of Internal Control

Entity Controls

When designing a system of internal control, the nonprofit should start with the entity controls that form the foundation of the control structure and support the control activities for the various transaction cycles. Management will need to ask "What policies and procedures could we put in place to meet the objectives in the COSO framework?"

There is no one correct answer to that question. Chapter 2 discussed the questions dealing with governance that are asked in the Form 990. If the IRS took the effort to include questions about entity controls on Form 990, it implies that the IRS believes that the controls that are the subject matter of the questions are important. However, if an organization has only those controls, it will not generally be sufficient to meet the objectives identified in the COSO framework. Certain vendors of tools and templates, including the AICPA[7] and Practitioner's Publishing Company,[8] offer products with examples of internal controls that could be implemented at the entity level. Management should consider the options available and make decisions on the design and implementation of entity level controls considering the size and complexity of the organization.

The next example shows how an organization used internal control products to choose the controls that were right for it and document them. Controls that are not documented are less likely to be consistently followed.

Example

A nonprofit historical society had $25 million in revenue. Its primary revenue sources were memberships and contributions from donors. In addition, the organization had a gift shop, offered workshops and programs on topics of historical interest, and sold admissions to its museum. In 2010, a new ED was hired. Prior to joining the historical society, she worked with a charitable organization that placed a high priority on its internal controls. One of the first things she did was ask the CFO to perform an evaluation of the organization's entity level internal controls. The new ED was concerned because she knew that nonprofits faced scrutiny from the IRS, Charity Navigator, GuideStar, and others. She also knew that donors prefer to give to organizations they feel they can trust to do the right thing.

The new ED believed that once the foundation for the control structure was solid, the organization could then undertake an evaluation of each of its transaction cycles. The CFO purchased the COSO's *Internal Control over Financial Reporting—Guidance for Smaller Public Companies* and used it to get suggestions on controls that would be effective for her organization. In fact, the organization already had some very good controls. They just weren't sufficiently documented. The CFO created a new structure that not only documented the controls already in place but also included controls that would fill what she believed to be the gaps or holes in the historical society's controls. The resulting table follows.

7 ControlsDoc is a control documentation product that can be purchased through the AICPA's store at www.cpa2biz.com/index.jsp.

8 Practitioner's Publishing Company is the Tax and Accounting Business of Thomson Reuters. Their products can be purchased at ppc.thomson.com/sitecomposer2/.

Control Environment (Controls with * indicate that they are also included in Form 990 questions)	
Principle	**Controls Identified by the CFO From the COSO Framework**
Integrity and ethical values establish management's intent that the conduct of the organization is transparent and above reproach; that the financial statements are free of misstatement; and the organization complies with all laws, regulations, grant requirements, and donor restrictions.	• The organization has a code of ethics and conflict of interest policy. Employees are trained on the policy and are expected to sign an acknowledgement each year of their understanding. (*) • The organization has a whistleblower policy and an anonymous reporting mechanism. Employees are trained to know where to report instances of suspected fraud or noncompliance with laws, regulations, contracts, and grant agreements. (*)
The board of directors understands its roles related to the oversight of the financial reporting function and internal control.	• Two-thirds of the board members are independent. (*) • The board signs the code of ethics and conflict of interest policy. (*) • The board reviews the financial statements and Form 990 before they are released. (*) • The board consistently performs budget to actual, current period to prior period, and other reviews of financial information on a monthly basis. • The board meets with the external auditor at least yearly and on an as-needed basis. • The board is aware of the need for effective internal controls and discusses their effectiveness with management. • The board includes at least one financial expert.
Management's philosophy and method of operating are conducive to effective controls. Management does **not** exercise inappropriate levels of control, take inordinate business risks, or expect employees to achieve unrealistic or unethical operating results.	• The organization publishes a newsletter, and it is used to reinforce executive management's and the board's view of accurate financial reporting and ethical values. The newsletter reminds management and the employees of their responsibility to the organization and gives them a place to turn if they feel pressured.
The organization is committed to retaining competent employees in the areas of financial accounting and reporting.	• Training programs are held for employees so they are current on requirements and policies affecting their job. Performance appraisals are performed and reviewed with employees yearly.
Human resource policies and procedures support effective internal control over financial reporting.	• Background and credit checks are performed on new employees. • Employees who are in financial positions are bonded.
Risk Assessment	
Principle	**Controls Identified by the CFO From the COSO Framework**
Risk assessments are performed to understand where the organization is vulnerable. This includes internal and external risks.	• Management and department heads identify areas of risk to the organization and provide input to senior management's risk assessment. • Senior management and the board meet to discuss risks to the organization. Input from middle management and department heads is considered.
Information and Communication	
Principle	**Controls Identified by the CFO From the COSO Framework**
The organization has adequate information technology to support accurate accumulation of financial information, financial reporting, and compliance with laws and regulations.	• The information technology is appropriate to the size and complexity of the organization. • The organization has the appropriate controls over the input to the system and output from the system. • Information security, including passwords, is evaluated yearly. Passwords are changed every 90 days.

(continued)

(continued)

Information and Communication	
Principle	Controls Identified by the CFO From the COSO Framework
The organization has sufficient communication among the board, management, staff, external auditors, regulatory bodies, and others to allow for the exchange of information that would allow accurate and transparent financial reporting to take place.	• Information from regulatory bodies and changes to the organization's internal controls and policies are provided to staff on a timely basis to assist them in their duties. • See board controls in the preceding "Control Environment" section.

Monitoring	
Principle	Controls Identified by the CFO From the COSO Framework
Monitoring of the organization's activities takes place at the board level, the executive level, and at the individual account balance level.	• Monitoring of the organization's activities takes place at the board level. The board performs analysis on the financial statements on a monthly basis. • Board reviews Form 990. (*) • Senior management monitors financial metrics on a monthly basis. • Reconciliations of asset and liability accounts are performed on a monthly basis. • See other board monitoring activities in the preceding "Control Environment" section.

Control Activities

Control activities are important to prevent or detect and correct errors and fraud at the level of the transaction cycles. As discussed in this chapter, although there could be others, common transaction cycles are revenue and cash receipts, expenses and disbursements, payroll, and investments. It is important to document not only the processes involved in the accounting for these transactions but also the internal controls within the processes.

Even properly trained employees can make inadvertent errors, and that is why reconciliations of account detail to the general ledger, spot checking the work of employees, and analytical procedures are very important. But these controls alone will not be sufficient to prevent or detect fraud. There are excellent products[9] on the market that can provide management with examples of control activities that, along with segregation of duties, will more specifically address the risk of fraud.

The AICPA's Audit and Accounting Guide *Not-for-Profit Entities*[10] provides examples of areas in which it is particularly important to have good internal controls because the risk of error or fraud is higher in these areas:

- Identification, acceptance, and evaluation of donor–restricted contributions
- Valuation and recording of promises to give (pledges)
- Valuation and recording contributions of noncash assets (services, goods, utilities, use of long lived assets, and the like)
- Compliance with grantor requirements
- Compliance with accounting principles such as those related to the allocation of expenses by function as well as natural classification or joint cost allocation, agency transactions, and the like (see discussion of accounting in chapter 5)

9 ControlsDoc is a control documentation product that can be purchased through the AICPA's store at www.cpa2biz.com/index.jsp. Practitioner's Publishing Company is the Tax and Accounting Business of Thomson Reuters. Their products can be purchased at ppc.thomson.com/sitecomposer2/.

10 *Not-for-Profit Entities* (New York: American Institute of Certified Public Accountants, 2010).

• Identification and accounting for new programs

The following example illustrates how an organization could document the design of internal controls.

◼ Example

The ED of a private school was concerned about the internal controls over revenue. In particular, she wanted to ensure that contribution revenue was properly recorded and that payments by donors were recorded completely. She also wanted to be sure that the tuition being paid was posted to the correct student account. Some parents paid quarterly, some paid monthly, and some paid in advance for the year. There were also discounts associated with the advance payments. The school was small, and there were only two employees in accounting to keep up with the work.

She began by identifying the segregation of duties over revenue. Her documentation follows:

Segregation of Duties Over Revenue at Jordan Lewis Preparatory School

We believe that we have appropriate segregation of duties for the size and complexity of our organization. All cash comes into one central location. The mail is opened by two people, and a check log is prepared. Cash receipts in the form of checks are scanned in through the I Stream System and reconciled to amounts received by the Bank of the South. The ED and the board of directors monitor the levels of revenue analytically. There is follow-up on variances from budget. Bank reconciliations are performed and reviewed independently from the handling and posting of cash. A table summarizing the segregation of duties follows.

Revenue Source	Initiating Transaction	Cash Handling	Posting Transaction	Supervision and Monitoring
Academic programs	Academic program administrator handles registrations. All discounts are approved by the academic program administrator and the executive director.	Accountant 1 processes checks by scanning them into the IStream system. Accountant 1 processes credit cards.	Accountant 2 posts revenue and cash receipts. Accountant 2 mails statements to students' parents and follows up on complaints.	Accountant 1 performs bank reconciliations. Executive director reviews bank reconciliation monthly. Executive director reviews receipts analytically monthly.

(continued)

(continued)

Revenue Source	Initiating Transaction	Cash Handling	Posting Transaction	Supervision and Monitoring
Donations	Development department initiates some donations; others are unsolicited. Donations are made online. Development department writes acknowledgement letters from information provided by accountant 1 and for pledges received.	Accountant 1 processes cash receipts by scanning into the IStream system. Accountant 1 processes credit cards.	Accountant 2 posts cash received and credit cards. Accountant 2 posts pledges.	Reconciliation performed between fund-raising database (Raiser's Edge) and general ledger by accountant 1. All donations reviewed by executive director and board of directors (lists analytically reviewed). Executive director signs the acknowledgements and reviews general ledger classification for appropriate restrictions.
Special events	Person in charge of the specific special event adds the event to Raiser's Edge and records list of checks received related to the event.	Accountant 1 processes checks by scanning them into the IStream system. Accountant 1 processes credit cards.	Accountant 2 posts to accounting records.	Reconciliation performed between Raiser's Edge and general ledger by executive director.
Merchandise sales— Bookstore	Parents and students purchase books in bookstore. Bookstore personnel process credit card payments. Bookstore personnel reconcile the cash drawer daily and provide reconciliation and detail tape to accounting.	Accountant 1 processes cash and checks by scanning them into the IStream system. Accountant 1 reviews reconciliation.	Accountant 2 posts activity to the general ledger.	Executive director monitors cost of goods and sales margin through monthly analytical review.

Following are the controls in place to prevent or detect misstatement in revenue.

Revenue Source	Assertions Covered	Internal Control	Monitoring
All Forms of Revenue	Existence, occurrence, completeness	**Control 1:** Checks are endorsed with a "Bank of the South" stamp as they are run through the check scanning machine. The accountant places a red "POSTED" stamp on the face of the check.	
All Forms of Revenue	Existence, occurrence, completeness, valuation	**Control 2:** Deposits of cash are made by the receptionist on Tuesday and Friday. The checks are locked in the safe while they are waiting for deposit. Currency with denominations of $20 or more are tested with a counterfeit pen.	**Control 2:** The executive director goes online with Bank of the South to compare the amount of the deposit with the amount on the reconciliations from the development director, store, and accountant 1.
All Forms of Revenue	Accuracy, existence, occurrence, completeness	**Control 3:** The bank statement is reconciled by accountant 1.	**Control 3:** Bank statement is reviewed by the executive director.
All Forms of Revenue	Completeness, accuracy, existence, occurrence	**Control 5:** Accountant 1 attaches documentation to the computer-generated deposit slip and forwards it to accountant 2 for review after the cash receipts have been posted.	**Control 5:** These are reviewed again by the executive director when posted to the general ledger for completeness and accuracy.
All Receivables	Valuation	**Control 6:** Follow-up is performed on past due receivables by the academic program administrator and adjustments are made as needed for tuition. Follow-up is performed on pledges by the development director, and adjustments are made as needed.	**Control 6:** Accountant 1 proposes a journal entry based on the input from the academic program administrator. These are reviewed quarterly with the executive director.

(continued)

(continued)

Revenue Source	Assertions Covered	Internal Control	Monitoring
Special Events	Existence occurrence, completeness, cutoff	**Control 7:** Special event revenue is recorded in the general ledger by accountant 2.	**Control 7:** The executive director compares the monthly schedule of events to revenue posted to the general ledger and follows up with the special events coordinator if an event is listed on the schedule but revenue and expense have not been recorded. Further monitoring is performed by the board.
Merchandise at Stores	Existence, occurrence, completeness	**Control 8:** Cash registers are used at the bookstore. Cashiers have access sign in and sign out codes.	
Merchandise at Stores	Existence, occurrence, completeness	**Control 9:** The bookstore manager has access to the register tape compartment and occasionally reviews the tape if there is a question about a transaction.	

Antifraud Programs and Controls

Nonprofits, like other small organizations, are vulnerable to fraud. The ACFE describes three categories of fraud:

- **Fraudulent financial reporting.** Improperly reporting transactions and events in the financial statements. This could include overstating or understating account balances, failure to make required disclosures, or making misleading disclosures.
- **Asset misappropriation.** Theft of assets. Assets may be cash or noncash assets.
- **Conflicts of interest.** Use of an employee's position in a way that violates the employer employee relationship. Examples are bribery, extortion, and conflicts of interest.

The most prevalent fraud scheme reported in the *2010 Report to the Nations on Occupational Fraud and Abuse* is theft of assets.[11] In fact, 90 percent of respondents to the survey reported

---

11 Association of Certified Fraud Examiners (ACFE), *2010 Report to the Nations on Occupational Fraud and Abuse*, available at www. acfe.org. Note that the ACFE's survey included 1,843 cases of occupational fraud that occurred in 106 countries between January 2008 and December 2009. Sixty percent of those cases were from the United States.

it. The median loss ($90,000 per incident for nonprofits in the survey) is far less than for fraudulent financial reporting ($4,000,000 per incident for all companies—nonprofits were not separately identified in this category), but the occurrence is far more frequent.

The ACFE *2010 Report to the Nations on Occupational Fraud and Abuse* highlights the fact that smaller organizations are more likely to be touched by fraud, primarily because they are lacking in antifraud programs and controls. Antifraud programs and controls have shown to be effective in reducing the magnitude of frauds and the length of time it takes before the fraudster is caught.

In its Statement on Auditing Standards (SAS) No. 99, *Consideration of Fraud in a Financial Statement Audit,*[12] the AICPA states that there are three important elements to consider when evaluating the possibility of fraud. The first is the incentive or pressure that an individual has to commit fraud. The second is the opportunity. The third is the ability to rationalize the act.

Misappropriation of Assets

Lindsey works for a charitable organization. She has 3 children, and one of them is very ill. The medication for her child is very expensive, and Lindsey makes too much money to qualify for public assistance. Her husband was just laid off from his job. At her job, Lindsey opens the mail by herself and makes a list of the incoming cash and checks. She knows that frequently a $10 or $20 bill will come in with nothing more than a note saying, "Thank you for the good work that your organization does for the disadvantaged." No name, no address, and no way to write an acknowledgement. The pressure on Lindsey to help her child is significant, and she decides that she, too, is disadvantaged and takes the money.

Incentive or Pressure: Lindsey sees her child suffering and feels desperate because she can't pay for the medication.

Opportunity: Lack of controls. Lindsey has no one watching her open the mail, and the cash is an easy thing to steal. Further, the cash is unsolicited, and the donor is not expecting an acknowledgement.

Rationalization: Lindsey believes her family is disadvantaged in its circumstances and she may even believe that she will pay back the money once her husband gets work.

Fraudulent Financial Reporting

Grace works for a private school in its development department. The expectation is that she will raise 20 percent more in donations this year than the last. The economy is not good, and Grace is having trouble getting new donors. There is a foundation that is willing to give the organization a matching grant if Grace is able to raise $100,000 by the end of the fiscal year. Grace goes to several existing donors with multiyear pledges and asks them to extend their pledges one year. Five of them are willing to do it, and these additional pledges provide the organization with $50,000 in donations toward the $100,000. This is not enough for the match.

---

12 Statement on Auditing Standards (SAS) No. 99, *Consideration of Fraud in a Financial Statement Audit* (AICPA, *Professional Standards*, AU sec. 316), October 2002.

Desperate to meet her goal, Grace goes to the accounting department and tells them that they need to write off pledges in the amount of $50,000 from multiyear donors. About a week later she reports an additional $50,000 in pledges. There are no new pledges; Grace is just reinstating the pledges written off the prior week. The people in the accounting department do not understand the significance of what they have been asked to do, and they are reluctant to question Grace who is their friend. Grace files a report with the foundation claiming credit for (1) the amounts she raised in the fiscal year and (2) the fraudulently written off and reinstated pledges. She receives the matching grant and meets the expectations of the ED and the board. This is clearly fraud perpetrated on the foundation that will provide the matching grant.

Incentive or Pressure: Grace is afraid that she will not meet the expectations of the board.

Opportunity: Lack of controls. Grace knows that the accountants have limited knowledge and training and do not understand what they are being asked to do. There is insufficient review of journal entries at all levels where this activity could be detected.

Rationalization: Grace believes that what she is doing isn't really stealing because the foundation has so much money and because her organization is deserving of the funding.

Revenue Recognition and Management Override

SAS No. 99 states that there are two areas that are presumed to be significant risks of fraud. The first is misstating (recognizing) revenue. The primary reason a nonprofit would do this is so that it could show larger results, thereby making the nonprofit appear that has more revenue than it actually has. For many organizations, this is an easy place to misrepresent financial results. Management could

- record fictitious pledges,
- represent that revenue is collectible when it is not (instances in which the donor is not likely to honor the pledge), or
- represent revenue as eligible to be spent on operations as opposed to restricted to spending for a specific purpose or time period.

Management override is also presumed to be a significant risk of fraud because management could

- have access to all parts of the system and record transactions that do not exist or do not accurately reflect the situation. This is a violation of the segregation of duties that the organization may have.
- put pressure on employees to make inappropriate entries to the system knowing they will do it for fear of reprisal.
- ask employees to make inappropriate entries knowing that the staff does not have the experience to know the entries are improper.
- create estimates that are biased.

- improperly record unusual transactions or those with little business rationale believing that the board will not question them.

Antifraud programs and controls should be designed to prevent or detect these sorts of actions.

The AICPA provides a list of entity level controls that are good antifraud controls in the appendix to SAS No. 99.[13]

Control Environment

- Code of conduct or code of ethics
- Ethics hotline and whistleblower program (hotline can take many forms)
- Hiring and Promotion Guidelines—background and credit checks
- Oversight by the audit committee and board
- Investigation of ethical violations and prompt punishment and remediation of control deficiencies

Fraud Risk Assessment

- Management's identification of fraud risks and implementation of antifraud measures
- Board's assessment of the potential for management override of controls or other inappropriate influence over the financial reporting process

Information and Communication

- Appropriate internal controls to prevent unauthorized changes to programs or master files
- Communication between management and staff, management and the board, management and the auditors, the auditors and the board, and, if there are internal auditors, communication between them and the board
- Ethics hotline (or equivalent for smaller organizations)
- Open door policy
- Collaborative board

Monitoring

- Board receives and reviews periodic reports describing the nature, status, and eventual disposition of alleged or suspected fraud and misconduct
- An internal audit plan (if the nonprofit is large enough) that addresses fraud risk and a mechanism to ensure that the internal auditor can express any concerns about management's commitment to appropriate internal controls or report suspicions or allegations of fraud
- Involvement of other experts—legal, accounting, and other professional advisers—as needed
- Review of accounting principles, policies, and estimates used by management in determining significant estimates

---

13 Adapted from the appendix of Statement on Auditing Standards No. 99, *Consideration of Fraud in a Financial Statement Audit* (AICPA, *Professional Standards*, AU sec. 316).

- Review of significant nonroutine transactions entered into by management
- Review of functional reporting by internal and external auditors to the board and audit committee

The *2010 Report to the Nations on Occupational Fraud and Abuse*[14] showed that those completing the survey had antifraud controls as follows.

Antifraud Control	Percentage of Those That Had the Control
Code of conduct	76.1
Internal audit department	69.9
Management review of internal control	52.2
Independent audit committee	48.6
Employee support programs	44.9
Fraud training for managers and executives	41.5
Fraud training for employees	39.6
Antifraud policy	39.0
Surprise audits	28.9
Job rotation and mandatory vacation	14.6
Rewards for whistleblowers	7.4

Joseph Wells, the founder of the ACFE, acknowledges that internal controls will not ever completely prevent or detect fraud. However, in an interview[15] with Kim Nilsen, he discussed the results of the survey and noted that the median time it took to detect occupational fraud was 18 months. The *2010 Report to the Nations on Occupational Fraud and Abuse* notes that the most frequent way that fraud is detected is by a tip. In fact, 40.2 percent of the nonprofit respondents to the survey indicated that this was how the frauds in their organizations were detected. A tip may come from an employee, vendor, or funding source. Management's review was another way that frauds were caught (15.4 percent), followed by internal audits (13.9 percent), by accident (8.3 percent), by account reconciliation (6.1 percent), by document examination (5.2 percent), by external audit (4.6 percent), and by other methods (6.3 percent). This suggests that a strong whistleblower program, frequent account reconciliation, review of documents, and an external audit may be very beneficial to the nonprofit considering the cost.

Joseph Wells suggests that preventive controls are the key to combating the cost of occupational fraud. His advice is summarized in the antifraud check-up tool that follows.

---

14 ACFE, *2010 Report to the Nations on Occupational Fraud and Abuse*, available at www.acfe.org.
15 Kim Nilsen, "Keeping Fraud in the Cross Hairs," *Journal of Accountancy*, June 2010.

Antifraud Provision	Questions for Board Members to Ask	Response
Training	Do employees receive training that helps to educate them about the following: • What constitutes fraud? • Costs of fraud, such as job loss, publicity issues, loss of donor funding, and so forth? • Where to go for help if they see something suspicious or unusual? • Is there a zero tolerance policy for fraud and has it been communicated?	
Reporting	Does the organization have an effective way for employees to report fraud or suspicious behavior? Is there an anonymous reporting mechanism for employees to use? Do employees understand that those issues reported will be investigated?	
Perception of detection	Does the entity seek knowledge of fraudulent activity? Is there a message sent that that there will be tests made to look for fraud? • Are there surprise audits? • Is software used to identify issues from data?	
Management's tone from the top	Does the organization value honesty and integrity? Are employees surveyed to determine whether they believe that management acts with integrity? Have fraud prevention goals been set for management, and are they evaluated on them as an element of compensation? Is there an appropriate oversight process by the board or others charged with governance?	
Antifraud controls	Are any of the following performed? • Risk assessments to determine management's vulnerabilities • Proper segregation of duties • Physical safeguards • Job rotation • Mandatory vacations • Proper authorization of transactions	
Hiring policies	Are the following incorporated in the organization's hiring policies: • Past employment verification • Credit check • Criminal and civil background check • Education verification • Reference check • Drug screening	
Employee support programs	Are there any programs in place to help struggling employees with financial issues, drug issues, or mental health issues? Is there an open door policy so that employees can speak freely? Are anonymous surveys conducted to assess employee morale?	

One of the most important things that a board member or member of management can do is to become aware of the ways that fraud can be accomplished. The next section discusses some of the most common ways that fraud can occur and internal controls that might be implemented to either prevent or detect it at the transaction level.

Corruption	25.5%
Noncash	14.7%
Payroll	13.4%
Financial statement fraud	5.6%

Billing Schemes, Check Tampering, and Expense Fraud

Billing schemes, check tampering, and expense reimbursement were the most prevalent type of fraud against small businesses, occurring 28.7 percent (billing schemes), 26.1 percent (check tampering), and 16.8 percent (expense reimbursement) of the time with a median duration of 24 months. In billing schemes, the fraudster submits fictitious invoices for payment. With check tampering, the fraudster steals checks and makes them out to him- or herself or another organization under his or her control or steals outgoing checks to a vendor and deposits them in his or her bank account.

🗔 Example

Marie and Carolyn worked for a nonprofit organization that provided meals to the elderly. Marie worked in operations, and Carolyn worked in accounting. The nonprofit spent thousands of dollars each week to purchase food, to package food, and to reimburse volunteers for gasoline and automobile mileage. Marie and Carolyn did not work together and did not know each other very well, but their cubicles were very close together. Although not an eavesdropper by nature, Marie frequently overheard Carolyn defending herself to what sounded like bill collectors. But one day, she noticed that Carolyn wasn't getting as many calls anymore and was glad that she appeared to have solved the problem. One day, Marie noticed Carolyn slipping what appeared to be a check in her purse. Because it looked like a business check, Marie's curiosity was piqued. A week or so went by, and Marie noticed Carolyn putting another check in her purse. She thought it was odd but couldn't understand how Carolyn would have access to checks made out to the company because she worked in accounts payable.

Marie was bothered by these incidents. She was aware of the organization's open door policy. The policy said that all unusual events should be reported to the internal auditor. She took advantage of the opportunity and discussed the situation with the internal auditor. The internal auditor began to watch Carolyn and put the pieces of the puzzle together.

The Scheme: Carolyn was responsible for approving invoices for payment. She would look to see if the vendor was on the approved vendor list, review the documentation supporting the invoice, and, if the math was correct and the receiving documents agreed, then she initialed the invoice and approved it for payment. There were some invoices, though, that did not have supporting documentation. These were invoices for consulting or other professional services. Carolyn was also responsible for vendor relationships, so she received any checks that came to the organization representing repayments for overpayments to vendors. If an invoice was paid twice, or if for some other reason a vendor wrote a check to the nonprofit, the procedure called for Carolyn to notify accounts payable and give the check to the person in charge of preparing the daily deposit.

Carolyn knew that the information system did not detect duplicate payments. And she knew that monitoring was weak. To perpetrate the fraud, as she was approving the invoice she made a duplicate of it. One she knew the invoice was paid, she submitted the duplicate for payment. When the vendor refund came in, she put it in her purse and deposited it to her own checking account through the ATM.

Fraud Scheme: Duplicate payment scheme

Example

Jerry and Donna both worked for a nonprofit clinical research organization. Jerry was involved in performing research, and Donna worked in the accounting department. They got to know each other very well and decided to form an informal partnership.

The Scheme: Jerry created a company, JEH Consulting, and printed up fictitious invoices for computer consulting services. He actually used a post office box to receive payment but had a bogus address on his invoice that purported to be the address of JEH Consulting. Donna set up a fictitious vendor in the accounting system and approved Jerry's invoices and sent them through accounts payable. The team started small, and the invoices were below any threshold that would have alerted company personnel to the fact that computer consulting was higher than expected. However, over the 18 months, which included 2 audit cycles, Jerry began to make his invoices larger and larger until, on the second audit cycle, the amount was above the threshold for investigation by the external auditor who was performing analytical procedures. The auditor was aware that often fraudsters create service companies so that there is no need for fictitious receiving documents. The fraudulent payments also tend to get larger over time. He also knew that remittances to post office boxes could be a red flag. The auditor pulled the invoices for the consulting services. Using Google Maps, he determined that the address of JEH Consulting was actually a vacant lot.

Fraud Scheme: Fictitious invoices

Example

Sandra was a bookkeeper for a church. She had been the bookkeeper for about 20 years. Sandra had little oversight of her work because the pastor of the church believed she was an honest person. Sandra had been defrauding the organization for years.

The Scheme: She was paying the utilities and other operating expenses of the church and also paying her own. Because she had been doing it for so long, the auditor's analytical procedures did not show any unusual increases. This went on until one day the pastor went into the hospital for an extended period of time. The treasurer of the governing board wanted to see the support for the checks that Sandra wrote rather than just sign them the way the pastor did. Sandra's game was over. Unfortunately, the church chose to let her go quietly rather than prosecute. This is a failing of many nonprofits that do not want adverse publicity. When her activities were investigated, the governing board discovered that she had stolen approximately $600,000 over a 10 year period. In addition to writing checks from the church account to pay her bills, up until the current year she was also reimbursing herself for office supplies and other items from petty cash. In the current year, she began using the debit card that the church treasurer got because he thought it was better than Sandra using petty cash. Sandra realized that when she purchased office supplies, she could get cash back. No one ever saw it because only the name of the vendor showed up on the bank statement. Sandra destroyed the receipts.

Fraud Scheme: Excess purchasing scheme, fictitious (inflated) invoices

---

 Example

Justin had the complete confidence of the chief executive of an international nonprofit. He had the ability to initiate payments to be made to grantees in other countries by wire transfer. He said he needed to do this to keep the payments flowing. The chief executive was often overseas himself. In addition, Justin had very little oversight and complete custody of the assets. The only duty he did not perform was to sign the outgoing checks. The nonprofit used UPS to send packages to the grantees, and the UPS bill was very large. Justin made payments to UPS every two weeks but never reconciled the vendor statement, and no one asked to look at it. Circumstances changed in his life and he needed some cash.

The Scheme: He set up a bank account for his "new" company, UPS Roofing. After the check to UPS had been signed, he stole it and altered the payee. He deposited the check. So many checks were written to UPS that UPS never complained. The nonprofit was a steady customer. After a while he stole another. The board wondered why the organization was so short of cash and hired a consultant to come in and investigate. At that point Justin's fraud was uncovered.

Fraud Scheme: Check tampering

Billing schemes may be the easiest to accomplish because it is very easy to create invoices. It is also very easy to deposit checks made out to another company into a personal account through an ATM. Bank controls are not sufficient to prevent this activity and banks, would prefer to pay back money for those incidents brought to their attention than to put in costly controls.

Following are internal controls that could be put into place in the organization to prevent or detect billing and other cash disbursement schemes. Note that this is not a comprehensive list of all possible internal controls that could be implemented. For a more complete list, consult the tools referenced in preceding sections.

Control	What Types of Occurrences This Could Help to Prevent or Detect
Bond employees that have access to purchasing, cash disbursements, and accounts payable processing. Employee theft bonds can be obtained through insurance companies. The website www.suretybonds.com/employee-theft-bonds.html provides additional information and sources.	This technique will not prevent or detect fraud but will help to compensate the company should fraud occur.
Require employees to take two consecutive weeks of vacation near the end of an accounting cycle. Someone else should perform the duties during that time. If two-week vacations are not feasible, rotate duties so that the person generally performing the function will not have the same access for a period of time.	Fictitious invoices, altering invoices, duplicate payment schemes, and stealing checks
Require documentation of the receipt of goods (that is a receiving report) or services (a signature by the individual who had the service performed). This should be independent of the person who approves the invoice for payment. Documentation could be electronic. Management should determine the form that is acceptable to them.	Fictitious invoices, altering invoices, duplicate payment schemes, and stealing checks
Management should approve all vendors on the approved vendor list. The list should be reviewed periodically to ensure that no vendor has been added without approval.	Fictitious invoices
Reconcile the disbursements records to the accounts payable open invoice file. Reconcile the accounts payable detail to the general ledger. Management should review reconciliations.	Fictitious payments
Use of positive pay. *Positive pay* is a feature that can be added to an organization's account in which the bank will only pay those items that have previously been identified by name and amount.	Fictitious payments and stealing checks
The following duties should be separated: • Check preparation • Check signing • Ability to change the master vendor file • Approval of invoices for payment • Accounts payable processing • Cash disbursements • Mailing checks (do not give checks back to the employee who wrote them or the accounts payable clerk.)	Fictitious checks, excess purchasing, duplicate payments, and stealing checks Note that although locking up the check stock is a good control, today many frauds are committed when fraudsters obtain bank account information and print their own. Technology has come a long way, and it makes legitimate and fraudulent commerce easier.
Reconcile the bank account promptly and investigate all old reconciling items. Stop payment on items older than 90 days and reissue checks. Bank reconciliations should be reviewed promptly as well.	Fictitious payments

(continued)

(continued)

Control	What Types of Occurrences This Could Help to Prevent or Detect
Stamp invoices "paid" to prevent repayment.	Duplicate payment schemes
Management should perform analytical procedures comparing budget to actual, current period to prior period.	Fictitious invoices, altering invoices, duplicate payment schemes, stealing checks, inappropriate wire transfers, and check tampering
Purchase orders, check requests, checks, and receiving documents should be prenumbered and the series accounted for by an independent person.	Fictitious payments and stealing checks
Payments to employees should be authorized by management.	Excess purchasing schemes
Wire transfers and other electronic payments should be reviewed by management and, if large enough, by two people.	Wire transfer schemes and electronic payment schemes
Manual (hand-written) checks should not be used. If they must be used, senior management should approve them.	Fictitious invoices
Invoices should be approved and supported by receiving documents, purchase orders, bills of lading, check requests, or other support. Invoices should be summed and the quantities challenged for reasonableness.	Fictitious invoices and excess purchasing schemes

Use of Analytical Techniques to Identify Unusual Disbursement Transactions for Investigation

Today there are several software programs that can help management run tests that will help to identify usual transactions. ACL, IDEA, and even Excel are such software programs. Data from the organization's general ledger can be downloaded into these programs and certain tests run in a very short period of time. Running such tests sets the tone that employees are being watched, and, according to Joseph Wells, this is a deterrent to fraud. Management could run the following queries:

- Which employees have the same addresses as vendors?
- Which vendors use post office boxes to remit payment?
- Which vendors have initials in their names?
- To which vendors are the most payments made?
- Search for duplicate payments (by invoice number and by payment amount)
- Run Benford's law to identify unusual patterns in expenses.

In 1938, Frank Benford conducted a study dealing with digit frequencies in data. From that study, he found that there is a probability in numbers that certain digits will be the first, second, third, fourth, fifth, and so on number in the string of digits a certain percent of the time. He built a table that has been used in analytical procedures ever since. An excerpt from Benford's table follows.[16]

---

16 Theodore Hill, "A Statistical Derivation of the Significant-Digit Law," *Statistical Science*, vol. 10, no. 4, Nov., 1995, p. 354–363.

Position of Digit	Proportion as First	Proportion as Second	Proportion as Third	Proportion as Fourth
0		.11968	.10178	.10018
1	.30103	.11389	.10138	.10014
2	.17609	.10882	.10097	.10010
3	.12494	.10433	.10057	.10006
4	.09691	.10031	.10018	.10002
5	.07918	.09668	.09979	.09998
6	.06695	.09337	.09940	.09994
7	.05799	.09035	.09902	.09990
8	.05115	.08757	.09864	.09966
9	.04578	.08500	.09827	.09982

This information can be used to investigate occurrences. Not all anomalies in data mean that there is fraud.

Example

Wayne James Nelson worked for the state of Arizona as a manager in the state treasurer's office. He was convicted of fraud against the state in 1993.

The Scheme: He created several fictitious vendors and began writing checks to it, depositing the amounts in his own account. Over a very short period of time, he wrote 23 checks. The first was $ 1,927.46. The amounts became larger and larger. However, the checks were always under $100,000 because another level approval would have been needed. The total checks written from October 9, 1992, through October 19, 1992, were $1,878,687.58. When Benford's law was run on these data, the pattern in the checks was almost the opposite of what Benford's law would show. Most people do not know that there is this pattern in numbers. Many of the checks written began with the numbers 7, 8, and 9. According to the chart, it is evident that these numbers are less likely to be the first digit in a series of numbers. Nelson argued that he did this as a test to show that the accounting system did not have the appropriate level of controls.*

---

* Mark Nigrini, "I've Got Your Number," *Journal of Accountancy*, May 1999.

Skimming and Larceny

The two most prevalent schemes in the area of cash receipts and revenue are skimming and cash larceny. According to the *2010 Report to the Nations on Occupational Fraud and Abuse*, skimming and larceny occurred in 21.6 percent and 12.3 percent of the cases reported, respectively, with a median duration of 18 months.

Skimming is harder to identify than larceny because cash receipts are stolen before they are recorded in the books and records. In a nonprofit, many contributions that the organization receives are not solicited. In addition, contributions are not like operating revenue in that sometimes there are more than at other times, so the amounts are less predictable, and analytical procedures are practically impossible to perform. With cash larceny, the payment comes into the organization and is recorded in the books; it just never gets to the bank.

 Example

Howard works for a nonprofit charity. He is responsible for opening the mail and preparing a list of the checks for deposit. The checks on the list are stamped "for deposit only." That is, if they make it to the list. Howard also has access to the organization's stationary. He knows that donors expect an acknowledgement letter, and, if they don't get it, they call the ED and make inquiries.

The Scheme: Howard started taking the currency that came in because many times there was no indication of who gave them money. Then he became bold because he didn't get caught and stole checks for which the donations were unrestricted. He wrote each donor an acknowledgement letter on the nonprofit's stationary and mailed it to them promptly. Like many fraudsters, Howard became greedy and stole more and more cash receipts. He became worried that the bank would identify the checks made out to the organization going into his checking account. After the golf tournament for the year was finished and all the receipts and disbursements were accounted for, he was asked to close the account when he went to the bank to make the deposit. Instead he left it open and began depositing the stolen checks into that bank account. He used the money to pay his mortgage and other bills. Howard got caught when the auditors wanted to confirm the closure of bank accounts that were supposed to have been closed.

Fraud Scheme: Skimming

 Example

Jim was responsible for performing the bookkeeping for a pledge drive at his organization. A fund-raiser was held, and approximately $500,000 in pledges was made by enthusiastic donors. Sue, the development director, added up the pledges, wrote the letters thanking the donors for their pledges, and gave the pledge list to the cash receipts clerk to post as contribution revenue. She also gave the list to Jim along with the donors' addresses and phone numbers for follow-up after the event. The organization had reliable donors, and the cash started coming in. Jim identified the checks that were related to the campaign and began to mark the donors on the list as paid. He gave that information to the cash receipts clerk to post to the accounting records, and he prepared a deposit slip to take them to the bank.

The Scheme: Around the second week after the fundraiser, a check came in for $5,000. Jim was tempted to take the check and deposit it into his account. He listed it in the cash receipts to give to the clerk but never deposited the check into the organization's account. Instead he deposited it into his own. He rationalized that he only needed the money for a short period of time and fully intended to pay it back before anyone could find out. He volunteered to reconcile the bank account for the month and his offer was gratefully accepted. He listed the check as a reconciling item on the bank reconciliation to make the account balance to the general ledger.

Jim was not able to pay the money back. The ED was supposed to review the bank reconciliation. Although she was two months behind, at the end of the quarter she asked to see them. She also asked Jim why he was performing someone else's function. Upon review of the reconciling items, she wondered how a deposit in transit could be so old. Jim was caught.

Fraud Scheme: Larceny

Following are internal controls that could be put into place in the organization to prevent or detect cash schemes. Note that this is not a comprehensive list of all possible internal controls that could be implemented. For a more complete list, consult the tools referenced in the preceding sections.

Control	What Types of Occurrences This Could Help to Prevent and Detect
Management should perform analytical procedures comparing budget to actual and current period to prior period.	Cash larceny and skimming
Reconcile the bank account promptly and investigate all old reconciling items. Deposits in transit should not be any more than one or two days old. Bank reconciliations should be reviewed promptly as well.	Cash larceny and skimming
Keep amounts not deposited in a safe.	Stealing deposits and skimming
Consider a lockbox where there is a lack of segregation of duties and large volumes of cash.	Cash larceny and skimming
Use multipart deposit forms and reconcile the deposit to the amounts posted in the general ledger. Use prenumbered deposit slips.	Cash larceny and skimming
Reconcile receivables to the general ledger.	Cash larceny and skimming
Bond employees with access to cash.	Cash larceny, skimming, and stealing cash on hand (petty cash)
Management should review the receivables (pledges or accounts) for collectability and follow up.	Cash larceny and skimming
Have a mechanism for donors to report issues.	Cash larceny and skimming
Two people should count cash. Surveillance could be used in cases where there is a significant amount of cash.	Cash larceny and skimming

(continued)

(continued)

Control	What Types of Occurrences This Could Help to Prevent and Detect
Segregate the following duties: • Opening the mail and logging the receipt • Posting the cash • Depositing the receipts in the bank • Handling complaints from donors • Performance of bank reconciliations • Writing acknowledgement letters • Following up on aged receivables • Reviewing bank reconciliations	Cash larceny and skimming

Payroll Fraud

As noted in this chapter, payroll fraud is not as prevalent as fraud involving cash receipts and cash disbursements. However, awareness of payroll fraud is important. Typical fraud schemes are

- ghost (fictitious) employees and
- paying more than the appropriate salary.

 Example

Zeke needed cash. His job was to review the payroll and withholdings and post the summary information to the general ledger. However, because duties were segregated, he did not have the ability to create a new employee in the system. Hannah was his friend, and she had responsibility for entering new employees in the master payroll file and making changes to the file for pay rate increases and changes to withholding. The accounting manager reviewed the payroll analytically each month, but, because Zeke had been with the nonprofit so long, her review was cursory.

The Scheme: Zeke started visiting Hannah's cube and talking to her more at work. He was trying to see if he could determine her password to the master payroll file. But Hannah typed in her password too quickly for him to see it. The organization had a policy of changing passwords every 90 days. One day Zeke initiated a conversation with Hannah about this control. Hannah told him that she could never keep up with all her passwords so she wrote them in her calendar and kept them in her desk drawer. This gave Zeke the information he needed to steal the password and give himself a raise. About 6 months later, because he had not been caught, he entered a new employee into the system. He used the social security number of a deceased person he found on the internet. He set the withholdings to zero and made sure the employee number was outside the range of the other employee numbers so that the ghost employee would not appear on the summary that the accounting manager reviewed. Because he had responsibility for posting to the general ledger, he spread the salary over several different account numbers so that none would appear unusual when the accounting manager performed analytical review.

Fraud Scheme: Failure to deposit withholdings and misappropriating them

Example

Shirley worked for a food bank, and she was experiencing a personal cash flow problem. She was the only administrative employee. The organization was in the process of searching for a new ED, so there was no segregation of duties. The board was not working very hard to replace the ED; because the organization was so small, the board believed Shirley could easily handle the work. After all, the less paid out for administrative expenses, the more money was available for the program. The majority of the employees were in operations.

The chair of the board reviewed the results of operations each month, so Shirley was afraid she would get caught if she put a fictitious employee on the payroll. And she couldn't think of a way to take incoming cash or write checks to herself. The organization had few cash transactions, receiving only one grant check each quarter, which paid for the operating expenses.

The Scheme: One day, when preparing to make the deposit to the IRS for payroll withholdings, she decided to deposit the check in her account instead. After all, no one looked at the regulatory correspondence to the organization, so she believed that she had a long time before anyone noticed. She really intended for this to be a temporary loan.

Fraud Scheme: Additional checks or bonus paid to employees; Expense report fraud

---

 Example

Dean was the administrator of a nursing home association. He was one of the most influential people in the state and lobbied extensively for the organization. The board believed he could never be replaced. There were 50 employees in the organization.

The Scheme: Dean not only abused the travel and entertainment policy, but he also created fictitious expenses and submitted them without guilt. He believed that because of him the nursing home industry was fairly treated by insurers and the state Medicaid agency. He also thought he could get a lot better compensation if he worked for a commercial entity. The board was aware of what he was doing because it had brought to their attention by accounting personnel, but no one was willing to do anything about it. This is not only a case of expense fraud but also an issue that tests the moral courage of the board. Moral courage is more fully explored in chapter 9.

Following are examples of controls that could be used to prevent or detect payroll schemes.

Control	What Types of Occurrences This Could Help to Prevent or Detect
Analytically review the payroll expense divided by number of people on the payroll. Compare budget to actual.	Ghost employees, overpaying employees, and writing additional checks to employees
Compare the number of people in the organization to the number of checks written.	Ghost employees, keeping terminated employees on the payroll, and writing additional checks to employees
For those organizations that still have manual checks, once a quarter or year, hand out the paychecks so that ghost employees are identified. ID should be shown to collect the check. For those with direct deposit, the pay stub could be handed out.	Ghost employees, keeping terminated employees on the payroll, and writing additional checks to employees
Segregate the following duties: • Master payroll file • Reconciliation of payroll and related withholding and benefit accounts • Review of payroll and bonus checks • Preparation of checks • Signing checks • Approval of expense reports • Posting payroll to the accounting records	Ghost employees, writing additional checks to employees, keeping terminated employees on the payroll, inflating payroll checks, keeping terminated employees on the payroll, giving out unauthorized bonuses, and expense report fraud
Review timesheets for excess hours.	Overpaying employees and paying for hours not worked
Require time-reporting mechanisms.	Overpaying employees and paying for hours not worked
Use direct deposit. Have an independent person review information that goes to the service organization. Use an imprest account.	Overpaying employees, stealing paychecks, writing additional checks to employees, and keeping terminated employees on the payroll
Lock up personnel files.	Ghost employees
Require original receipts and review for reasonableness, compliance with policies, and so forth. Authorizing personnel should not review their own expense reports.	Expense report fraud
Use positive pay.	Employees writing additional checks to themselves and stealing paychecks
Restrict the use of manual checks.	Employees writing additional checks to themselves
All changes to payroll need to be approved.	Ghost employees, writing additional checks to employees, keeping terminated employees on the payroll, inflating payroll checks, and keeping terminated employees on the payroll.

Controls Over Noncash Items

Noncash items can be stolen very easily from a nonprofit. Noncash items can range from supplies to laptop computers to other portable items. In some nonprofits, such as thrift stores and food banks, the level of noncash assets is proportionally higher. It may be tempting to believe that noncash items are of low dollar value, and some may be, but there have been fraud cases involving the theft of millions of dollars of noncash items over a period of time. When the fraudster sells the goods to others, this is referred to as "back door" sales. In one high profile fraud, approximately $26 million was stolen from a thrift store type of organization. Surveillance is the best option for a control because this type of fraud is difficult to analytically review.

When Processing is Outsourced

Nonprofit organizations often find it beneficial and less costly to outsource certain processes to other entities. Outsourcing provides the organization with the ability to allow a company with expertise in the area and robust technology to process its transactions for a fee, thereby enhancing segregation of duties and eliminating the need for additional employees. Payroll is a good example of such a process. Another process frequently outsourced relates to processing investment transactions.

When processes are outsourced, it is very important for management to ensure that they understand the capabilities and quality of the service organization performing the processing. Management and the board are still responsible for the existence, accuracy, completeness, and valuation of the information that is processed by other entities. One way to do this is to obtain a Statement on Standards for Attestation Engagements (SSAE) No. 16, *Reporting on Controls at a Service Organization*, report.[17] The outside service organization will pay for an independent auditor to perform an audit of its controls on selected processes, and the resulting report is the SSAE No. 16 report. Management should review the report to determine if

- the opinion on the system controls is other than unqualified.
- there were no exceptions in testing that would significantly affect the processing so that management believes the controls are not sufficient for their purposes.
- the controls specified by the service organization that should be implemented by the user entity (the nonprofit) to prevent or detect and correct errors related to input of the data and output of the information are in place and functioning effectively. This is very important because a service organization can only be responsible for the activities in its system. What happens before the inputs reach it and what happens when the information leaves it can only be monitored by management of the user organization.
- the time period over which the controls are either understood or tested is adequate for the user organization's purposes. The SSAE No. 16 reports generally span a 6 month period, and the more overlap there is in the user's year and the period tested by the service auditor, the better.

---

17 Statement on Standards for Attestation Engagements (SSAE) No. 16, *Reporting on Controls at a Service Organization* (AICPA, *Professional Standards*, AT sec. 801). Note that for service organization reports with periods ending on or after June 15, 2011, the professional standards governing the audit of the service organization are in SSAE No. 16. The literature up to that point was SAS No. 70, *Service Organizations* (AICPA, *Professional Standards*, AU sec. 324).

Example

A nonprofit used a service organization to process payroll. The nonprofit submitted a tape containing the payroll information to the service organization to perform the processing. The service organization has no control over the contents of the tape. If, for example, a fictitious employee was entered, or if withholding information was not changed by the nonprofit before the tape was sent, the service organization would have no way of knowing that what was being processed was incorrect. In addition, in its list of user controls, the service organization states that the user is responsible for the review of the information processed and should bring errors to the attention of the service organization.

Internal Controls Evolve

Internal control should continue to evolve as the organization changes. The evolution of organizations could be compared to a house that was built when a couple married. They liked the house, so when they were preparing for a child, they added an additional room. As the family grew, additional rooms were added. Later the house was remodeled. Although the renovations accommodated the growing family, the internal structure was insufficient to support the growing house. Organizations evolve the same way, but often the internal controls are not reexamined to determine whether they are still sufficient and meet the needs of the organization. Policies and procedures may change but are not always updated in the organization's policy and procedure manuals. With all there is to do and with pressure to do more with less, sometimes this important area gets minimal attention. However, as noted, if employees don't understand what they are supposed to do and why they are supposed to do it, lack of consistency surely follows. And if a new employee comes in to take the place of one who has worked with the process for some time, the new employee will have a difficult time knowing exactly what duties management wanted performed. The internal controls lose effectiveness.

Example

Josh is the ED of a small membership organization. In fact, he founded it in 1970 and is very proud of all it has accomplished. Nearing 65, Josh is preparing to retire and talks about how this important trade group that has achieved such good results for its members is his legacy. During the audit of the financial statements, his auditor asked him, "Do you want this organization to be around for years to come after you leave?" Josh was surprised at the question and said, "Of course, why do you ask?" The auditor said, "All the policies, procedures, and processes are in your head; they have never been written down. How will anyone know what to do if you are not around to tell them?"

The external environment may change the way organizations view internal control. For example, when enacted in 2003, the law referred to as Check 21 streamlined the way that checks were processed. However, in the process, it took away the customer's ability to have its cancelled checks returned, and an important internal control was lost. There was significant value in being able to review the front and back of cancelled checks to look at the signature of the endorser. But evolving technology also gave organizations the ability to institute a positive pay system. As discussed in this chapter, positive pay enables management to notify the bank of the check numbers and amounts of checks that are authorized to be paid. Any items presenting that are not a part of the list are declined by the bank. This helps to segregate duties without adding additional people. Organizations should consider new technologies when evaluating their systems of internal control.

In the fall of 2010, COSO announced that it is embarking on modernizing its original framework that was published in the early 1990s. This project is not intended to supplant the existing framework but to make it more relevant to the environment today and changing needs to regulators and other stakeholders.[18] COSO also intends to tie this framework into a system of enterprise risk management, which was discussed in chapter 6.

Internal controls are very important to the success of an organization. Not only do they prevent and detect error and fraud, but they also help safeguard the reputation of the organization.

Conclusion

Although people don't want to believe that they or their organization will have a problem from fraud or suffer errors that are more than trivial, the examples of fraud schemes and errors presented in this chapter demonstrate both that no one is immune and that the effects of these problems can be more far reaching and damaging than one might anticipate. Implementing specific controls to address the risk of fraud and error can improve an organization's assurance that such issues will be prevented or at least detected sooner. The examples in this chapter provide a business case for why internal controls are important. The illustrations of specific controls designed to mitigate the risk of fraud or error provide suggestions for how a system of internal control can be improved. With this knowledge, board members and executives can be better prepared to participate in the design and implementation of an effective system to help protect their organization from these types of risks.

---

18 "COSO Announces Project to Modernize Internal Control—Integrated Framework," COSO Press Release, November 2010, www.coso.org/documents/COSOReleaseNov2010.pdf.

Chapter 8

Focus on Tax Exempt Status

John and Kay, 2 audit committee members of Companions for the Blind, a charitable nonprofit organization, were making a final review of the proposals for tax work submitted by 3 public accounting firms. John thought about the presentations that each of the firms made to Companions of the Blind about their expertise in preparing the Form 990. Wayne, a tax partner in one of those firms, made a particularly compelling case for using his firm's services. Wayne's presentation included an explanation to the board about why the proper preparation of Form 990 was so important. He also discussed the complexities involved in completing the form and how important it was for the board or its designated committee to review and approve it.

In the meeting, Wayne said, "Over the past decade, there has been significant focus by legislators such as Senator Charles Grassley, watch dog agencies such as Charity Navigator and Board Source, and government agencies such as the IRS on the tax exempt status of nonprofits. Nonprofits benefit by not having to pay federal income and excise taxes and, in many states, by not having to pay state income, property, and other taxes. Some nonprofits also use their tax exempt status to issue bonds at lower rates because the interest is not taxable to the bond holders. These benefits can save a nonprofit significant money, which can then be spent on programs that benefit the community. But abuse of tax exempt status, poor internal controls, and lack of board oversight over the years has caused the IRS to focus more on areas in which issues have occurred. Compensation practices and board governance are of particular interest to them right now, and the information tax return (Form 990), which was redesigned in late 2007* for fiscal years beginning in 2008 (note that most of these fiscal years end in 2009), focuses significant attention on compensation paid to officers, directors, trustees, key employees, and highly compensated individuals, not to mention the dozen or so questions on the organization's governance practices. The tax exempt organization is required to answer questions pertaining to its governance practices by checking a box 'yes' or 'no' and in some instances providing explanations of its policies or procedures. This technique forces the tax exempt organization to either implement the

(continued)

* The form was redesigned in later 2007 to be used by tax exempt organizations beginning in 2009.

(continued)

governance policies and procedures or admit that it doesn't have them. The IRS is the only organization I know of that has a no cost system of 'enforcement.' Each day thousands of people, including contributors, supporters, employees, state attorneys general, watchdogs, newsgroups, data gatherers, and other organizations go to the Guidestar website and other web-based sources to view the Form 990s that are of interest to them. They make funding and other decisions based, in part, on what they see in the form. Therefore, governing boards, whose members are listed in the organization's Form 990, need to be very concerned about the thoughtfulness and accuracy with which the Form 990 is prepared and review it carefully."

John said to Kay, "Maybe we better look past the fee to the expertise of the firms. What Wayne said made a lot of sense, and I for one do not want my name associated with an organization that does not appear to be concerned with tax compliance. I never knew the thing was so complicated or that it could be seen by so many people." Kay said, "You're right. It sounds like the IRS is concerned about abuses by tax exempt organizations, and if it took the effort to redesign the form to gather specific information then there's probably more to it than we even know."

This chapter is designed to provide board members with an understanding of the issues that nonprofits must consider related to obtaining and maintaining tax exempt status. Although the chapter discusses the various forms that must be completed by tax exempt organizations, it is not intended to provide instruction as to how to complete or file the forms. This chapter provides scenarios to illustrate some of the more typical situations that a tax exempt organization might encounter. Tax regulations are complex, and those related to information tax return Forms 990, 990–EZ, 990–N, 990T, and 990PF are no different. It is always important to obtain and read the instructions for each form before completing it. When in doubt, it is a good idea to consult a tax professional.

Nonprofit Organizations and Tax Exempt Status

The terminology and definitions dealing with concepts related to nonprofit organizations can be confusing. *Nonprofit* is a type of organization, *not-for-profit* is a type of activity, and *tax exempt* is a status granted through sections of the Internal Revenue Code that are then recognized, or not recognized, by the IRS.[1]

There are many types of tax exempt organizations. Following are the most prevalent.

Type	Examples of What They Do	IRC Code Section
Charities, educational, religious, scientific, literary, testing for public safety, fostering amateur sports competition, and prevention of cruelty to children or animals	Conduct activities consistent with their descriptive class	501(c)(3)

---

1 Bruce R. Hopkins, *Starting and Managing a Nonprofit Organization: A Legal Guide* (Hoboken: John Wiley & Sons, Inc., 2009).

Type	Examples of What They Do	IRC Code Section
Private foundations	Can be either operating or nonoperating. Operating foundations operate their own programs, whereas nonoperating foundations provide funding to charities and other nonprofit organizations and governments for charitable purposes.	501(c)(3)
Civic leagues and social welfare organizations	Civic associations, health maintenance organizations and volunteer fire departments	501(c)(4)
Labor, agricultural, and horticultural organizations	To improve the conditions of work or to improve products or efficiency	501(c)(5)
Business leagues, chambers of commerce, and real estate boards	To improve business	501(c)(6)
Social and recreational clubs	For pleasure, recreation, and social activities	501(c)(7)
Fraternal beneficiary societies and associations	Payment of life, sickness, accident, or other benefits to members	501(c)(8)
Voluntary employees beneficiary associations	Payment of life, sickness, accident, or other benefits to members	501(c)(9)
Domestic fraternal societies and associations	Type of lodge that devotes the net earnings to charitable, fraternal, and other purposes. Not permitted to pay life, sickness, or accident benefits to members	501(c)(10)
Teacher retirement fund associations	Pay retirement benefits to teachers	501(c)(11)
Benevolent life insurance associations, mutual or cooperative telephone companies, and mutual ditch or irrigation companies	Offer benefits to members	501(c)(12)
Cemetery companies	Burials and incidental activities	501(c)(13)
State chartered credit unions	Offers banking and other financial services to members	501(c)(14)

More detailed information may be found in section 7.25, *Exempt Organizations Determinations Manual*, of the IRS' Internal Revenue Manual in exhibit 7.25.1-1, "Table of Organizations Exempt Under Section 501," at www.irs.gov/irm/part7/irm_07-025-001.html#d0e331.

Holding companies for exempt organizations are classified as 501(c) (2) organizations.

IRS Filings

Tax exempt organizations are required to file many forms with the IRS and with state agencies. The forms noted in the next paragraphs will be discussed in this chapter. Appendix B to the chapter identifies other forms that these organizations must file. This information is for returns filed generally in 2011 for tax years beginning in 2010. Churches are not required to file Form 1023 or 990 but many do in order to give comfort to their donors that the organization is tax exempt.

IRC Code Section	Annual Gross Receipts	Assets	Information Tax Return	Application For Recognition of Tax Exempt Status
501(c)(3)	Normally not more than $5,000	Any	990N	No requirement
501(c)(3)	Normally less than $50,000	Any	990N	1023 required
501(c)(3)	$50,001 to $199,999	And < $500,000	990 EZ	1023 required
501(c)(3)	$200,000+	Or $500,000+	990	1023 required
501(c)(3) Private Foundation	Less than $5,000		990 PF	1023 required
Other code sections listed in preceding table	Thresholds listed previously apply.	Thresholds listed previously apply.	Types of returns vary by threshold.	1024 recommended

Form 990-T is also required to be filed when the organization has gross unrelated business income (UBI) (gross receipts before cost of goods sold) of $1,000 or more from a regularly carried on trade or business. Form 990-T is also used for the payment of proxy tax on lobbying expenditures or other taxes. Even organizations that are exempt from filing a Form 990, such as churches, are subject to the same Form 990-T filing requirements.

The information tax returns are required to be filed by the fifteenth day of the fifth month after its fiscal year end. There are 2 3-month extensions available for those organizations filing the Form 990-EZ, 990, or 990-PF. These returns are posted on the Guidestar website (www.guidestar.org) within approximately 2 months.

Example

Fiscal year end	Due date of return	Due date with 1st 90 day extension	Due date with 2nd 90 day extension
June 30, 2010	November 15, 2010	February 15, 2011	May 15, 2011

If the exempt organization has $10 million or more in total assets, and if it files at least 250 returns of any type during the calendar year ending with or within the organization's tax year, then it will be required to file the Form 990 or 990-EZ electronically. As noted in appendix B, there are many types of returns that the organization will be required to file. These include income, excise, employment tax, and information returns. Note that each W-2 that an organization completes is considered a return.

Private foundations and nonexempt charitable trusts are required to file Form 990-PF electronically, regardless of their asset size, if they file at least 250 returns of any type annually.

If an organization must file its return electronically but does not, it is considered to have not filed its return. In addition, late filing can result in substantial monetary penalties and even loss of exempt status.

Differences Between Nonprofit and Commercial Organizations

The fundamental difference between a nonprofit organization and a commercial entity is not the fact that a nonprofit makes no profit and a commercial entity (also referred to as a for-profit entity) was created to make a profit. If *profit* is defined as the excess of revenues over expenses, all entities that wish to remain viable must make a profit. The phrase "no margin, no mission" is often used in nonprofit organizations to describe the need to have residual earnings.

The distinction between a commercial entity and a nonprofit is that the nonprofit organization is subject to the private inurement doctrine. The IRS discusses avoidance of private inurement in Publication 557, *Tax Exempt Status for your Organization,* as one of the characteristics that must be upheld by a nonprofit in order to be recognized as tax exempt. It states that "no part of the net earnings of a nonprofit can inure to the benefit of any private shareholder or individual."[2] Basically this means that excess of revenues over expenses of the organization, along with its assets, should be used to conduct the activities of the organizations and not to enrich a private party.

An IRS General Counsel Memorandum (GCM)[3] states that private inurement is likely to arise when "the financial benefit represents a transfer of the organization's financial resources to an individual solely by virtue of the individual's relationship with the organization and without regard to accomplishing the tax exempt purpose." Another GCM[4] explains that private inurement is prohibited to prevent anyone in a position to do so from siphoning off any of an exempt organization's income or assets for personal use.

In order for private inurement to be present, the private party (also known as an *insider* in federal tax law)[5] must have the ability to control or otherwise influence the actions of the charitable organization. For purposes of private inurement, an insider would be an officer, director, trustee or key employee, family members of those individuals, and certain entities that are controlled by them. Private inurement can occur when

- compensation is paid to an individual.
- there is a sale or lease of property between the organization and an individual.
- loans are made to individuals by the organization.
- goods or services or facilities are furnished to the organization by an individual or vice versa.

A Guide to Federal Tax Issues for Colleges and Universities provides several examples of case law in which private inurement was said to have occurred either resulting in failure to recognize the tax exempt status of the organization or revocation of the organization's tax exempt status.

---

2 IRS Publication 557, *Tax Exempt Status for Your Organization,* www.irs.gov/pub/irs-pdf/p557.pdf.

3 IRS General Counsel Memorandum (GCM) No. 38459, July 31, 1980.

4 IRS GCM No. 39862, December 2, 1991.

5 *A Guide to Federal Tax Issues for Colleges and Universities,* Section 300, Private Inurement and Excess Benefit Transactions, NACUBO, www.federaltaxissues.com.

🔲 Example

Jeremy is about to be offered a position as the CFO of HIV-Aids Partners, a nonprofit charity. The compensation committee of HIV-Aids Partners is in the process of determining his compensation package. Because he will work for the organization, the payment of compensation is permissible. However, when deemed excessive, it may be considered private inurement because he would be deemed an insider. The committee performed some research into whether the amount it wanted to offer Jeremy as compensation would be considered reasonable. This included not only the cash compensation but also fringe benefits he would receive in the form of insurance, deferred compensation, and retirement benefits.

🔲 Example

After a significant amount of deliberation, the board of directors voted to make an emergency loan to the executive director. The loan was to be for a period of 9 months, and the board performed research to determine the market rate of interest commensurate with the risk involved. The board chair had this statement put into the minutes: "We must be very careful to monitor the repayment of this loan and to document all of the consideration we gave to the issue in deciding to make it. We must also not make this a precedent for future actions because it is our policy not to grant loans to those who would be considered insiders. We understand that this loan will be disclosed on the Form 990 and must be prepared for any inquiries from donors or others."

When an individual receives a benefit in excess of what is provided to the organization, it is considered an *excess benefit*. If the person is considered a disqualified person, then the IRS can impose intermediate sanctions on him or her.

A *disqualified person* is defined by the IRS as a person who was in a position to exercise substantial influence over the affairs of the applicable tax exempt organization at any time during the five year period before the excess benefit transaction occurred. It is not necessary for the individual to exercise substantial influence for an excess benefit transaction to have occurred. They only have to be in a position to do so.

Examples of a disqualified person[6] are as follows:

- A voting member of the governing body
- A person who has responsibility for implementing the decisions of the governing body or for supervising the management, administration, or operation of the organization

---

6 www.irs.gov/charities/charitable/article/0,,id=123300,00.html.

- A person who has ultimate responsibility for managing the finances of the organization
- The person who founded the organization
- A substantial contributor to the organization
- A person whose compensation is based primarily on revenues derived from organization activities that the person controls
- A person who has or shares authority to control or determine a substantial portion of the organization's capital expenditures, operating budget, or compensation for employees
- A person who manages a discrete segment or activity of the organization that represents a substantial portion of its activities, assets, income, or expenses
- A person who owns a controlling interest in a corporation, partnership, or trust that is a disqualified person
- A person who is able to exercise substantial influence over a supporting organization (under Internal Revenue Code section 509(a)(3))

Family members of the disqualified person and entities controlled by the disqualified person are also disqualified persons. In making this determination, *control* is defined as owning more than 35 percent of the voting power of a corporation, more than 35 percent of the profits interest in a partnership, or more than 35 percent of the beneficial interest in a trust.

The intermediate sanctions are imposed on the disqualified person and not the nonprofit. The disqualified person who received the excess benefit is subject to an initial tax of 25 percent of the amount of the excess benefit. He or she also has to return the excess benefit amount to the organization. If an organization manager knowingly participated in an excess benefit transaction, then that person is subject to an initial tax of 10 percent of the excess benefit. And additional taxes could be levied—equal to 200 percent of the excess benefit—in situations in which corrective action was not made.

 Example

Sunshine Home increased the pay of its executive director to $450,000. The board approved the compensation. When Form 990 was prepared, the compensation was properly listed on the form. A reporter from Channel 3, Eye on You News, was working on a story about inappropriate use of charitable assets and pulled the Forms 990 for 25 charities in the area, one of which was Sunshine Home. Based on the research performed by the reporter, executive directors in similar commercial and nonprofit organizations earned as much as $250,000.

(continued)

(continued)

If the IRS reviewed the situation and determined that $250,000 was reasonable compensation,* then $200,000 would be considered the excess benefit. The executive director is a disqualified person.

Compensation paid to disqualified person	$450,000
Compensation held to be reasonable	$250,000
Excess benefit	**$200,000**
Initial tax to disqualified person (25%)	$ 50,000
Tax on each board member who signed off on the compensation assuming they knew it was an excess benefit (10%)	$ 20,000
Payback on part of disqualified person	$200,000
Second tier tax if the situation is not remediated. This is leveled on the disqualified person (200%).	$400,000

There is an exception for the first time a payment is made to a disqualified person. The amount must be a fixed payment or calculated using a fixed formula specified in the contract. In addition, the person could not have been a disqualified person prior to entering into the contract.

* Treas. Regs. §53.4958-4(b)(1)(ii) states that the excess benefit is the amount over the value of services that would ordinarily be paid for like services by like enterprises (whether taxable or tax-exempt) under like circumstances (reasonable compensation).

Closely related to private inurement is private benefit. It comes from statutory law that charities must be operated primarily for their tax exempt purpose.[7] This occurs when individuals receiving a benefit are not members of the charitable class and when the benefit is not incidental. For a benefit to be incidental, it must be necessary in that the exempt objectives cannot be achieved without also benefitting private individuals. A charitable organization will not qualify as tax exempt if its primary purpose is to provide a private benefit. The benefit does not need to be provided to insiders to constitute a private benefit.

Example

Helping Hands is a nonprofit, tax exempt organization that helps lower income patients apply for Medicaid and refers them to physicians who take patients with Medicaid. In doing so, it indirectly provides benefits to physicians, including the physicians who sit on its board. However, because it would be impossible to carry out its tax exempt purpose without indirectly providing this benefit to physicians, the benefit is deemed to be incidental.

---

7 Treas. Reg. §1.501 (c)(3)-1(c).

> **Example**
>
> Starving Artists is a charitable organization that promotes the arts by
> encouraging young artists. It holds monthly functions at which the work
> of young artists is displayed, allowing the artists to gain exposure and sell
> their work. Recently, the organization began holding events at which its
> members could showcase and sell their work. The organization's tax advisor
> advised them to stop the practice immediately because the members were
> not considered to be part of the charitable class. If the members had been
> willing to donate their work to the organization where it could be sold and
> the proceeds used for the organization's programs, this would be a different
> situation.

Most tax exempt[8] organizations are nonprofits, but not all nonprofits are eligible to be tax exempt. To be tax exempt, the organization must qualify. In order to be tax exempt, the organization needs to meet the statutory requirements that provide for its exempt status. Charities, credit counseling agencies, and certain employee benefit organizations are required to file with the IRS. Social welfare agencies, labor organizations, trade groups, professional associations, and social clubs are not required to file. The filing for charitable organizations is Form 1023. Other organizations file a Form 1024. Some 501 (c) (3) organizations such as churches are not required to file for exemption. However, many do because it gives the donors an additional layer of comfort knowing that their contributions are tax deductible.

Recognition of Tax Exempt Status

As noted in this chapter, unless the nonprofit is a church and elects not to file Forms 1023 or 1024 for recognition of tax exempt status and has no more than $5,000 in gross receipts, the IRS requires that the form be filed within 27 months of the date that the nonprofit was formed. Along with the form, the organization must attach its Certificate of Incorporation and By-laws. For those entities wishing to obtain tax exemption under section 501(c) (3), there are some important considerations. The organizing documents should clearly show that

- the entity is organized for charitable, educational, or religious purposes or one of the purposes described in the preceding paragraph related to that code section.
- no part of the organization's net earnings will inure to the benefit of private shareholders or individuals.
- the organization will not substantially attempt to influence legislation and will not participate in any political campaign of candidates for public office.

8 State and local governments are tax exempt but are not considered nonprofits.

The third bullet point does not mean that the organization cannot perform lobbying activities. However, they are limited as discussed subsequently in this chapter.

The organizing documents (for example, articles of incorporation) must also limit the purpose of the organization to one of those described in section 501(c) (3). However, it is not enough to say that the purpose is within the code section; the document must state the purpose specifically.

 Example

New Horizons was drafting its organizing documents and identified its purpose as "assisting the home-bound elderly with activities of daily living regardless of their ability to pay."

Also important in the organizing documents is the dissolution clause. If the organization were to be dissolved, the assets must be distributed to another organization for an exempt purpose under section 501(c) (3).

 Example

New Horizons was drafting its organizing documents. Management and the board were trying to decide whether it was better to leave the dissolution clause very broad or whether to name a specific organization. Its tax advisors noted that it may be better to leave them broad because the specific organization named would need to be a section 501(c)(3) at the time of dissolution, and so an alternative would also need to be named just in case. New Horizons drafted the language as follows:

> Upon the dissolution of New Horizons, its assets shall be distributed to Hope Valley Home for the Aged. If Hope Valley Home for the Aged is not a section 501(c) (3) at the time of New Horizon's dissolution, then its assets shall be distributed for one or more exempt purposes within the meaning of section 501(c) (3) of the Internal Revenue Code, or corresponding section of any future federal tax code, or shall be distributed to the federal government or a state or local government for a public purpose.

Form 1023 requires the organization provide the following information:

Requirement	Caution
Description of the organization's activities	It is important to be sure that the narrative is well thought out. The Form 1023 is open to public inspection. In addition, this information is expected to agree to the information in Form 990.
Description of public charity status	IRC Code Section 509(a) (1) and 170(b) (1) (A) (i)—a church or a convention or association of churches. (Complete and attach Schedule A of Form 1023).
	509(a) (1) and 170(b) (1) (A) (ii)—a school. (Complete and attach Schedule B of Form 1023).
	509(a) (1) and 170(b) (1) (A) (iii)—a hospital, a cooperative hospital service organization, or a medical research organization operated in conjunction with a hospital. (Complete and attach Schedule C of Form 1023).
	509(a) (3)—an organization supporting either one or more organizations or a publicly supported section 501(c) (4), (5), or (6) organization. (Complete and attach Schedule C of Form 1023).
Compensation and financial arrangements with officers, directors, trustees, employees, and independent contractors	In 2006, the form was revised to add more disclosure on the arrangements with insiders and certain vendors. As noted earlier, the IRS has placed significant focus on private inurement in the interest of good governance. Some of the questions deal with whether the compensation arrangements of the person approving the arrangements are documented; what objective standards were used to determine the reasonableness of the compensation; and whether the organization will have dealings with organizations owned more than 35 percent by an officer, director, or trustee. In case such arrangements exist, how they will be made at arms-length must also be specified.
Conflict of interest policy	The organization's conflict of interest policy must be attached, along with a description of the approval procedures for the policy. Although it is not necessary to have a conflict of interest policy, it is something that the IRS will see as unfavorable if the organization does not because it is an element of good governance.
Lobbying	As noted earlier, a charitable organization can only perform limited lobbying activities. The Form 1023 asks if the organization attempts to influence legislation and, if so, whether it has made an election under Section 501(h) to measure its activities by expenditures. There is an additional form that the organization completes if this is the case. The general rules are noted in a subsequent section, but the answer to this question is a tip to the IRS about whether the organization's tax exempt status should be recognized. If the election is not made, the organization must attach a description of the activities to Form 1023.
Political activities	Charitable organizations cannot participate in partisan political activity.
Fundraising	Information on how fund-raising is conducted.
Other financial information	Balance sheet and projected statement of revenues and expenses. If the organization has been in existence over 1 year and up to __ years, then it will provide up to __ years of statements of revenue and expenses.

Lobbying

Many 501(c) (3) organizations attempt to influence legislation through lobbying. However, lobbying cannot be a substantial portion of a charitable organization's activities without jeopardizing its tax exempt status. But the word *substantial* is not well defined.

The IRS makes it relatively easy to determine the amount of lobbying that would not be considered substantial by use of an expenditure test. This test is not required, but if the organization elects to use it, this test provides comfort to the organization that the objective results will determine whether its lobbying activities are substantial. Charitable organizations other than churches can lose tax exempt status if their lobbying activities are substantial. This is defined as more than 150 percent of the lobbying nontaxable amount.

The organization will pay a proxy tax of 25 percent on its excess lobbying expenditures. If the lobbying expenditures are sufficient to cause the organization to lose its tax exempt status, then it will still pay a tax that is equal to 5 percent on the lobbying expenditures that resulted in the organization being disqualified. It is also possible that the organization manager could be taxed. If the manager agreed to the expenditures knowing that they were likely to result in the loss of tax exemption, then the manager may have to pay a 5 percent tax. The manager will not pay a tax if the action was not willful and it was due to a reasonable cause.

Organizations such as civic leagues, horticultural or agricultural organizations, labor organizations, trade groups, and HMOs that are exempt under other code sections are permitted to make lobbying and political expenditures. However, they need to let the dues paying members know that the portion of the dues that were used for lobbying are not tax deductible. If the organization chooses not to notify the members, then a proxy tax will be paid equal to 35 percent of the lobbying or political expenditures. Form 990–T must be filed when proxy taxes are paid.

Lobbying can be conducted in two ways: grass roots lobbying and direct lobbying. Grass roots lobbying is conducted at the level of the community to try to cause the population's opinion on issue to be swayed to support the organization's cause.

▣ Example

An Alzheimer's association wants to bring an awareness of the seriousness of the disease to the public and inspire them to write to their representatives to obtain more federal or state dollars for Alzheimer's research. The association sends out materials describing the disease and the devastating effects it can have on the afflicted individuals and their families. The communication also includes a call to action.

Direct lobbying would include any attempt to influence legislation by contacting a member of a legislative body or the member's staff or any other government official or employee who would participate in drafting or voting on legislation.

Example

A charitable organization concerned about Multiple Sclerosis (MS) sends a person to Washington, D.C., to discuss a bill that would reduce the amount of funding that would be devoted to MS research. The lobbyist makes direct contact with the members of the committee that drafted the legislation.

There are certain activities that would not constitute lobbying:
- Sending a nonpartisan research report out to interested parties
- Evaluating social issues such as teen pregnancy or violence against women
- Defending the organization against a threat to its tax exempt status, deductibility of contributions, or other such issues at a hearing or meeting with a legislative body
- Communicating with legislatures on nonlobbying related matters
- Providing information or technical advice or answering questions to a legislator or member of his or her staff

Example

Your Sight, a charitable organization, participates in both grass roots and direct lobbying. The organization's exempt purpose expenditures were $5,384,504. Of those expenditures, $567,500 were spent on lobbying. Of the $567,500, $25,000 was spent on grassroots lobbying. The organization elected to use the objective measure under section 501 (h). In its first year, Your Sight made the following evaluation of its lobbying expenditures. The evaluation resulted in the organization paying a proxy tax of $37,069.

Objective Test for Lobbying Activities

Evaluation of Lobbying Expenditures	
How much was spent on grassroots lobbying?	$ 25,000
How much was spent on lobbying, including grassroots lobbying?	$567,500
Calculation for Nontaxable Lobbying Expenditures	
Amount of exempt purpose expenditures (do not include amounts paid or incurred for a separate fund-raising unit or other organization or amounts to organizations if primarily paid for fundraising, but do include lobbying expenditures)	5,384,504
Are the exempt purpose expenditures < $500,000? Multiply the amount of expenditures by 20%. This is the lobbying nontaxable amount.	N/A
If NO, then: Are the exempt purpose expenditures between $500,000 and $1,000,000? Multiply the amount over $500,000 by 15%. Add $100,000 to compute lobbying nontaxable amount.	N/A
If NO, then: Are the exempt purpose expenditures > $1,000,000 but not over $1,5000,000? Multiply the amount over $1,000,000 by 10%. Add $175,000 to compute lobbying nontaxable amount.	N/A

(continued)

(continued)	
If NO, then: Are the exempt purpose expenditures > $1,5000,000? Multiply the amount over $1,500,000 by 5%. Add $225,000 to compute lobbying nontaxable amount.	419,225
Calculation for Nontaxable Grassroots Lobbying Expenditures Calculate the grassroots nontaxable amount (multiply lobbying taxable amount by 25%)	104,806
How much of the amount spent on grassroots lobbying is > the nontaxable amount?	NONE
How much of the amount spent on lobbying is > the lobbying nontaxable amount?	148,275
Compute Tax: If the organization spent more on lobbying than the grassroots or lobbying nontaxable, multiply that amount by 25%.	**$ 37,069**

Public Charity or Private Foundation

Form 1023 asks whether the organization is a public charity or a private foundation. A public charity receives a substantial amount of its support from the public, including funding from governmental units. There are three main types of public charities:

- Publicly supported organizations
- Those organizations that support publicly supported organizations (referred to as *supporting organizations*)
- Organizations that operate exclusively for public safety testing, such as SBCCI Public Safety Testing and Evaluation Services that tests building products

A supporting organization is one that is organized and operated exclusively to benefit or perform certain functions for a publicly supported charitable organization. It must also be operated, supervised, or controlled by or in connection with a publicly supported charitable organization.

 Example

New Trends, a private school, wanted to raise money for expansion. To do this, it created New Trends Foundation to benefit only the school, to raise money for it, and to manage the money. The private school qualified as a public charity. Therefore, New Trends Foundation is a supporting organization.

A charitable organization, unless it is a church, educational institution, hospital or a medical research organization operated in conjunction with a hospital, endowment fund operated for the benefit of state and municipal colleges and universities, or governmental unit, has to meet certain tests to determine if it is publicly supported. Otherwise it could be classified as a private foundation. A private foundation is often funded by few sources and often by an individual, family, or company. The expenditures of a private foundation are funded generally from the earnings on the assets contributed by those sources. There are operating foundations that conduct their own programs (operating foundations), but more often the foundation gives to other charities. The IRS imposes additional requirements on private foundations:

- Private foundations are subject to a tax on the net investment income. This can be either 1 percent or 2 percent depending on the foundation's operations.
- The foundation must document its grant making procedures on Schedule H of Form 1023 and have them approved in advance.
- Private nonoperating foundations are required to annually spend at least 5 percent of the net fair market value of noncharitable-use assets on qualified distributions for charitable purposes. If they fail to do so, a 30 percent penalty is imposed. For those that do not remediate the situation, an additional 100 percent penalty is imposed on the shortfall. Qualifying distributions can be made to public charities, private operating foundations, or governments to be used for charitable purposes. These are typically referred to as *grants*. Grants cannot be made to organizations that are related to or controlled by the private foundation.
- The private foundation files information tax return 990-PF instead of Form 990

Donors will generally prefer to give to public charities and private operating foundations because the deduction for individual contributions is limited to 50 percent of the donor's adjusted gross income. Donations to nonoperating foundations are more limited. Depending on the type of contribution, the maximum is either 20 percent or 30 percent of the donor's adjusted gross income.

Public Support Test for Charitable Organizations

Before September 9, 2008, the IRS had an advance ruling process. After that date, the IRS automatically classifies a new 501(c) (3) organization as a public charity as long as the financial information provided in the Form 1023 shows that it could reasonably expect to be publicly supported. During the first 5 years of the charity's life, the IRS reviews the results of the support test described in the next section. After the charity's first 5 years, if it fails the test in 2 consecutive Form 990s, it will be classified as a private foundation. There is no retroactive assessment of private foundation taxes on the organization.

A public charitable organization has several opportunities to meet the public support test. Based on the types of support and revenue the organization receives and earns, it will elect Test 1 or Test 2. Test 1 was constructed for those organizations that receive a large amount of contributions and do not provide services for which they charge a fee. Test 2 was constructed for those organizations that derive a significant amount of their revenue by charging fees for services. However, there are limitations, as discussed in the next section.

Test 1 (509(a)(1))—Compute the Public Support Percentage

The public support tests are made over a 5 year period including the current year. After deducting amounts from a substantial contributor at start up (unusual gifts), public support will equal the sum of

1. the remaining gifts, grants, contributions, and membership fees received (contributions of services are not included unless they are furnished by a governmental unit, as noted subsequently in this chapter),
2. tax revenues levied for the organization's benefit and either paid to or expended on its behalf, and
3. value of services or facilities furnished by a governmental unit to the organization without charge,
4. **Less** those gifts and contributions from an individual or organization that equal more than 2 percent of total support for the 5 year computation period. Note that the total support must be computed first to determine the amount to subtract from public support.

This amount is divided by **total support**, which represents list items 1–3 plus gross income from interest, dividends, payments received on securities loans, rents, royalties and income from those types of sources, net income from unrelated business activities even if it is not regularly carried on, and other income. Capital gains, contributions of services, and unusual grants are excluded from the denominator. Fees for services that are related to the tax exempt function are **not** included in total support.

If the organization has been in existence for 6 years, it will compute the public support percentage for the current year and also document the public support percentage computed in the prior year. If the organization's public support percentage is not 33⅓ percent or more, then it has the opportunity for another test. This is called the *facts and circumstances test*. In this test, the organization could still be considered a publicly supported charity if meets 10 percent of the support requirement and if it shows attraction of public support. *Attraction of public support* means that it is organized and operated in such a way that it will attract new support from the public or the government on a continuous basis. It will need to have a fundraising program.

If the organization has not been in existence 5 years, then it will end the test because it has 5 years to meet the requirements. It is presumed to be a public charity until 5 years have passed and it has failed both of the public support tests discussed in the preceding paragraph for 2 years in a row. If it fails the test 2 years in a row, then it is considered to be a private foundation.

⬛ Example

Julia, the CFO of Westchester's Mental Health Outreach Association (WMHOA), was making an evaluation of the organization's charitable status. She believed the organization would qualify under 509(a) (1) because of the amount of donations the organization received from various sources. WMHOA also charged fees for its services on a sliding scale. And because of an endowment, WMHOA had a significant amount of interest income.

During the 5 years covered by the 2010 Form 990, the organization had the following:

Contributions from the public	$4,000,000
Interest income	740,000
Net income from unrelated business activities	1,350,000
Income from seeing clients (tax exempt purpose)	2,500,000
Total support and revenue	**8,590,000**

Evaluation of public charity status:

Donations that were over 2% of total support coming from individuals and foundations	1,500,000
Public support (less amounts excluded because of 2% large donation requirement)	2,500,000
Total support	**$6,090,000**
Support percentage	41.05%

Julia was very happy to see that the organization met the test. For the past several years, it had received very large contributions from individuals and foundations that were over 2 percent of the organization's total support over the 5 year period, which were deducted from public support. Although the organization met the 10 percent facts and circumstances test, they worked diligently to increase the number of donors, and, over the last 2 years, the number of donors had increased. This year, they met the test.

Test 2 (509(a)(2))—Compute the Public Support Percentage

This test includes the elements discussed in the preceding paragraphs with the following additions or changes:

- Gross receipts from activities that are related to the tax exempt mission are added into the calculation of public support.
- The 2 percent disallowance described in the preceding section is **replaced** with the following. Amounts of gross receipts from the organization's exempt purpose activities that are received from any one payor (which represent greater than $5,000 or 1 percent of the organization's total support for **any** of the 5 taxable years, including the current year) are not included in the computation of public support. This does not include amounts from disqualified persons.
- The organization also has to meet an investment income test, so the investment income is included in total support but not public support. It may not have an investment income that is greater than 33⅓ percent of total support.
- There is not a 10 percent facts and circumstances test.

As with Test 1, capital gains are excluded from the calculation as are contributions of services in Test 2. The calculation considers 5 years including the current year. If the organization has not been a 501(c) organization for 5 years, it does not need to evaluate the public support percentage. And, also like Test 1, it takes 2 years of failing the test to be classified as a private foundation.

 Example

Jared, the CFO of Hawthorne Health Clinic, was making an evaluation of the organization's charitable status. He knew that Julia was evaluating public support under 509(a) (1), but he knew that his organization had substantially more fee-for-service income and many fewer donations. He thought he would qualify under 509(a) (2). He was not concerned because he had few large payments and because the investment income was only about 5 percent of total support. He made the following evaluation.

During the 5 years covered by the 2010 Form 990, the organization had the following:

Contributions from the public	$6,450,000
Internet income	400,000
Income from seeing clients (tax exempt purpose)	6,500,000
Total support and revenue	**7,350,000**

Evaluation of public charity status:

Payments that were over $5,000 or 1% of total support except amounts from disqualified persons for any of the years	15,000
Public support (less amounts excluded because of 1% large payment requirement)	6,935,000
Total support	**$7,350,000**
Support percentage	94.35%
Investment income percentage	5.44%

Supporting Organizations

As noted, supporting organizations may qualify for public charity status. There are three types of supporting organizations, and they are referred to as Type I, Type II, and Type III. The important aspect of the supporting organization is that the charitable organization must maintain control of the supporting organization. In effect, the charitable organization is sharing its tax exempt status with the organization that supports it.

A supporting organization cannot be controlled directly or indirectly by disqualified persons other than foundation managers. These might be contributors to the foundation or a family member, owners of more than 20 percent of the combined voting power of a corporation that is a substantial contributor to the foundation, a beneficial interest of a trust or unincorporated business that is a substantial contributor, a corporation, partnership, trust, or estate of which more than 35 percent of the interest is owned by any of the mentioned persons. A foundation manager and family members are also disqualified persons. However, the foundation manager is not included in the prohibition against disqualified persons.

Type I and Type II organizations differ only in that Type I organizations are operated, supervised, or controlled by one or more publicly supported organizations. The officers, directors, or trustees of a Type I supporting organization must be selected by the supported organization's governing board, officers, or membership. Type II organizations are supervised or controlled in connection with one or more publicly supported organizations. The same persons would supervise or control the supporting and supported organization. Both Type I and Type II organizations need to meet two tests:

1. **Organizational Test.** The Articles of Organization must limit the purposes of the supporting organization to the one that is being supported.

2. **Operational Test.** The supporting organization would be recognized as one that supports one or more publicly supported organizations if its activities are limited to those that provide support to the supported organization(s). The supporting organization is not required to pay out all of its income to the supported organization, but it must ensure that its income carries on some activity or program that benefits the supported organization.

A Type III supporting organization needs to meet a test that shows that it is operated in connection with the publicly supported charitable organization:

- **Organizational Test.** The Articles of Organization must limit the purposes of the supporting organization to the one that is being supported. And the supported organization must be specified by name. If the organization chooses, it can also designate a class or purpose of organization that would be a substitute if the named organization was dissolved or lost its tax exempt status. There also needs to be a historic relationship between the two organizations.

- **Responsiveness Test.** The supporting organization must be responsive to the needs of the supported organization. The supported organization must elect, appoint, or maintain a close and continuous working relationship with the officers, directors, or trustees of the supporting organization. This helps to ensure that the officers, directors, and trustees of the supported organization have a voice. All IRS-required information must be provided to the supported organization.

- **Integral Part Test.** The supporting organization must maintain involvement in the operations of the supported organization because the supported organization needs to be dependent on the supporting organization. In other words, the supporting organization is an integral part of the supported organization. There are two ways to satisfy this test:

  1. The activities carried on by the supporting organization are ones that **"but for" the supporting organization** the supported organization would need to perform them.

  2. The supporting organization makes payments of substantially all of its income to or for the use of the supported organization. The amount received has to be large enough to ensure that the publicly supported organization is attentive to the activities of the supporting organization.

- **Operational Test.** If the supporting organization meets the integral part test, the only thing that it can do to fail this test is to conduct activities of its own that would not meet the "but for" test.

Example

Genessee Foundation was formed to support the activities of Genessee Shelter, a 501(c) (3) organization. Its organizing documents state that it was created solely to manage the property of Genessee Shelter and to raise funds for and manage its endowment. When it raises money for the shelter, it recognizes contribution revenue. All of the revenue is used on services to support the foundation or is distributed to the organization. The shelter's board selects a majority of the supporting organization's officers, directors, or trustees. The foundation is a Type I supporting organization.

 Example

Creative Solutions was formed to provide record keeping and other administrative services to five small tax exempt organizations. It charges lower fees to these organizations than they would otherwise pay to commercial organizations. The nonprofits would have to perform these services "but for" the fact that Creative Solutions performs them. Each of the five tax exempt organizations has representation on Creative Solutions' board. Creative Solutions is considered functionally integrated because it operates as a part of each of the five tax exempt organizations it serves. It is a Type III supporting organization.

Charitable Contributions

Donors give to charitable organizations because they care about the cause. But in return, most are also very interested in the tax deduction they get for their donations. To qualify as a donation, the gift must be given voluntary and without the expectation of receiving any benefits from the charitable organization, such as services or property of equal value. This is called *donative intent*. The organization to which the contribution is given must be considered qualified in order for it to be tax deductible to the donor.

One of the reasons to ensure that the Form 1023 is properly filed and that the organization passes the charitable support tests is so that the organization will be qualified. Generally, only organizations that are organized under U.S. tax laws are qualified. Exceptions are certain charities that are organized under the laws of Mexico or Canada that fall under a treaty with the United States.

Churches and religious institutions such as associations of churches or integrated auxiliaries of a church (such as a men's or women's organization, religious schools, mission societies, or youth groups) are automatically qualified, but donors need to know that some entities that call themselves "religious organizations" may not meet the definition for IRS purposes. For that reason, it is probably a good idea for a religious organization to apply for recognition of tax exempt status. A donor can go online to search for charities, schools, hospitals, religious organizations, and other 501(c) (3) organizations that have been recognized as tax exempt at www.irs.gov/app/pub–78/.

Contributions can be cash, securities, or other property. Donors are responsible for identifying the fair value of their donations. The IRS has an excellent publication that can be accessed online at www.irs.gov/publications/p561/ar02.html that will help donors determine the fair value of their gifts. Donors often provide services to a 501(c) (3) organization, but these are not tax deductible. Only the mileage and out of pocket expenses are deductible. The IRS rate for mileage that can be deducted for each mile driven in service of charitable organization for 2011 is 14 cents.

Although it is the donor's responsibility to obtain one, nonprofits should expect to provide an acknowledgement for charitable donations they receive. The IRS does not require a standard acknowledgement, but the donor needs the following in order to substantiate his or her contribution.

Contributions <$250	• Bank record with the name of the qualified organization and the amount and date of the contribution **or** • Contemporaneous written acknowledgement of the contribution (for example, a letter or receipt). The content of the acknowledgment is discussed later.
Contribution that is $250 or more	• Contemporaneous written acknowledgement of the contribution
Payroll deduction for a single contribution of $250 or more	• Pay stub, form W-2 **and** • Pledge card with the name of the organization. The pledge card must also state that the organization does not provide goods or services in return for contributions.
Payroll deduction for a single contribution <$250	• Pay stub, form W-2 **and** • Pledge card that states the name of the organization

When the donor receives goods or services for making the donation, the nonprofit will need to provide an acknowledgement to them. The term *contemporaneous* refers to the timing of the written acknowledgement. An acknowledgement is considered contemporaneous when it is received by the earlier of the date on which the donor filed his or her tax return or the extended due date of the return.

Form 1771 (www.irs.gov/pub/irs-pdf/p1771.pdf) contains sample acknowledgements for a nonprofit to use. The required content of the acknowledgement is as listed:

- The name of the qualified organization.
- The amount of the contribution for those that are cash.
- A description of the property (note that it is the donor's responsibility to value the property for his or her deduction). The nonprofit also has a valuation issue that is related to recording the donation at the fair value at the date of donation. This was discussed in chapter 5.
- The amount, if any, of goods or services provided to the donor by the nonprofit. This is referred to as a *quid pro quo* contribution. The rules associated with these goods or services and the responsibility to the donor are discussed in the next few paragraphs.

Nonprofit organizations will often offer premiums to donors in a pledge campaign. When this happens and the donors accept the goods or services offered by the nonprofit, an acknowledgement must be provided if the quid pro quo donation is $75 or more. The requirements of the acknowledgement are

- the amount of the contribution that is deductible and
- an estimate of the fair value of the goods or services.

When the benefits that are provided in exchange for a contribution are of intangible religious benefit that are not sold, such as attendance at a religious ceremony or free religious education that does not lead to a degree, then the acknowledgement should state this.

There are exceptions to the quid pro quo rule for low cost items. If the goods or services did not exceed (1) 2 percent of the payment or (2) $96, then no disclosure statement is necessary. Also, (1) if the payment by the donor is at least $48,[9] and (2) the only items provided were items bearing the organization's name such as mugs or pens or address labels, and (3) the cost is $9.60 or less, then no disclosure statement is necessary.

Another exception is the membership benefits exception. A member benefit would be considered insubstantial when the annual payment is $75 or less and the privileges are items that may or may not be used, such as free or discounted admissions to the facilities (such as a museum), discounts on purchases, or free or reduced rate parking. If the event is a members-only event, then the "per person" cost to the organization, not including overhead, is within the limitations mentioned for low cost items.

If the nonprofit is going to solicit quid pro quo donations, then a disclosure statement needs to be included in such a way that it will be apparent to the donor and not buried in small print.

Jack, the development director of Save the Barred Owl, a 501(C) (3) organization, was drafting acknowledgement letters to send to donors. Two examples follow.

Letter to Mrs. Aurora for her contribution of goods—no goods or services received by donor

Thank you for your donation of 3 pairs of Bushnell PowerView 20x50 Super High-Powered Surveillance Binoculars on January 15, 2011. We appreciate your support of Save the Barred Owl. No goods or services were provided in connection with this donation.

Letter to Mr. Walker for his contribution of cash—goods or services received by donor

Thank you for your $2,000 donation on January 15, 2011. We appreciate your responsiveness to our pledge drive and your support of Save the Barred Owl. In appreciation for your gift, we are sending you a CD featuring natural bird sounds called *Bird Song Ear Training Guide* that is valued at $12.

---

9 *Charitable Contributions: Substantiation and Disclosure Requirements*, (2010). Retrieved from www.irs.gov/pub/irs-pdf/p1771.pdf on April 16, 2011.

Nonprofits need to ensure that acknowledgements are provided and that they meet the requirements mentioned. The penalty for noncompliance is $10 per contribution, not to exceed $5,000 per fundraising event or mailing. This can only be abated if the charitable organization shows that the failure to meet the requirement was due to a reasonable cause.

Filing Form 990

Filling out the Form 990, the information tax return, is a time consuming process, but it is critically important that the tax-exempt organization devote sufficient resources to preparing and reviewing it. As discussed in this and preceding chapters, the form was revised to include a significant section related to governance. The sections of the form related to governance will be heavily scrutinized by the IRS and watchdog agencies, not to mention funding sources. See appendix C for a handy checklist of those items.

The Form 990 consists of a core form with 11 parts and 16 schedules. Not all of the schedules will be required of each organization.

Elements of the IRS Form 990 Core Form	
Part I	Summary (mission and significant activities and summary information about the revenues, expenses, and net assets of the organization)
Part II	Signature Block
Part III	Statement of Program Service Accomplishments (program services and accomplishments, changes in programs and services, and three largest programs by expenses)
Part IV	Checklist of Required Schedules
Part V	Statements Regarding Other IRS Filings and Tax Compliance
Part VI	Governance, Management, and Disclosure (including a section on policies) (see Appendix C for a list of the policies referred to in Form 990 and its schedules.)
Part VII	Compensation of Officers, Directors, Trustees, Key Employees, Highest Compensated Employees, and Independent Contractors
Part VIII	Statement of Revenue
Part IX	Statement of Functional Expenses
Part X	Balance Sheet
Part XI	Reconciliation of Net Assets
Part XII	Financial Statements and Reporting
Form 990 Schedules		
Schedule A	Public Charity Status and Public Support	Public support tests
Schedule B	Schedule of Contributors	Requires contributions to be identified in detail if they are 2% of contributions or $5,000 if the organization is a 501(c) (3). The threshold for all others is $5,000.
Schedule C	Political Campaign and Lobbying Activities	Questions related to involvement in political activities and calculation of excess lobbying expenditures

(continued)

(continued)

	Form 990 Schedules	
Schedule D	Supplemental Financial Statements	Information about donor advised funds, conservation easements, collections of art and historical treasures, trust, escrow and custodial arrangements, endowment funds, land, buildings and equipment, securities, program related investments, other assets and other liabilities, request for text of the Uncertain Tax Position footnote, reconciliation of change in net assets from Form 990 to financial statements, reconciliation of revenue per the audited financial statements with revenue per return, and reconciliation of expenses per audited financial statements with expenses per the return
Schedule E	Schools	Questions about schools related to racial discrimination and financial aid from governmental agencies
Schedule F	Statement of Activities Outside the United States	Questions about grants made to individuals and organizations as well as activities conducted outside the United States
Schedule G	Supplemental Information Regarding Fundraising or Gaming Activities	Questions about fund-raising activities, fund-raising events, and gaming activities
Schedule H	Hospitals	Includes information about the organization and its charity care, bad debts, joint ventures and management companies, and information about the community benefit it provides
Schedule I	Grants and Other Assistance to Organizations, Governments, and Individuals in the United States	Information on grants and assistance provided to those inside the United States
Schedule J	Compensation Information	Although certain questions on compensation exist in the core form, Schedule J requires more information about compensation for certain parties at certain levels. Included here are benefits, such as first class air travel, club dues, use of personal residence, along with retirement and other benefits.
Schedule K	Supplemental Information on Tax-Exempt Bonds	Bond issues, proceeds, and private business use
Schedule L	Transactions With Interested Persons	This schedule will help the IRS pay closer attention to those that might have excess benefit transactions. The items covered in this schedule are loans, grants, or assistance to interested persons.
Schedule M	Noncash Contributions	Types of property; donated services are not included.
Schedule N	Liquidation, Termination, Dissolution, or Significant Disposition of Assets	To be completed when the organization is terminating
Schedule O	Supplemental Information to Form 990 or 990-EZ	To be completed with explanatory information when necessary
Schedule P	Related Organizations and Unrelated Partnerships	Provides information about related organizations

See appendix A for a checklist that could be used for the board's review of Form 990.

Unrelated Business Income

Organizations that are exempt under section 501(C) (3) are subject to tax on UBI. The tax applied is at the regular corporate rate. As noted, organizations that have gross income from businesses unrelated to their tax exempt mission of $1,000 or more are required to file Form 990–T. If the organization believes that it will have net UBI of $500 or more, then it should be making estimated payments every quarter. Estimated payments are due by the 15th day of the 4th, 6th, 9th, and 12th months of the tax year.

UBI is the income from a trade or business that is carried on regularly by an exempt organization when the purpose of the activity is not substantially related to its tax exempt purpose. The purpose of this requirement is to ensure that tax exempt organizations do not compete unfairly with commercial enterprises. Even if the net proceeds from the trade or business will be used to further the organization's tax exempt mission, it is still UBI.

 Example

Saint Francis, a nonprofit school, holds a Halloween Carnival each year. Although this activity may compete with commercial carnivals, it is an activity that happens once a year. To qualify as UBI, the business activities must be carried on regularly, which would generally mean throughout the year. Therefore, the carnival would not give rise to UBI.

Example

Durham Rehabilitation Center provides overnight accommodations for those individuals trying to improve their lives who currently are homeless. In addition, the center provides a handyperson service that employs the current residents of the center for a period of up to six months. The profits from this business are used to finance activities of the center. Although the center's handyperson service is a business that is regularly carried out, the income is not UBI because the business contributes to the organization's mission to help rehabilitate homeless individuals.

There are several activities excluded from the definition of UBI. Some of the most common are as follows:

- **Volunteer work force.** If the activity is conducted with a volunteer work force, then the income is not UBI even if the business is regularly carried on and not related to the organization's tax exempt purpose. Examples are a thrift store and dances at which the workers are volunteers.

> **CAUTION:** Nonprofits should be careful. There have been cases in
> which the volunteers were given free meals and, in some cases, tips.
> This can negate the exclusion.

- **Convenience of members.** If the activity is operated for the convenience of members, students, patients, officers, or employees, then it would be exempt from UBI. Examples are a cafeteria in a school and a pharmacy in a hospital.

> **CAUTION:** In some cases in which others are using the services, the
> services may not be considered "for the convenience" services. For ex-
> ample, if a nonprofit hospital has a pharmacy that is in the hospital, then
> it is not likely that anyone other than the patients would use it. But if it
> were free standing in a shopping center with easy access to the public,
> people who are not patients might use it.

- **Sponsorship payments.** When a nonprofit receives a payment from a sponsor and the only benefit the sponsor derives is the inclusion of his or her company's name or logo or use of products, this is a qualified sponsorship payment, and there is no UBI. An example is a fundraising event like a golf tournament at which sponsors names are displayed on banners.

> **CAUTION:** If the sponsor is sponsoring a trade show or convention, this
> may be UBI.

- **Selling donated merchandise.** When substantially all of the merchandise being sold in a business activity is donated, it does not result in UBI. Examples are a thrift store and used book store.

> **CAUTION:** Nonprofits sometimes find opportunities to buy merchandise
> at deeply discounted prices. If a used book **store, for** example, decides to
> sell both donated and purchased merchandise UBI could result.

- **Pole rental.** Pole rentals are not considered unrelated trade or business when rented by a mutual or cooperative telephone or electric company described in section 501(c) (12).

What may not be considered UBI in one setting may be considered UBI in another setting.

> ### ■ Example
>
> Asparagus Fern Science Center has an auditorium where it shows films related to natural science to schools and other groups. It charges a small fee on top of the entrance fee for admission. In addition, to bring in more money when the science center is closed, the theater shows movies that are 40 to 50 years old to the public. They found that many people appreciate seeing movies from the 60s and 70s on a big screen. The science center does not have UBI when it shows the scientific films during normal operating hours, but it does have UBI when it shows the old movies after hours.

More examples can be found in the IRS publication 598, "Tax on Unrelated Business Income of Exempt Organizations," which can be accessed at www.irs.gov/pub/irs-pdf/p598.pdf.

There are also several types of income that are excluded from UBI:

- Dividends, interest, annuities, and other investment income
- Income from lending securities
- Royalties
- Rents (there are certain exceptions)
- Income from research
- Gain or loss on disposition of property
- Income from services provided under federal license
- Member income of mutual or cooperative electric companies

Income that is derived from debt-financed property is considered UBI even though it might otherwise be excluded. There are exceptions to this as well. If the property is substantially related (85 percent or more) to the tax exempt purpose, then the property is not treated as debt-financed property. Other exceptions are if the property is leased to a medical clinic and the lease is primarily for purposes related to the lessor's exercise of its tax exempt mission, and the property is used in research activities. Nonprofits should read IRS Publication 598 to ensure that they are aware of all the exceptions.

Where there is a business there are also costs of conducting the business. Nonprofits should keep good records of all the possible expenses that could be deducted against UBI including overhead.

IRS Audits

There are many issues that could trigger an IRS audit. The IRS can make office and correspondence examinations, field examinations, and team examinations, all of which tie up the nonprofit's resources, including valuable time. Recently, the primary issues appear to be

- Tax exempt status
- Public charity or private foundation classification
- Excessive advocacy activities

- Payroll tax related issues
- Involvement in conservation easements, donor advised funds, and joint ventures
- UBI issues
- Political campaign activities
- Executive compensation
- Community benefit for hospitals
- Excess benefits
- Fundraising costs
- Tax exempt bond recordkeeping
- Charitable giving scams

The best thing a board can do related to tax issues is to ensure that management is well versed in these issues and complies with all laws and regulations. In organizations in which the staff is not sufficiently knowledgeable, there is no substitute for a tax professional who has a deep understanding of the issues affecting tax exempt organizations. A tax professional maintains current knowledge and has resources at his or her fingertips to help the organization protect and, if necessary, defend its tax exempt status.

Conclusion

Board members need an understanding of the issues that nonprofits must consider related to obtaining and maintaining tax exempt status in order to perform important monitoring activities. Although this chapter provides the board member with an overview of the most important aspects related to an exempt organization's tax status, it is no substitute for the assistance and advice of a tax professional who specializes in the area. Tax regulations are voluminous and complex, and they are subject to change. A tax professional keeps abreast of not only the issues but also the IRS hot buttons that will be areas of risk to the tax exempt organization. Nonprofit board members and executives can use the information in this chapter to participate intelligently in a board in review of the Form 990 and to know when additional consultation with a tax professional is necessary.

Appendix A
Guide for the Board's Review of Form 990

Core Form		
Part	Description	Important Questions for Board's Review
Part I	Summary (mission and significant activities and summary information about the revenues, expenses, and net assets of the organization)	1. Is the mission described accurately? 2. Would the description attract potential donors? 3. Does it agree to the Form 1023/1024? 4. Are the data comparable with the prior year? If not, why not? Is it favorable or unfavorable?
Part II	Signature Block	N/A
Part III	Statement of Program Service Accomplishments (program services and accomplishments, changes in programs and services, and three largest programs by expenses)	1. Is the description of the program services consistent with its mission, the Form 1023/1024, and the website? 2. Are the services described in enough detail to assist the user in understanding them?
Part IV	Checklist of Required Schedules	1. Is the organization engaged in some activity, such as conservation easements, donor advised funds, gaming, or other types of activities, that are the subject of additional scrutiny by the IRS? 2. Did the organization answer "yes" to lines 25a, 25b, 26, or 27 relating to excess benefit transactions and loans, grants or assistance to officers, directors, key employees, or substantial donors? If so, should policies be examined?
Part V	Statements Regarding Other IRS Filings and Tax Compliance	1. Has the organization followed the IRS rules related to classification of personnel as employees versus independent contractors? 2. Have all the payroll taxes been deposited on a timely basis with the IRS? 3. Were any other required filings made on a timely basis (also see Appendix B)? If not, this could indicate poor internal controls. 4. Were the rules related to donor acknowledgement followed, and were acknowledgements provided on a timely basis so that donors could substantiate their deductions? 5. Is there a likelihood that the organization is subject to interest and penalties? Examine lines 3b, 6b, 7h (should be answered yes) and 5a, 5b, 8, 9a, and 9b (should be answered no).
Part VI	Governance, Management, and Disclosure (including a section on policies) (see Appendix C for a list of the policies referred to in Form 990 and its schedules.)	1. Are the written policies and procedures covered in this section adopted by the organization, and is the board certain that the documentation is available? 2. Is the organization conducting activities in multiple states, and, if so, has it been registered?
Part VII	Compensation of Officers, Directors, Trustees, Key Employees, Highest Compensated Employees, and Independent Contractors	Consider the compensation of the persons listed on the form and evaluate whether the compensation appears reasonable. Is there documentation available to support it? How would a member of the donor community, or the organizations potential donors and funding sources, view the compensation related to that of other organizations of similar size?

(continued)

(continued)

Core Form		
Part	**Description**	**Important Questions for Board's Review**
Part VIII	Statement of Revenue	Examine the sources of revenue to ensure that the organization is appropriately diversified. Are there actions that should be taken to cushion the risk to the organization?
Part IX	Statement of Functional Expenses	1. Consider the expenditures in terms of how the resources are being expended. Evaluate in the light of prior years. 2. How large a percentage is compensation and benefits? 3. Has the board specified a procedure for approval of nonroutine and nonfixed expenditures in excess of a certain amount? 4. Consider the propriety of amounts spent for outside management services, legal and accounting, investment management fees, advertising, travel, rent, lobbying, and professional fundraising services. 5. How would a donor or funding source view the percentage of expenditures spent on management in general and fundraising?
Part X	Balance Sheet	1. Is there excess cash, and is it in an interest bearing vehicle? 2. Are there significant related party loans? Is there adequate oversight? 3. Are receivables being monitored for collectability? 4. Are liabilities being held too long due to cash flow issues? 5. Are restrictions on net assets being met?
Part XI	Reconciliation of Net Assets	Was a reconciliation of net assets performed?
Part XII	Financial Statements and Reporting	1. Should the organization consider an independent audit if it doesn't presently have one? 2. Do the auditors report to the audit committee or to the governing board? 3. Does each member of the governing board or group overseeing the audit receive a copy of the letter(s), including significant deficiencies, material weaknesses, or constructive service comments?
Schedules		
Schedule A	Public Charity Status and Public Support	1. Is the organization in danger of becoming a private foundation? 2. What could it do to increase the amount of public support?
Schedule C	Political Campaign and Lobbying Activities	1. Is the organization in danger of too much lobbying? What steps could it take to reduce the amount and still be effective? 2. Is the organization participating in activities that could jeopardize its tax exempt status?
Schedule D	Supplemental Financial Statements	Are there activities under IRS scrutiny in which the organization should review the adequacy of its internal controls and documentation?
Schedule E	Schools	Does the school have the appropriate controls in place to prevent discrimination?

	Schedules	
Schedule G	Supplemental Information Regarding Fundraising or Gaming Activities	1. Are there any activities, such as those with professional fundraisers, that need additional evaluation? 2. Does the board approve contracts with professional fundraisers? 3. Do the gaming activities constitute unrelated business income because of indirect compensation of volunteers?
Schedule H	Hospitals	Is the hospital collecting the appropriate information? Is any valuable information being missed? Is the hospital in danger of not meeting the community benefit standard?
Schedule J	Compensation Information	1. If any of the boxes on line 1a are checked, is the benefit really warranted? 2. Is there strict accountability for expense reimbursement? 3. Does the organization set compensation with an appropriate method?
Schedule L	Transactions With Interested Persons	Has the organization disclosed all the direct or indirect transactions or relationships required?
Schedule O	Supplemental Information to Form 990 or 990-EZ	1. Has Schedule O been used to its best advantage by providing explanatory material to "no" answers? 2. If any fraud was detected in the organization, was it described? 3. Was the way information is made public disclosed on Schedule O? 4. Are transactions with interested persons disclosed? 5. Does the schedule describe the Form 990 board review process?
Schedule R	Related Organizations and Unrelated Partnerships	Are all required relationships disclosed?

Appendix B
Important Filings for Tax-Exempt Organizations

Independent Contractors and Lessors			
Return or Form	To Report or Pay	Frequency	When Due
1096	Transmittal form for 1099s	Annual	Feb 28
1099-INT	Report payments of interest to unincorporated entities of $10 or more in a calendar year	Annual	Payee: Jan 31 IRS: Feb 28
1099-MISC	Report payments of $600 or more to unincorporated entities for the following: • Services • Rent • Commissions, fees, royalties • Other nonemployee compensation (trade or business)	Annual	Payee: Jan 31 IRS: Feb 28

Employment Related			
Return or Form	To Report or Pay	Frequency	When Due
940, 940-EZ	Employer's federal unemployment tax	Annual	Jan 31
941	To report employer social security taxes and income and social security taxes withheld from employees	Quarterly	Apr 30, Jul 31, Oct 31, Jan 31
943	Farm worker wages and withheld payroll taxes	Annual	Jan 31 (Feb 10 if timely deposits)
1099-R	Distributions from retirement or profit sharing plans, IRAs, simplified employee pensions, insurance contracts	Annual	Payee: Jan 31 IRS: Feb 28
5500, 5500-C/R	Employer-maintained employee benefit plan information report	Annual	Jul 31 (or last day of 7th month after end of plan year if fiscal year)
W-2	Report wages, other compensation, withheld and employer-paid payroll taxes (income, social security, Medicare)	Annual	Payee: Jan 31 Social Security Administration: Feb 28
W-3	Transmittal form for W-2s	Annual	Feb 28

Other Tax Returns			
Return or Form	To Report or Pay	Frequency	When Due
720	Various federal excise taxes	Quarterly	Apr 30, Jul 31, Oct 31, Jan 31
990-T	Unrelated business taxable income (if gross income $1,000 or more), or Internal Revenue Code (IRC) Section 6033(e)(2) proxy tax	Annual	15th day of 5th month after tax year-end
990-W	Calculate estimated tax payments on unrelated business income and private foundation net investment income	Quarterly	Payments: 15th day of 4th, 6th, 9th, 12th month of tax year Form: Retained by taxpayer

	Other Tax Returns		
Return or Form	To Report or Pay	Frequency	When Due
1041	Filed by Sec. 4947(a)(1) charitable trusts if any taxable income or gross receipts $600 or more	Annual	15th day of 4th month after tax year-end
1120	Filed by 501(c) organization if not a political organization and has Sec. 527(f)(1) political organization taxable income	Annual	15th day of 3rd month after tax year-end
1120-POL	Filed by Sec. 527 political organizations if political organization taxable income over $100 OR gross receipts over $25,000	Annual	15th day of 3rd month after tax year-end
4720	By Sec. 501(c)(3) organizations, managers, tax related to the following: • Certain lobbying, political activities • Personal benefit contract premiums • Excess benefit transactions Also by private foundations for certain excise taxes	Annual	15th day of 5th month after tax year-end

	Other Forms		
Return or Form	To Report or Pay	Frequency	When Due
945	Report nonpayroll income tax withholding	Annual	Jan 31 (Feb 10 if timely deposits)
1098	Report mortgage interest received in a trade or business from an individual or sole proprietor if $600 or more	Annual	Payee: Jan 31 IRS: Feb 28
1098-C	Report contribution of a qualified vehicle over $500. Copy B to donor to attach to income tax return.	Annual	IRS: Feb 28 As acknowledgment to donor, 30 days after arms-length sale or if to be improved, used, or sold cheaply to needy individual, then 30 days after contribution
1098-E	Report $600 or more of student loan interest from an individual in the course of a trade or business.	Annual	Payee: Jan 31 IRS: Feb 28
1098-T	Eligible educational institutions: Report tuition for each student with a reportable transaction	Annual	Payee: Jan 31 IRS: Feb 28
1099-B	Broker or barter exchange: Report certain transactions	Annual	Payee: Jan 31 IRS: Feb 28
1099-C	Organizations in the trade or business of lending money: Report $600 or more of debt cancellation	Annual	Payee: Jan 31 IRS: Feb 28
3115	Apply for a change in accounting method	N/A	With Form 990 or Form 990-EZ, AND on or after 1st day of year of change but not later than when tax return filed
3800	Claim certain tax credits	Annual	With Form 990-T
4562	Report depreciation and amortization	Annual	With Form 990-T
8275, 8275-R	Disclose positions taken in Form 990-T contrary to Treasury regulations	Annual	With Form 990-T

(continued)

(continued)

Other Forms			
Return or Form	**To Report or Pay**	**Frequency**	**When Due**
8282	Report disposition of donated property valued over $5,000 and held less than 3 years	N/A	125 days after disposition
8283	Report noncash charitable contributions	Annual	With Form 990-T
8300	Report receipt of cash in trade or business (except charitable contributions) of $10,000 or more	N/A	15th day after receipt of cash
8868	Request extension of time to file Forms 990, 990-EZ, or 990-PF	N/A	By 15th day of 5th month after tax year-end (initial)

Other Tax Returns			
Return or Form	**To Report or Pay**	**Frequency**	**When Due**
8870	Information report on certain personal benefit contracts	Annual	Charitable remainder trust: Apr 15 Others: 15th day of 5th month after tax year-end
8886-T	Report participation in a prohibited tax shelter transaction	Various	Various
8899	Charitable donee: Report net income from qualified intellectual property to its donor and IRS	Various	Last day of 1st month after donee's tax year-end
SS-4	Organization's application for employer identification number	N/A	No deadline, but the sooner the better
W-2G	Report charitable fundraising event prizes of $600 or more each	Annual	Following year— To winner: Jan 31 To IRS: Feb 28
W-9	Request tax ID number of winner of prize of $600 or more	N/A	Before prize awarded
TD F 90-22.1	Report financial interest in, or signature or other authority over, a foreign financial account if aggregate value over $10,000 at any time during the calendar year	Annual	June 30

Appendix C
Governance Policies and Procedures

Does the organization have this policy or procedure?	Yes	No	If no, why not?	Where documented?
Independent directors				
Meetings of the governing board and committees that represent those charged with governance				
Adequate Form 990 review process				
Whistleblower policy				
Conflict of interest monitoring policy				
Public disclosure of documents policy				
Endowment spending and accumulation practices				
Appropriate footnote for uncertain tax positions attached to Form 990				
Financial statements compiled, reviewed, or audited				
Policy against discrimination (schools)				
Charity care policy for hospitals				
Bad debt policy for hospitals				
Thorough disclosure of community benefit activities for hospitals				
Collection practices for patients known to qualify for charity care or financial assistance				
Gift acceptance policy				

Did the organization have this issue?	Yes	No	N/A	What controls will be put in place to remediate the deficiency?
A material diversion of assets				
Inadequate policies over donor advised funds				
Inadequate policies over conservation easements				
Failure to require substantiation of expenses				
Inadequate level of documentation for compensation decisions				
Inadequate documentation for transactions with related organization or interested parties				

Chapter 9

The Courage to Lead

Cal is the founder and recently retired CEO of a Fortune 100 company. He is also a patron of many philanthropic organizations. He recently joined the board of a small, local nonprofit focused on the arts and education. He brings both substantial financial means and the operating style that served him well in the corporate world. Orders are issued; invectives fly. Fellow board members are demeaned and resign. New members (nominated by Cal, who is also the organization's largest donor) are sycophants and toadies. Initiatives are railroaded through. Corners are cut. Sam, the board president, and Sally, the CEO, have spoken with Cal about civility, mutual respect, governance, and board processes. These conversations initially brought nominal change but lately have been dismissed with umbrage.

Following her last discussion with Cal, Sally has given up on efforts to confront him. She chalks up his behavior to "differences in style" and maintains that the financial ends justify the interpersonal and strategic means. Sam maintains that the price being paid for the donor's largesse is too high. He believes that Cal is driving off potential trustees and donors, and he is concerned that all of Cal's suggestions are unanimously supported and pursued, regardless of whether they are meritorious, legal, or in keeping with the organization's mission.

Vast pressures face today's executives, managers, board members, and employees. A core capacity for successful leadership is the willingness to act on principle in the service of the organization, even if it means taking positions that are unpopular. As we have discussed throughout the book, knowledge and skills are required for nonprofit leaders to detect and redress financial impropriety or other areas of organizational risk. A vital third component, though, is the willingness to act, based on knowledge and skills, in order to lead with integrity. This chapter examines the concept of moral courage and the barriers that can impede ethical action and provides tools and exemplars to overcome those barriers.

Moral Courage

Courage is a familiar concept. One common meaning refers to it not as the absence of fear but as action despite fear. The word courage conjures up acts of bravery: a firefighter carrying a child from a burning building, a police officer approaching a stopped car on a dark street, civil rights marchers facing down fire hoses and attack dogs. In these instances, the fear overcome is that of risk to personal safety or, indeed, the risk of death. For those who act with moral courage, the fear may be less profound but no less daunting: the loss of a job, friends, reputation, or advancement.

Moral courage is often defined as action on behalf of principle.[1] It is "the capacity to overcome the fear of shame and humiliation in order to admit one's mistakes, to confess a wrong, to reject evil conformity, to renounce injustice, and also to defy immoral or imprudent orders."[2]

People often associate the term *moral courage* with whistleblowers, those people who have spoken out publicly to reveal a wrong. Whistleblowers portrayed in film include Erin Brockovich's advocacy for safe drinking water, Jeffrey Wigand and suppressed cigarette risk research, Frank Serpico and police corruption, and Karen Silkwood and nuclear dangers. The drama that made these such compelling movie characters came from not only the risks they endured to get their stories out but also the prices they paid for doing so. With the possible exception of Erin Brockovich, who appeared to thrive after her courageous acts, these stories, full of tribulation and adversity, are unlikely to encourage would-be whistleblowers to step up and act.

The good news is that whistleblowing is only a small subset of the array of acts that constitute moral courage. Consider the following:

- The shopper who speaks up when a mother viciously strikes her child in the checkout line
- The office worker who sees a youngster kicking a goose by the pond outside her window and rallies her coworkers to join her in confronting him
- The nurse who pulls a doctor aside to point out a medication error in the orders he has just written
- The student who reports a cheating network in his high school's advanced placement exams
- The driver who leaves a note after accidently hitting a parked car
- The teacher who speaks up in the break room when others are making fun of a student's presumed sexual orientation

These are not grand acts worthy of a movie script, but each is an act of courage. You may even recognize situations like this from your own life, regardless of whether you responded to the dilemma in the same way. These everyday acts of courage have parallels in nonprofit governance as well, like these examples:

- The lone trustee who questions the basis for a significant increase in CEO compensation

---

1 Rushworth M. Kidder, *Moral Courage: Taking Action When Your Values are Put to the Test.* (New York; William Morrow, 2005).

2 William I. Miller, *The Mystery of Courage* (Cambridge; Harvard University Press, 2000).

- The new consumer representative to a board who asks for background information on a motion before participating in a vote
- The trustee who recuses herself from a vote because it could be perceived as a conflict of interest with her position in a local business
- The executive who overhears derogatory comments about the agency's clientele at a board meeting and speaks up, educating trustees about the needs clients face and the agency's culture of acceptance

If our personal and professional lives offer so many opportunities for moral courage, why is it not more common? Why is it considered exceptional (and exceptionally risky) to speak truth to power? What, in individuals and in their organizations, keeps people from standing up for principle?

Barriers to Ethical Action

If the opportunities for ethical action are plentiful, so are the deterrents. Consider the prevailing norms in our organizations and communities, captured with adages like "Snitches get stitches," "Go along to get along," "It's easier to ask forgiveness than permission," "The ends justify the means," "It ain't cheating if you don't get caught," and "Don't bite the hand that feeds you." Each speaks to a different yet powerful rationale for inaction. Let's look at seven in more depth.

The first barrier is **moral ambiguity**. Action on behalf of principle first requires identification of a principle that is being violated. Some people may be unaccustomed to operating under ethical standards, and others may reject principled conduct outright. However, a more common reason for moral ambiguity is relativism, the belief that there are no commonly held principles. Rather, each person must decide what is right for him—or herself. This thinking is reflected in the phrase, "Well I wouldn't ever tell an offensive joke like that, but who am I to suggest he shouldn't?" Years of work by the Institute on Global Ethics gives the lie to this fallacy.[3] Across nations, cultures, industries, and socioeconomic strata, the institute has identified core values such as respect, responsibility, and honesty. Organizations and other groups of individuals create norms of conduct and expectations for accountability when members violate those norms. Clear community standards, principled leadership, and shared responsibility create ethical clarity and offer a foundation for morally courageous action.

The second barrier is **discomfort**. No one likes to be the skunk at the garden party. No one likes to be the one on the committee, in the midst of apparent consensus for a swift decision, who speaks up and says, "Perhaps we haven't considered all the alternatives." Few of us would find it easy to say, "I'm uncomfortable with that" after one colleague treats another disrespectfully or a trustee makes a racially offensive joke. Yet these daily acts of courage help us train for the big event, the time when acquiescence is not an option. In the words of the legendary character Dumbledore, "It takes a great deal of bravery to stand up to our enemies, but just as much to stand up to our friends."[4]

---

3 Rushworth M. Kidder, *Moral Courage: Taking Action When Your Values are Put to the Test.* (New York: William Morrow, 2005).

4 J. K. Rowling, *Harry Potter and the Sorcerer's Stone.* (New York, Scholastic Press, 1997) p. 306.

Related to discomfort is the phenomenon of **groupthink**. Drawn from the principle of nondissent, it can be thought of as collective discomfort. Anyone who ever spent time on the playground knows that the group exercises a powerful influence on behaviors of the individual. The peer pressure of childhood and adolescence has analogous effects in adulthood when groups overtly or covertly influence individual members. In groupthink, differences of opinion are quelled, driven underground, or papered over. Decision-making processes that emphasize consensus can yield nominal agreement that overlooks meaningful and relevant dissent. Individuals may believe that they alone have qualms or questions about a given direction. In their silence, decisions evolve that appear to be unanimous but are in fact only superficially so.

The third barrier to ethical action is the **bystander effect**, which yields restraints on individuals similar to those of groupthink. Diffusion theory suggests that the more people are exposed to any event, the less likely it is that any one of them will act on it. Think of it as collective irresponsibility. From the Holocaust, to the Kitty Genovese murder, to the recent crisis in Darfur, there is evidence that the group exerts a powerful psychological influence to restrain individuals from action. This influence mitigates our sense of personal responsibility, dampens our resolve, and provides us security along with the illusion that someone else will act if we choose not to.

The next deterrent to ethical action is the **presumption of futility**. "I'm not going to speak up if it won't make a difference." "It'll go nowhere." "Nothing will change." "It's a no-win situation." People compute a risk-benefit formula and often decide that if they can't have the desired outcome, they won't expend the effort to chance it. This is an understandable calculus. We often focus on results and outcomes in our work lives. We consider the consequences of our actions in our professional and personal interactions or, in other words, the return on our investment. Still, there are several problems with predicating action on the likelihood of success.

Outcomes are hard to predict. Hopelessness, optimism, powerlessness, skepticism, and naïvete can all cloud the crystal ball in predicting the future. And outcomes are not always the result of rational, linear processes. Change can be accidental, immediate, delayed, or incremental; the gratification for action may be deferred or denied. Change is difficult, intransigent problems may not cease on the basis of one voice or one act of courage. If success is a precondition for acting, it will always be a mighty deterrent. The final problem with the futility mindset is that it diminishes the importance of the action itself. If something is the right thing to do, it is right irrespective of the impact. Accounts by people who have acted with moral courage repeatedly indicate that they are glad they did what they did, reasoning it was better to have done what conscience demanded and failed than not to have tried at all.

The fifth impediment to ethical action is our own **socialization**. One study referred to the phenomenon as being "groomed for submission" in explaining why nurses failed to report medical negligence they had observed. A 2006 Institute of Medicine study on medication errors noted the phenomenon as deference to "the authority gradient:" the greater the disparity of level in the hierarchy, the less likely the subordinate is to speak up when an error is detected.[5] But this is not just an artifact of our professional socialization or our

5 Philip Aspden, Julie A. Wolcott, J. Lyle Bootman, and Linda R. Cronenwett (Eds.), *Preventing Medication Errors: Quality Chasm Series*. Institute of Medicine, Board on Health Care Services (Washington DC: National Academies Press, 2006).

societal deference to the powerful. It is also a result of culture, gender, and social class. It is the result of a thousand messages internalized and lived, such as "if you can't say anything nice, don't say anything at all" and "respect your authority."

Interestingly though, some people manage to act on ethics despite their socialization. In a recent study of negligence in health care settings, the Association of Critical Care Nurses discovered that though 48–88 percent of the 1,800 physicians, nurses, and allied health professionals studied had observed incompetence, troubling errors, or dangerous shortcuts, only 10 percent had acted on those observations. Nevertheless, this "skilled minority" had the highest morale and greatest job satisfaction of the subjects studied. Although their happiness is a good outcome, the report's title, "Silence Kills,"[6] is a reminder that there are far greater reasons for ethical action than personal well-being. Inaction in deference to authority can sometimes be a matter of life and death.

The sixth barrier is that of **personal cost**. This goes beyond the social or acceptance cost associated with the barrier of discomfort. Personal cost is about the loss of jobs, security, and personal well-being. People of courage often pay a high price for taking ethical action. This seems a particularly cruel and unjust penalty for the risks incurred in the efforts to right a wrong. Paradoxically, many people who act with moral courage ultimately dismiss the price they paid for their actions. "It was the right thing to do." "I was so focused on keeping that job I had lost sight of the toll having it took on my soul." "Regardless of what happened, I can still look my kids in the eyes and look at myself in the mirror."

In contrast, those who use personal risk as a rationale for inaction often inflate the costs of action and diminish the costs of inaction; it's what the literature refers to as **moral cowardice**. Out of fear of the consequences, people fail to consider the price they pay for not living their principles and for looking the other way in times of crisis. As John McCain puts it, "Remorse is an awful companion. Whatever the unwelcome consequences of courage, they are unlikely to be worse than the discovery that you are less a man than you pretend to be."[7]

Although remorse **is** a poor companion, it may also be a precursor for action. The disappointment people carry from times of cowardice can strengthen their resolve not ever to feel that way again. It provides an opportunity to reflect, even with regret, on the opportunity lost and the steps that might have been taken. In doing so, individuals of conscience prepare for the next opportunity and appreciate that, whatever we do, at the end of the day, we live with ourselves and our decisions.

 Example

In the nonprofit sector, the case of William Aramony and the United Way of America (UWA) aptly illustrates the damage created by failings in moral courage. Aramony was the visionary and charismatic CEO of the national UWA for over two decades, shaping it into one of the largest nonprofits in

(continued)

---

6 "Silence kills," *Nursing*, vol. 35, issue 4 (2005) p. 33.

7 John McCain, *Why Courage Matters: The Way to a Braver Life* (New York: Random House, 2004).

(continued)

the country. During his tenure, he instituted a number of innovations in the field of philanthropy and in the organization itself: the creation of employer-based annual donor appeals, corporate partnerships (as with the National Football League to advertise UWA causes), and internal talent identification and cultivation.

Unfortunately, this meteoric growth was also accompanied by other excesses: first class international travel, chauffeur service, lavish gifts to young girlfriends, extravagant vacations. Early opportunities to intercede in the scandal were stymied by familiar barriers to moral courage: discomfort, moral ambiguity, futility, personal cost, diffusion of responsibility, and deference to authority.

Some people failed to act because they did not identify Aramony's actions as improper, concluding that the expenses were legal and therefore acceptable. Board members from the corporate sector, accustomed to the norms of their organizations, were ill-equipped to evaluate the effect of such practices in the nonprofit sector. Other trustees explicitly assumed that the CEO knew the field of social welfare better than they did, and thus they deferred to Aramony's judgment. Others refused to pass judgment on what they considered personal conduct. Who had the right to criticize the CEO as long as he was doing his job? The first class trips were not a secret and therefore must have been appropriate; otherwise, wouldn't someone do something about them?

Staff with long-time ties to UWA may have considered Aramony's behavior unseemly for a high profile nonprofit CEO but found little traction in making a case against it:

- Staff members and affiliate leaders who raised questions were marginalized and ridiculed. Others were compromised by their personal loyalty and debt to the CEO.
- If the organization was exceeding its goals, perhaps the ends justified the means.
- The CEO was powerful and had powerful allies on the board. Why rock the boat?
- The board was responsible for the CEO, and if the governing body approved his actions, why should lesser staff question it?

An anonymous tip to the board chairman in 1990, followed by internal complaints and media inquiries, resulted in an outside investigation, narrowly drawn to examine accounting practices. Although the audit revealed no personal enrichment on Aramony's part, it served as a tipping point for outrage throughout the organization, resulting in the CEO's resignation in 1992. Later that year, Aramony and other executives were indicted for defrauding UWA of over a million dollars though misuse of leave salary and retirement benefits and improper billing of private expenses. Ultimately he was sentenced to seven years in prison on more than two dozen counts of tax and fraud charges.

More than 30 years later, the UWA scandal offers more than a caution-ary tale about moral courage. On the positive side, it gave rise to increased sensitivity and accountability, particularly in executive compensation, administrative costs, and return-on-investments. However, it also damaged the UWA brand and that of related charities, irretrievably undermined donor confidence, and cultivated enduring skepticism about the virtuous inten-tions of the nonprofit organizations.[*, **, †]

* Cushman, J. J., Jr., *Charity Leader's Success Was Also His Undoing* (New York: New York Times, 1992).
** Glaser, J. S., *The United Way Scandal: An Insider's Account of What Went Wrong and Why* (New York: John Wiley and Sons, 1993).
† Kellerman, B., *Bad Leadership: What It Is, How It Happens, Why It Matters* (Boston: Harvard Business School Press, 2004).

Strategies for Ethical Action

If overcoming the barriers to moral courage requires the cultivation of the will, successful ethical action requires cultivation of the way. This section addresses the skills and resources individuals can draw upon to "do the decided."

Have a Clear Compass

Whether derived from faith, personal moral codes, professional standards, or some other source of principles, clarity of purpose is an essential element of ethical action. Being mind-ful of one's individual and institutional values is the foundation for taking a stand on those values. Without this framework, as the saying goes, "if you don't stand for anything, you'll fall for anything." In addition, basing action on principle—something larger than the whims and preferences of the individual—empowers both the actor and the act of courage.

In the case at the outset of the chapter, Sam's objections to Cal should be rooted in prin-ciples such as integrity or fairness, or on organizational values such as respect and good gov-ernance, rather than on Sam's personal offense at Cal's demeanor or personality differences between the two. That way, Sam is standing up for something bigger and more enduring than himself.

Know Your Objective

Beyond having a foundation for action, a person of courage needs an objective for action: what is it that he or she wants to achieve by an act of courage? Clarity is important because vague goals ("I just want us to get along") lead nowhere, and different objectives will call for different strategies. If the objective is to encourage more respectful discourse, group conversation and ground rules about the concern would be appropriate. If the objective is to encourage more respectful behavior by an individual, a private, one-to-one conversation by an influential peer might be called for. If the intent is to avoid crippling conflicts of interest on the board, a policy or structural change might be in order, relegating major donors to "ambassador" or other positions rather than trustee roles.

What does Sam want? To promote a thorough airing of issues in group discussions? To diversify the board? To foster organizational transparency? To halt improper practices? To encourage self-awareness in others when troubling things are said or done? Originally, Sam's objective may have been to increase Cal's sensitivity and encourage him to change for the sake of the board. The strategies of talking to him and having Sally talk to him have not worked. Sam must either change his strategy to achieve the same objective or change objectives. Perhaps it would be more fruitful to focus on strengthening the board so that it can carry out its fiduciary responsibilities irrespective of Cal's actions and statements. This objective might entail several strategies:

- Securing consultation or education for the board
- Selectively reinforcing input of other members
- Utilizing a board development subcommittee to seek and prepare strong, objective candidates for trustee positions
- Conducting exit interviews with trustees who have resigned or retired and using the findings to improve board functioning

Seek Advisers and Allies

Moral courage involves individual acts, but there is no need to go it alone. People of action need others to serve as their sounding boards, sustainers, advisers, and allies. Different people play different roles. Some are inspirational—they encourage the problem solver to be strong, to take risks, and to live his or her principles. Others are strategists—they offer suggestions, help weigh tactics, rehearse conversations, and play out reactions to worst-case scenarios. Some are supporters—they offer comfort and affirmation even in light of adversity. Still others are partners in change—they share the concern, agree on the need for action, make their voices heard, and take part in strategies.

In the arts agency case, Sally and Sam have come to an impasse about Cal. Sally does not want to take further action, apparently in the fear of antagonizing a wealthy donor and powerful leader. Sam feels the situation is untenable in that Cal is using his influence to discourage sound governance. Beyond that, his behavior is at odds with the principles of integrity and the values of the board.

Sam needs both advisors and allies. He should think about past board members who are familiar with the situation and who might offer advice on strategies. He should consider current board members who share his concerns and could serve as partners in change. Sam's area association for nonprofits might have individuals available for confidential consultation. Sam's spouse or partner, mentor, therapist, and other confidantes are further resources for support and suggestions.

Hopefully the board has well-established job descriptions and governance policies for board members, periodic peer or self-evaluations, and a board development or governance committee to address relationships among board members and between the board and the CEO.[8] How would Cal's performance on the board be viewed in light of these documents? Is he living up to the expectations of all board members? What does feedback indicate about

8 Ram Charan, *Owning Up: The 14 Questions Every Board Member Needs to Ask.* (San Francisco: Jossey-Bass, 2009).

his role and demeanor? How has the governance committee addressed poorly performing board members in the past? Is there a reason why they are not acting in Cal's case? Can they be mobilized to speak with Cal or to raise the "board climate" issue at a future meeting? To the extent that these documents set forth agreed-upon expectations and processes for dealing with board matters, Sam can refer to them when determining his strategy and use them to bolster his position about the risks facing the board.

Walk the Walk

In the boardroom, like the classroom and the living room, more is caught than taught. Humans learn by example. In fact, research shows that most people are just about as ethical as the people around them. Leaders have a powerful capacity to create courage by example, to establish an organizational climate that lives the values it espouses. Ethical action is not easy, but it can be practiced; it can be taught. Those who aspire to act with moral courage serve as powerful examples to others and thus must be sure that their actions are congruent with their words, that they live the code of ethics established for the organization, and that they model the behavior they desire in others.

Hopefully, Sam's actions to date have represented the behavior he desires in Cal and the rest of the board: civil, ethical, fair, and so on. As he decides his next steps, he should continue to uphold those standards by respecting confidentiality in sharing his concerns with others, by taking steps in a proportionate and orderly fashion (rather than starting with the most severe actions at his disposal), and by treating others respectfully and putting the organization's interests ahead of his own wishes and feelings.

Understand Change Strategies

Not all situations that demand moral courage allow for planning and strategy. Some situations (the bigoted comment, the rushed vote, the abusive parent in a public setting) arise unbidden and demand action in the moment. Others though, including those in the organizational context, allow for, and even demand, thoughtful and well-planned action. Moral courage is the will to act, strategy is the plan for action, and skill is the capacity to carry out the plan.

There are a vast array of theories and mechanisms for organizational and behavioral change. Some involve incremental progress, negotiation, and compromise; others advocate the use of power and radical transformation. All require a careful assessment of the prospects for change: the timing and climate, the points where leverage may be used most effectively, the areas of resistance, and the motivations of various players. Chapter 10 expands on these concepts and supplies tools for change.

In possession of a clear objective, Sam might use a tool such as force field analysis to enumerate the factors that support or advance his cause and those that act as barriers. Restraining forces might be fear, loyalty, or ingratiation on the part of board members; Cal's financial power; ignorance about legal and ethical imperatives for nonprofit trustees; and an array of other factors. Factors that can drive change include Sam's position and his relationships with board members, the board's investment in the organization and their desire to avoid legal or reputational damage to the nonprofit, or the availability of other donors whose means and power might compete with Cal's if he retracts his support. After this analysis, Sam can decide which tactics will yield the greatest likelihood of success. These may include educating board members about the risks they incur from questionable decisions; recruiting other independent, powerful, and well-to-do individuals for the board; or even offering to resign if the troubling board processes continue.

Practice Considerate Communication

Communication is a fundamental skill for those who wish to act with moral courage. Faced with a bigoted comment, an individual might make a joke of the statement; berate the speaker; follow up individually at a later point; or react nonverbally, conveying astonishment, disgust, or offense. Some reactions will be effective, others incendiary. Some will encourage reflection, others defensiveness. Sometimes it is hard to predict how a communication will be received; it is, after all, up to the receiver to process what is communicated. Still, the sender can endeavor to maximize success by sending messages in a clear and sensitive manner. One suggested model is to follow an S–B–I format, conveying the **situation**, **behavior**, and **impact**. Under this format, for example, Sam might say, "At last month's meeting (S), when Cal criticized Linda's idea (B), the whole group stopped discussing options (I)." Another version of this communication style involves "I-statements" in which the communicator personalizes the impact of the action ("When you ___, I feel___"). In Sam's case, I-statements include (to Cal) "When you insist on your personal selections for the board, I fear we will lose balance and diversity" or "At today's meeting when you said, 'let's just get on with it,' I felt disrespected."

This style of communicating can seem awkward at first, but, like other skills, it can be cultivated to good effect. It avoids common communication pitfalls such as labeling, blaming, and over-generalizing and homes in on the specific concern in such a way that the receiver can hear it and act on it.

Conclusion

The capacity for moral courage is a leadership imperative. Leaders must make difficult decisions, endure criticism, model ethical behavior, and uphold organizational standards. All of these require courage and adherence to principle. Although a variety of individual, interpersonal, and institutional characteristics can serve as barriers to ethical action, that action flows from a will and a skill that can be cultivated. The willingness to act with moral courage fosters personal accountability, organizational integrity, and community well-being. Yet the will to act is not enough. To maximize their effect, people of good intentions must still possess the skills to intervene strategically and make their voices heard.

Chapter 10

Change Management

Dee-Ann is the long time executive director of the state affiliate of a national professional association. For well over a decade, both local board members and the staff at the national level have had serious misgivings about her performance. Some have complained that her foot dragging and ineptitude have sabotaged grants and other funding opportunities. Others allege that her parochialism and laziness protract and smother every discussion of new ideas, alienating energetic and creative board talent. Her liaisons at the national office are frustrated that her state affiliate has a disproportionately large attrition in membership and a stagnant financial and service profile. In fact, hers is the worst performing of all of the state chapters, across all benchmarks.

The most common refrain about Dee-Ann is "Oh, God, is she still there? Why doesn't the board do something?"

The reasons vary. Dee-Ann is a meek and genial person who is inoffensive interpersonally. As such, efforts to confront her seem like bullying, regardless of who is delivering the message. Further, she has benefited from the association bylaws, which mandate term limits. By the time board members assess her deficiencies, they lack the time or will to act. Dee-Ann has also taken a particularly active role on the board development committee. As a result, the board is usually populated with partisan, laissez faire, or ineffectual members who side with Dee-Ann against those with "aggressive plans" for the organization. Dee-Ann's annual evaluations have fluctuated around average. Typically, the board has tried to emphasize the strengths in her performance (her almost single-handed management of the office, her history with the organization, and her willingness to work for a modest salary), and they have minimized her deficiencies. Occasionally, change plans have been instituted, but turnover in leadership or sensitivity to Dee-Ann's feelings have resulted in anemic follow through and poor accountability by both Dee-Ann and the board.

Sonja has just been narrowly elected to a two year term as president following two years as a regional representative to the board. The predominant goal for her presidency is to deal with Dee-Ann, once and for all. Her assessment of the board members indicates that approximately one-third are fed up with Dee-Ann and want her fired. Another third will stand by Dee-Ann under all circumstances. The remainder consists of new members who have yet to perceive a problem and those who are aware of problems with Dee-Ann's competence but are divided about the best strategy to address it.

(continued)

> *(continued)*
>
> At Sonja's first meeting as president, the executive committee presented a proposal that had been tabled by the previous board. It called for an immediate and comprehensive growth plan for the organization. Though Sonja tried to facilitate broad discussion and questions and answers, Dee-Ann dominated the conversation, variously deriding it as too ambitious, risky, complicated, and out of character for an association of their size. Some board members repeatedly deferred to her "expertise" over the "opinions" of other board members. The plan is scheduled for a vote at the next board meeting, though Sonja is uncertain about the likely outcome and angry that this crucial decision might be sabotaged despite all the efforts and compromises that went into its creation.

Although detection of financial irregularities and control lapses are vital to nonprofit governance, other skills and knowledge are needed to institute structural and personnel changes to avoid and address such problems. This chapter introduces organizational change concepts, tools to evaluate change prospects, and affiliated strategies and skills required to manage risk and change.

Understanding Change

Change is inevitable, but it is rarely embraced. The reluctance is understandable. It requires doing something new or ceasing something familiar. Change involves risks. Will it work? Will it be beneficial? Will it be worth the time and effort required? Whether the change is desired or dreaded, massive or microscopic, resulting from opportunity or from catastrophe, it forces people from their comfort zones and thus engenders an array of emotions and reactions. Even when the changes are positive and desired, they are still difficult to sustain. New years' resolutions eagerly set at the beginning of January too often fall by the wayside by March. As William Bridges notes, change is situational but transitions are psychological.[1] What impedes enduring change? Why is it difficult for those in the midst of change to make the necessary transitions?

Three interlocking emotions typically accompanying change efforts: fear, exasperation, and distrust:

- **Fear** can arise from many sources. Particularly in a tenuous economy, organizational change may put jobs at risk, diminish financial security, or restructure roles in such a way that old skills and knowledge are no longer valued. Fear arises from this loss of the familiar, from powerlessness, and from threats to organizational turf and self-interests.

- Like fear, **exasperation** can be linked to feelings of powerlessness. It also arises when change means an additional burden on an already too full list of responsibilities.

- **Mistrust** emerges from a variety of sources. Sometimes workers doubt management's competence. Many have already experienced initiatives that ended in

---

1 William Bridges, *Managing Transitions: Making the Most of Change* (Philadelphia: Da Capo Lifelong Books, 2009).

disaster or maintenance of the status quo. Some distrust others' motives for change and suspect their access to decision makers. Do others have an inside track in information and opportunities? Why make change here? Why now? Why THIS change?

These feelings about change are manifested in a variety of responses that can derail the change effort:

- **Foot dragging** is a form of passive resistance. Rather than embrace the change or confront it, foot draggers wait out the initiative in the hope that it will just go away. Typically, people who respond in this fashion have endured many ill-conceived initiatives. The "wait and see" approach means they won't have to switch back to traditional practices if the current effort falters.

- **Nominal compliance.** In this strategy, staff members give lip service to the merits of the change effort and appear to endorse it while doing as little as possible to authentically enact the changes. Their efforts may be incremental or superficial—enough to give the impression of making changes without actual buy-in or action.

- **Talk it to death.** Although change is sometimes a process of "ready, aim, fire," in many organizations the process is "ready, aim, aim, aim, aim." Although change requires patience and time, many initiatives are undone by excessive examination. This over-attention to process may simply be part of organizational culture rather than an intentional effort to stymie transformation, but either way the result is the same. Board members and employees discuss, ponder, examine, and review all aspects, prognostications, bases, and data for a proposed change. They revisit decisions already made so that no decision is ever stable and reliable. They defer important decisions that impede forward progress. As a result, key personnel turn over, and the impetus for change is lost; institutional memory fades, the project is shelved or withdrawn, and change agents retreat in fatigue.

- **Bureaucracy.** A corollary to killing an initiative by discussion is to kill it with paperwork. Change in complex organizations requires widespread consideration and buy-in, but too many layers of review and input can turn a relatively straightforward proposal into an unrecognizable and untenable initiative.

- **Sabotage.** As opposed to the first four reactions, which are essentially forms of passive resistance, sabotage is a more proactive effort to resist change. It can take many forms but most often involves the use of alliances, rumors, and intentional incompetence to muster resistance and demonstrate the folly of the plan. Because there is always a gap between letting go of traditional processes and experiencing the benefits of new ones, there are ample opportunities to undermine change and tempt a return to the status quo.

- **Goal displacement** refers to focusing on the wrong things. Sometimes change efforts are doomed from the start because the problem and solution are misspecified. However, promising change strategies can also be undone when implementers direct their efforts to minor or superficial changes rather than those prescribed. For example, the board identifies issues with the lack of diversity and cultural competence in the organization, but the CEO's response is to task a manager as "chief diversity officer" and declare the problem resolved.

Clearly, the tactics to block change are varied and powerful. John Kotter, in his framework for change, devotes fully half of the recommended steps to dislodging the status quo before initiating the change itself.[2] Fortunately, abundant research exists to guide change efforts. The following nine guidelines are drawn from studies about individual change such as smoking cessation,[3] the transitions imbedded in change,[4] change from within organizations,[5] resistance to change,[6] leadership approaches,[7, 8] and a variety of tools and techniques needed to leverage change efforts. The recommendations for change are presented in the general order in which they should be carried out. However, because some steps are interlocking and interdependent, the change agent should move among different steps as needed.

Be Clear About What You Want

What needs to change? What vision is driving the change you desire? A clear, succinct, sensible vision is needed to help "direct, align, and inspire actions on the part of a large number of people."[9] Common failures at this stage involve either ambiguity or over-specification, delving so deeply into plans and processes that they are mistaken for a vision. Without a **clear** goal it will be difficult to diagnose the conditions that need to be influenced for change, communicate about the change, and evaluate the outcomes. In the absence of clear goals, how will you know when you've succeeded? A good litmus test for a precise vision is that it can be conveyed in less than five minutes to someone unfamiliar with the inner workings of the organization. Better yet, it can be conveyed in a few sentences during an elevator ride or in line at a coffee shop. To help put the goal in concrete terms, consider phrasing the goal as one of the following:

- We will stop doing ____.
- We will do more ____.
- We will begin doing ____.
- We will do ____ differently.

---

2 John P. Kotter, *Leading change* (Boston: Harvard Business Press, 1996).

3 Carlo C. DiClemente, Debra Schlundt, and Leigh Gemmell, "Readiness and stages of change in addiction treatment," *The American Journal on Addictions*, vol. 13, 2004, p. 103–119.

4 William Bridges, *Managing Transitions: Making the Most of Change* (Philadelphia: Da Capo Lifelong Books, 2009).

5 George Brager and Stephen Holloway, "A process model for changing organizations from within," Ralph M. Kramer & Harry Specht (Eds.), *Readings In Community Organization Practice*, (Englewood Cliffs, NJ: Prentice-Hall, 1983) p. 198–208.

6 Gerald Frey, "Framework for promoting organizational change," *Families in Society*, vol. 7, 1990, p. 142–147.

7 John P. Kotter, *Leading change* (Boston: Harvard Business Press, 1996).

8 Kerry Patterson, Joseph Grenny, David Maxfield, Ron McMillan, and Al Switzler, *Influencer: The Power to Change Anything* (New York: McGraw-Hill, 2008).

9 John P. Kotter, *Leading change* (Boston: Harvard Business Press, 1996) p. 6.

> ### 🔲 Example
>
> The Young Leaders Academy (YLA) was created 5 years ago to foster self-confidence and leadership abilities in 10 to 12 year old innercity youths. Two-thirds of YLA's funding comes from a state juvenile justice contract, and the rest comes from various municipalities and private donors. Last year, the local charter school started a similar program. At this month's YLA board meeting, members discussed the competitive threat posed by the new initiative. There is no shortage of youth to be served by the 2 agencies, but the board is concerned that YLA may lose the juvenile justice funds. After examining the challenges, the board concluded that YLA had a competitive advantage over the new program because of its relative longevity and success. However, to date, YLA has relied on anecdotal accounts and client testimonials to make the case for its effectiveness. The board asked the CEO to develop outcome measures for program effectiveness and a data collection and analysis plan. Anticipating push back from the staff about new forms and wasted resources, the CEO's goal was, simply stated, "To gather concrete information so we can more effectively tell YLA's story and assure its long term success."

Assess Before You Act

Change agents must understand the organization, its personnel, and the meaning the change will have before prescribing solutions or reaching for familiar, but perhaps ill-suited, strategies for change. Gerald Frey suggests 11 considerations for assessing the ease or complexity of a change effort.[10] The change agent must examine the following:

- **The perceived advantage of the change.** What are the benefits and negative implications? Who is most likely to be affected? If the advantages are not likely to pay off until sometime down the road, and the difficulties will be abundant, widespread, and immediate, the challenge to change will be great.
- **Effort.** This refers to the time and energy required for adoption and implementation. Do those affected perceive that the results will be worth the effort required to institute change? If they do not, change agents must regularly and broadly articulate and demonstrate the benefits (or the risks in not changing). Changes require buy-in and prolonged effort. Under these conditions, even the most fervent supporters may lose energy and interest. This possibility should be anticipated from the outset and mitigated through communication, attention to incremental gains, and other measures.
- **Risk.** What are the relative costs if the effort fails? What are the potential negative consequences? Can the initiative be implemented incrementally, or can it be reversed if it does not work?

---

10 Gerald Frey, "Framework for promoting organizational change," *Families in Society*, vol. 7, 1990, p. 142–147.

- **Sunk costs.** This refers to the money, time, and energy the change would cost the organization that it can't convert to other purposes if the initiative fails. Some sunk costs can be recouped or redirected to other activities, but others are so specifically targeted to institution of the new initiative that the outlays to achieve it are lost if the effort is unsuccessful.
- **Understandability.** This is linked to the clarity of the goal. Can change agents convey the intended results of change and the steps to be taken? Can they do so in language that is compatible with values of the audience? For example, the Young Leadership Program initiative on outcome data might be described as creating metrics, benchmarks, and a dashboard to track progress and effectiveness. Such language might confuse or alienate key constituents from the staff, volunteers, board, or donors. A more understandable message might say, "in addition to collecting success stories, we are also going to collect statistics so that we can depict, measure, and compare the results YLP gets."
- **Ability.** This refers to the organization or change agent's capacity to carry out the change. Are the proper skills, personnel, knowledge, and resources in place to carry out the initiative?
- **Depth.** This describes the extent to which an initiative changes an organization: more depth equals more resistance.
- **Distance.** This refers to the number of levels a proposal must travel to be accepted: more distance means more possible barriers and increased likelihood that the change message will become distorted. Changes that are localized to a unit or a team are easier to achieve than those that are broad based and affect the entire institution and beyond.
- **Idea and ideology.** How does the change proposal fit with the existing knowledge and attitudes of the organization? Innovations that are untested or at odds with the prevailing culture will meet greater resistance.
- **Need.** Why change? Is there a shared perception of a problem and the need for change? In the absence of broad based recognition of the problem, initial efforts must be made to educate key constituencies about the issues and the risks inherent in the status quo.
- **Generality.** This refers to the scope of the proposal or the size of the unit or organization affected: larger scope or size means there is greater potential for resistance.

Use of this framework has several advantages beyond helping to predict the challenges a change effort might face. By walking through the 11 elements, change agents are forced to think carefully about what they are proposing, anticipate the impact that it will have on those affected, and develop a thoughtful plan of action that begins not with the change but in laying the groundwork for the change and facilitating the personal transitions.

Example

Eden Academy is a hundred-year-old secondary school for girls. From time to time, there have been suggestions to admit male students, but those have typically amounted to half-hearted musings and have been set aside. Over the past five years, however, Eden has experienced a significant decline in applications and enrollments. As a result, tuition revenue is down, and the applicant pool is academically weaker. Focus groups with nonapplicants, applicants who turned down admission, alumnae, and other constituencies revealed that the lack of a coeducational learning environment was seen as a significant disadvantage of attendance at Eden. As a result of financial and competitive pressures, the board is weighing the question of male admissions. Ivan leads a subcommittee tasked with assessing the impact of the change. Using Frey's framework, Ivan's working group notes significant challenges.

Although the proposal is understandable, there is little perceived advantage in the change and limited understanding about the need to change, particularly among teachers and alumnae who are insulated from the effects of declining enrollment. Although the trustees alone have the power to make the decision, and in fact are the ones initiating the conversation, the change itself would be far reaching and would affect all elements of Eden's operations, particularly recruitment and fundraising. By and large, Eden has the capacities needed to integrate male students, and the effort and sunk costs required would be minimal. The greater problems lie in risk and ideology. As to risks, the effort to become a coeducational institution may weaken Eden's brand, put them in a new competitive market for students, and alienate applicants attracted to learning in an all-female environment. If the change does not improve the applicant pool, reverting to the old female-only model will have problematic effects on the school's reputation. More importantly, Eden is built on an ideology that learning is enhanced in an all-female environment. The proposed change directly contradicts that perspective. If the board casts aside that value, what will Eden's hallmark be? How will donors, alumnae, and applicants who embrace that feature react to the new Eden? How can the board mitigate these barriers if it chooses to go ahead with its proposal?

Create Awareness and Urgency

Frey's framework in the preceding section highlights the importance of perceptions. Those affected by change must embrace the existence of a problem to be solved, the merits of the change plan, the benefits in changing, and the risks in failing to change. Beyond their awareness of the problem, they must also possess a sense of urgency in order to overcome natural inertia and act in a targeted and timely manner. Kotter cautions not to confuse creating a sense of urgency with fueling anxiety.[11] The latter drives people further into their comfort

---

11 John P. Kotter, *Leading change* (Boston: Harvard Business Press, 1996).

zones and gives rise to avoidant behaviors. In contrast, creating urgency means broadly and frankly communicating the threats that give rise to change while offering a way forward to address those threats.

 Example

In 2010, federal health care reform prompted the widespread conversion of medical records from paper to electronic formats. The managers and staff at the Jones County Free Clinic have been aware of the change because other health care providers in the region have converted to the new system. However, the personnel at the clinic are overwhelmed with the volume of patients they must see and by the learning curve for undertaking the new system. For months they have deferred the switch, saying "not now." It appears that only the CEO possesses a sense of urgency about the change. As a result, she has embarked on a campaign to encourage others to understand the immediacy of the situation. To do so, she has shared accounts of the efficiencies other groups have experienced with the change, like tragic examples of paper files misplaced or destroyed in disasters and of patient care disrupted due to difficulties sharing information. She has capitalized on the staff's pride, cautioning them that Jones County will be left behind while other facilities advance. She has asked accreditors, Medicaid and Medicare liaisons, and key staff to spread the word about the benefits of electronic records compliance and the hazards of noncompliance. She has created and posted a timeline for the switch that depicts the number of days until the conversion. As a result, nearly three quarters of the staff perceive that the current recordkeeping procedures are untenable and must be changed.

Create a Powerful Coalition

Who wants the change? How many people want it? Are they powerful enough not only to push a change through, but also to have people engage in the transformation needed to make the change durable and successful? The larger the coalition supporting a change and the more social capital and legitimacy they have on the issue, the more compliance they will invoke in bringing the change to pass. Embedded in all of these elements is the issue of power. French and Raven have offered a classic typology by which we can understand types of power and their use:[12]

- *Expert power* arises from specialized knowledge or expertise (how to fix the copy machine, how to read a balance sheet, familiarity with state laws governing nonprofits, and organizational know-how).
- *Reward power* resides in the ability to provide benefits (vendor contracts, positive performance evaluations, and paid time off).

---

12 John R. French and Bertam Raven, "The bases of social power," In D. Cartwright (Ed.), *Studies in Social Power*. Dorwin Cartwright, ed. (Oxford: University of Michigan Press, 1959) p. 150–167.

- *Sanction power* is the capacity to impose negative consequences (dismiss staff, issue adverse audit findings, and withhold donations).
- *Referent power* arises by virtue of an individual's associations (golf partner with the CEO, secretary to the President, and daughter of the philanthropist).
- *Positional power* accompanies position in organization (president, CFO, and trustee).
- *Charisma* refers to power based on the traits of the individual (charm, magnetism, and vitality).
- *Legitimate* power is secured by formal process (election and selection through a search process).

These forms of power can be further divided into two subtypes: *functional powers* (for example, expert and referent power) reside in the person. They depend on what the person knows and can do. *Formal powers* are related more to the title the person holds and the power accorded to him or her because of that (for example, positional and legitimate power). Functional authority tends to legitimize formal power and make its use more easily acceptable.

Reward and sanction power can only be effective if the leader can keep close watch over personnel and stakeholders. Used alone, these forms of power tend to bring about compliance but usually only minimal levels of performance (as much as is necessary to avoid the punishment or attain the reward).

Expert, referent, and charismatic powers are more diffuse in their effects. They tend to bring about both attitudinal conformity (through enhanced motivation and internalized norms) as well as behavior change. Individuals responding to these types of power tend to perform beyond expectations and minimal requirements. The presence of these forms of power also increases the power of rewards, such as praise.

The power of those pushing the change can be harnessed to establish the urgency of the problem, promote the innovation itself, and reinforce and reward incremental steps. The powers held by those who will be on the receiving end of the change must also be considered. Those with a great deal of power have the least impetus for engaging in the change process because they can likely get their way without it or can withhold participation to maximize their power. On the other hand, when respected and powerful peers are on board, they can model, support, and advance change efforts.

Too often, change agents focus on positional or legitimate power at the expense of referent and charismatic powers. Although charm and connections will not necessarily triumph over substance, personal persuasion and networks can significantly affect the success or failure of transformation efforts.

Example

Eden Academy's decision to admit a coeducational student body requires a concerted effort to assure that the transition is smooth and the change enduring. Specific members of the staff and board were tapped to participate closely in the rollout of the new plan. Trustees who had attended the school used their connections with alumnae to explain the need for the change and the anticipated impact. As a longstanding employee, the provost possessed greater credibility than the headmaster or the director of finance, and thus her expertise and legitimate power were harnessed to make the case for change. Although the headmaster had the capacity to reward (or punish) employees for their responses to the transition, he chose to use those as levers of last resort, preferring to rely on charisma, expertise, and his links to the trustees, when needed, to move the process along. The headmaster's executive assistant and the director of alumni affairs were both well connected individuals, trusted by the rank and file. They served as important conduits of assurance and information to the staff and contributed useful insights to the change process.

Communicate

Communication is essential for successful transformations. Change agents must attend to the type, quantity, and substance of the messages sent. First, they must recognize that messages are sent through various channels: e-mails, newsletters, meetings, charts, and conversations in the break room. Messages are communicated intentionally and unintentionally. Leaders may portray a coalition that is publicly committed to a change, but if any of them behave in ways that reveal a lack of commitment, that will send a strong message throughout the organization. Actions must reinforce the messages sent. When respected "opinion leaders demonstrate vital behaviors, they are a powerful communication and motivation vehicle."[13]

Communications should also be frequent. Because staff are bombarded with messages, those focused on a change effort should constitute a large proportion of those sent overall.[14] Communications should also be attentive to the narrative emerging about the change. For example, if the theme of conversations is "all the board cares about is money," the corresponding messages should make the case for the ways that money is tied to the viability of the organization, staff retention, program effectiveness, and the like and not merely to the bottom line. This reframing of the message helps to "make the undesirable desirable,"[15] and it links potentially unsettling changes to values already embraced by the organization.

---

13 Kerry Patterson, Joseph Grenny, David Maxfield, Ron McMillan, and Al Switzler, *Influencer: The Power to Change Anything* (New York: McGraw-Hill, 2008).

14 John P. Kotter, *Leading change* (Boston: Harvard Business Press, 1996).

15 Kerry Patterson, Joseph Grenny, David Maxfield, Ron McMillan, and Al Switzler, *Influencer: The Power to Change Anything* (New York: McGraw-Hill, 2008).

Example

The Briar-Creek Animal Shelter has decided to expand into another county. Staff members fear that their workload may increase as volunteers and other scarce resources are stretched between the two sites. They also fear that they will be forced to commute to the other site if sufficient employees can't be found in the neighboring county. Most donors strongly identify with the first site and perceive the move as an abandonment of the shelter's commitment to Briar-Creek. Many of their gifts and other sources of funding are restricted to the original site. The new county has a less robust tradition of philanthropy, and only a handful of donors have emerged to support the shelter there. A subcommittee consisting of volunteers, board members, and staff with expertise in communications and marketing have created a comprehensive plan to keep all stakeholders apprised of the initiative and to respond to feedback. Their strategies have included regular presentations at staff meetings; town hall meetings with community members; updates on the website, Facebook, and other social media; feature articles in the local newspaper; and one-on-one meetings with donors, county leaders, and other prospective supporters. The committee has also worked to convey a message of inevitability—that the initiative will proceed and that everyone will work together to ensure that it adds to, rather than diminishes, the excellence created at Briar Creek. Although the committee has striven for consistency in their messaging, they have also swiftly addressed incidences of actions undermining messages, like when a board member told the county commissioners that he questioned the viability of the plan and would not support it financially until he was convinced.

Address Obstacles and Blockers

Building pro-change coalitions, engaging in active communications, and assessing power dynamics and the impact of the change will reveal forces that are pro-change and anti-change. Obstacles may come in the form of individual blockers or an array of other conditions such as limited resources, antagonistic organizational culture, weak leadership, and so on.

Social psychologist Kurt Lewin posited that conditions are held in place (dynamic equilibrium) by opposing forces.[16] For change to occur, the forces for change must be greater than the forces against change, or anti-change forces must be weakened for change to advance. The process for analyzing these elements is called *force field analysis*, and it is depicted in figure 10-1.

---

16 Kurt Lewin, "Defining the 'field at a given time,'" *Psychological Review*, vol. 50, 1943, p. 292–310.

Figure 10-1: *Force Field Analysis*

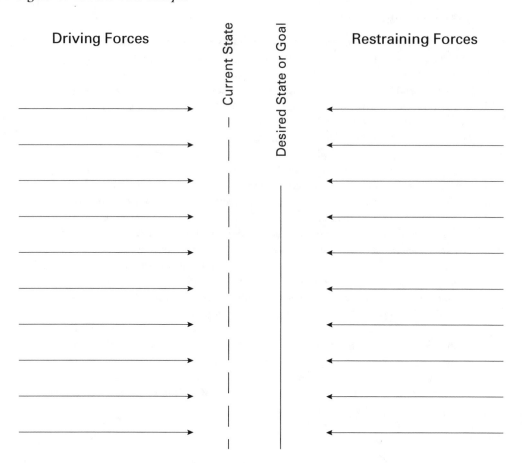

The steps in force field analysis are as follows:

1. Identify and chart the *desired state* based on the specific goal of the change effort.
2. Describe and chart the status quo or *current state* relative to the goal.
3. Identify and chart the forces driving change. These can be individual allies, statistics, current events, societal conditions, board actions—any factors that are considered to support and advance the move to change or innovation.
4. Identify and chart the forces resisting change. Again, these can encompass an array of factors, opponents, or conditions.
5. Review the various forces. Which factors are the strongest? Weakest? Which can be altered, and which are more fixed? Which would create counter-forces if they were flipped?
6. Consider the possibilities for reducing or removing some hindering forces. Strengthen or add new driving forces. Change the direction of the forces so that anti-change elements become pro-change.

![Example icon] Example

The Jones County Free Clinic was founded by a dedicated group of local residents. Its patients are predominantly African American and Latin American. The clinic also serves a large number of gay and lesbian young adults. Although the staff is largely made up of Caucasians, approximately 30 percent of the workforce (mostly at lower ranks) consists of persons of color. The clinic does not keep records on the sexual orientation of employees. These elements of change are analyzed in the following list using the steps in force field analysis:

- **Desired state:** the Diversify Board membership to include at least four representatives of racial, ethnic, or sexual minorities.
- **Current state:** the board has no members from minority groups.
- **Driving forces:**
  - The board development committee is committed to diversifying the board in the next round of nominations.
  - The population in Jones County is becoming increasingly diverse and is also an attractive retirement area.
  - Staff members are connected to an array of ethnic and cultural communities.
  - Fred, a clinic founder, is eager to see the board and staff better represent the clientele served.
  - Funding sources (including the state contracting agency) are concerned about the homogeneity of the board's current composition.
- **Restraining forces:**
  - The board development committee is not connected to minority networks that might generate board nominations.
  - Many local residents think the clinic is a public agency and are unaware of the board.
  - The clinic is perceived to serve immigrants and poor people. Citizens and activists who would make promising board members do not relate to those constituencies and do not envision themselves as volunteering for the agency that serves them.
  - Wilma, a clinic founder, is still on the board and is distressed at the clientele the organization is attracting. She believes that it is unnecessary to diversify the board and that doing so will bring more of "the wrong element" into the clinic.
- **Analysis.** Wilma is fixed in her resistance to diversification. However, other restraining forces may be weakened through better public education and by development committee outreach through staff to untapped communities. Fred is also adamant about his position in support of the change. He may be able to persuade other founders to ally with him, thus diminishing Wilma's capacity to hinder the change. He and committee members might tap into networks of newcomers and retirees to talk about the work of the clinic and the importance of an informed and connected board.

Create Short Term Wins

Leaders of change efforts must structure their plans so that there are early and steady examples of transformation. Until change takes hold and becomes self-reinforcing, there is the risk that motivations and energies will flag and that progress will stall or regress. In the absence of immediate successes, change agents must institute rewards and accountability mechanisms to foster nascent change efforts. Patterson, et al, recommend that these systems focus not on outcomes but on *vital behaviors*.[17] Allow people to experience the benefits of the changed behavior ("When I welcome potential board members visiting the agency, their enthusiasm for our mission increases and so does mine.").

The notion here is that when the proper behaviors are reinforced, the change will eventually follow. Thus, a board that wants to diversify might work on creating a welcoming climate for clients, visitors, and newcomers to the organization. To reinforce the vital behavior, people in power must notice the action, name it, and reinforce it through recognition. The reinforcement can be personal, such as in an e-mail or compliment ("It's great that you took the initiative to make the images of people on our website more diverse") or public ("This month's outstanding employee award goes to Gail for her efforts to make sure all visitors to the agency feel welcome here"). Aligned with this strategy, it is important to look at the current reward system to ensure that it doesn't obstruct the desired changes.

Give People the Tools to Succeed

Behavioral change is a prerequisite for any form of organizational transformation. Individuals or teams need to do something differently: use a new system for documentation, teach a coeducational class, solicit donors and board members from unfamiliar communities, or use statistics to evaluate program effectiveness. Sometimes these new behaviors are merely strange or uncomfortable. At other times, the demands go beyond existing cognitive, affective (emotional), social, or behavioral competencies. Leaders in change must ensure that the people implementing change have the tools to succeed. These tools may involve additional training or resources. They can also include rewards, reinforcement, and support through *partialization* (breaking the task into learnable bits and reinforcing incremental expansions in confidence and performance) and *coaching*.[18] Environmental changes (such as configuration of offices and free coffee in the break room) also help direct behavior change.[19]

---

17 Kerry Patterson, Joseph Grenny, David Maxfield, Ron McMillan, and Al Switzler, *Influencer: The Power to Change Anything* (New York: McGraw-Hill, 2008).

18 Ann Gilley, Pamela Dixon, and Jerry W. Gilley, "Characteristics of leadership effectiveness: Implementing change and driving innovation in organizations," *Human Resource Development Quarterly*, vol. 19, 2008, p. 153–169.

19 Kerry Patterson, Joseph Grenny, David Maxfield, Ron McMillan, and Al Switzler, *Influencer: The Power to Change Anything* (New York: McGraw-Hill, 2008).

> **Example**
>
> At the Jones County Free Clinic, the transition to electronic records was jumpstarted through a day-long, hands-on training during which all staff members were introduced to and became proficient with the technologies used to capture and track patient data. Of course a considerable amount of work had already gone on "behind the scenes" as consultants worked with IT staff to install new software and develop new processes for recordkeeping. For the rollout to those who would actually use the system, leaders closed the clinic for a day; acknowledged the trepidation about the new system; provided ample refreshments; and created an atmosphere of fun, collegiality, and success. The training was staffed by outside experts familiar with the technology and by clinic personnel, including the CEO, who had already become familiar with the new procedures. They were able to respond immediately when questions or difficulties arose and to offer ample feedback and praise to support skill development.
>
> Commencing the day after the training session, all vestiges of the paper system were removed. Forms and the stands they were held in were disposed of, paper records were removed from the front office, and clipboards were replaced with individual hand-held devices and terminals in each exam area.

Solidify Changes

Change is not secure at the point of implementation. In fact, this may be the point at which it is most vulnerable. The traditions and comfort of the former system are still familiar, and the challenges, kinks, and learning curve attendant to the new system are pervasive. As Kotter puts it, don't "declare victory too soon." "New approaches are fragile and subject to regression." And once urgency abates, "foot soldiers are reluctant to return to the front."[20] Planning efforts must anticipate backsliding as a natural part of the change process. Change agents can prepare for it by continued vigilance through the honeymoon phase, attention to interim goals, and use of communication vehicles that reinforce progress.[21] Through this phase, changes must be institutionalized, standardized, anchored in the culture, and linked to established organizational elements. Change only sticks when it becomes "the way we do things around here."[22]

---

20 John P. Kotter, *Leading change* (Boston: Harvard Business Press, 1996).

21 George Brager and Stephen Holloway, "A process model for changing organizations from within," R. M. Kramer & H. Specht (Eds.), *Readings in community organization practice*, Ralph M. Kramer and Harry Specht, eds. (Englewood Cliffs: Prentice-Hall, 1983) p. 198–208.

22 John P. Kotter, *Leading change* (Boston: Harvard Business Press, 1996) p. 14.

🔲 Example

In order to better position itself against challenges from a competing organization, the Young Leaders Program (YLP) has instituted a program evaluation plan that requires case workers, group leaders, and volunteers to collect data on
- youth who are selected for the program and those who are not;
- the services provided each YLP participant;
- a variety of outcomes, including quarterly grade and attendance reports and peer, teacher, and parent observations; and
- longitudinal data on program graduates.

Following the data collection maxim of "garbage in, garbage out," YLP administrators have emphasized that the success of the evaluation relies on the quality and accuracy of the data gathered. Spurred by fears of a program merger or acquisition, the staff initially accepted the new tasks and submitted timely and complete data forms. Three months into the effort, however, their interest flagged, and several began to push back against the additional work demanded by the initiative. Fortunately, the leadership team had anticipated this and had a plan. Respected leaders among the staff and volunteers communicated continually with their colleagues about the importance of this new, permanent responsibility. Change supporters discussed how the evaluation reflected YLP's values of accountability and excellence. Rather than taking time away from youth, it ensured that the services delivered to youth were effective and efficient. Monthly reports were generated to demonstrate how data collected would be used. New staff and volunteers were informed of the data collection responsibilities from the outset so that it was accepted as a natural element of YLP job descriptions. Within nine months, the innovation was a routine part of YLP operations.

Suggestions for Sonja

At the outset of the chapter, we presented the case of Sonja, the professional association board president who is attempting to institute a growth plan for the organization and address chronic performance problems on the part of the executive director, Dee-Ann. We will use her dilemma and her perspective to illustrate use of the nine recommended steps for effective change.

Be Clear About What You Want

Sonja is faced with two change initiatives: the growth plan proposed by the previous board and the question of what to do about Dee-Ann. An early strategic decision is whether she should undertake both activities simultaneously or sequentially, and, if the latter, which should come first. There are merits and drawbacks to each choice, but we recommend that Sonja table the growth plan for the time being. It seems unwise to impose a broad new initiative on a new board that did not participate in its design. Given Dee-Ann's opposition and the reticence the board demonstrated at the first meeting, it seems unlikely that the plan will pass in the near term, and a contentious process in the nascent board may compromise Sonja's leadership.

Once she has decided to focus her efforts on Dee-Ann's performance, she must be clear about her goal. It may be tempting to wish Dee-Ann could be fired or forced to resign, but Sonja should be mindful of the role of the goal as a rallying point to involve others in the change process. A goal that is perceived as hostile or harmful, no matter how warranted, will alienate potential allies and create backlash or unacceptable compromise positions. An alternative goal might be to "implement a performance appraisal process for all association employees based on best practice benchmarks set by the national association." The goal is clear, reasonable, and fair.

Assess Before You Act

Sonja has several constituencies to address in trying to institute meaningful, forthright performance appraisals. She must consider them all in thinking about how to sell the change effort. Dee-Ann is a significant stakeholder. Although institution of the appraisals is not up to her, given her relationships with the members and the trust some past and present board members invest in her, she has the capacity to undermine the plan. Other important constituents for the change process include the current board, opinion leaders in the membership, liaisons with the national office, former board members and officers, and potential board candidates.

Most of the stakeholders will perceive an advantage in instituting a performance appraisal system. It is likely that most constituents have experienced them in their own organizations and will view them as a common element of the modern workplace. It is not clear whether the board perceives the need for such a system, however. Some may find it an empty exercise in light of Dee-Ann's longevity; others may feel the change is overdue for exactly the same reason. Still others may think it is a good idea just because it is a standard practice.

Effort will be required by a subcommittee of the board to create the executive evaluation plan and adapt the benchmarks to their chapter. For example, if there are numerical targets for membership recruitment and retention, board surveys, or other feedback mechanisms, those must be created and implemented. Although the effort to create the evaluation should not be onerous, developing the board's capacity to do the evaluation may take extra effort. Board members may be familiar with conducting appraisals on employees in their workplaces but may not know how to implement them with a CEO whom they observe on only an infrequent and limited basis. Further, they may perceive Dee-Ann as a colleague and be reticent to pass judgment on her performance. If so, the organization's ability to undertake the change is mixed.

Sonja's push for a performance appraisal plan and the organization's adoption of it are rather low-risk endeavors. It can be incrementally implemented and refined over time, and the resources that went into creating and implementing it can be redeployed in future evaluations. A possible form of failure for the plan arises if it is developed but then carried out in a superficial fashion. If the appraisal fails to accurately portray Dee-Ann's strengths and shortcomings, the change effort and the evaluation itself will have been spent on a meaningless exercise or, worse, on one that gives a false impression of Dee-Ann's capacities. The latter would make it more difficult for Sonja and subsequent boards to hold her accountable for improving her work.

Sonja's goal is clear and understandable. The proposal and the assessment itself have limited depth and distance in that the responsibility for both resides with the board. The key to Sonja's successful change will rest, however, on the board 's ability to implement that change in a forthright and comprehensive manner. Therefore, she will have to create the conditions that help the board members to understand best practices in CEO performance and evaluations and the courage to apply those to their own organization. When framed as a mechanism for accountability, fairness, and proper governance, Sonja's proposal will be congruent with the values of the organization. Because Dee-Ann is the only employee of the organization, the proposal cannot be generalized to other units.

In all, Sonja's proposal is not novel, complex, or far-reaching. The mechanisms for passing it are straightforward, and the number of actors involved is minimal. On the other hand, risks include the uncertain capacity of the board to implement the change, even if they have embraced it, and the possibility of counterproductive effects if the evaluation is done shoddily.

Create Awareness and Urgency

Sonja can use feedback from the liaisons to the national office, respected former board members, and the literature on nonprofit governance to educate the board about the importance of appraisals for all nonprofits. In fact, most of the literature on governance ranks CEO selection and evaluation among the most prominent responsibilities of trustees. Some of this information may also be persuasive in regard to the necessity of acting immediately. Sonja and her supporters may point to the fact that evaluation is long overdue as a rationale for speedy action. However, members may counter that if it has taken this long, extra time to examine the merits of the proposal and various forms of appraisal should not be a problem. Pro-change forces may want to call on cautionary tales from a regional association of nonprofits, compliance demands from the national office, and other levers to foster a sense of urgency among board members.

Create a Powerful Coalition

Sonja needs allies to pass the plan and ensure that it is carried out thoroughly and accurately. She may draw these from any of the stakeholder groups, but she should be careful in creating a coalition made up solely of Dee-Ann's detractors, lest it engender backlash. In fact, people who are generally supportive of Dee-Ann but thought to be capable, fair-minded, and concerned for due process would have particular legitimacy on the issue.

Another promising ally would be a trusted former board member with expertise in human resource management. Such an individual might help to emphasize the necessity of timely action, chair a committee to develop the evaluation measures, and coach the board on conducting the evaluation itself.

As Sonja plans her change effort, she should consider the various bases of power possessed by her allies. Are people with positional or legitimate power overrepresented at the expense of people with referent power or other opinion leaders? Do some members of the pro-change coalition possess charisma and other persuasive capabilities? Can the national organization exert rewards or sanctions that might encourage timely action?

Address Obstacles

Sonja is in the best position to complete a precise force field analysis, but a cursory review suggests some options for action:

- **Desired state:** Institute comprehensive annual reviews of the association CEO.
- **Current state:** Evaluations are episodic and idiosyncratic. Dee-Ann is not given honest feedback about her strengths and weaknesses and is not held accountable for corrective action.
- **Driving forces:**
- — Sonja and one third of the board are concerned about Dee's performance.
- — Most of the board members endorse the need for CEO evaluations.
- — The national office wants the association to implement evaluations.
- — Board members and past members (initials J., S., L., and G.) have experience with evaluation metrics based on their work in human resources or in evaluations done on other boards of which they are members.
- **Restraining forces:**
- — Some supporters of the change effort are seen as "out to get Dee-Ann," and thus other members feel the need to protect her.
- — Dee-Ann is resistant to the evaluation.
- — Board members (initials A., C., and M.) are overly deferential to Dee-Ann's wishes.
- — Association membership is apathetic about the issue or hopeless that it will lead to change.
- **Analysis:**
- — Frame the change effort as in Dee-Ann's interests. This may soften her opposition and flip some hindering forces.
- — Solicit broad input, including Dee-Ann's, on the metrics to be evaluated. This may persuade some hindering forces of the fairness and transparency of the change.
- — Encourage the national office to leverage its power and expertise to encourage the change.
- — Make the case that this association's members are losing out on opportunities that members in other states have.

Communicate

As power players and countervailing forces are identified, Sonja and the pro-change forces should consider the types of communication, sources, frequency, and methods used. One-on-one conversations with board members seeking viewpoints and testing messages might be useful. Whether Sonja takes the lead in holding these discussions depends on her social capital and how her position on the matter is viewed. Other communication mechanisms could include presentations by national or regional nonprofit experts.

Create Short Term Wins

This step is perhaps the most difficult for Sonja, in that acceptance of the appraisal proposal and implementation of it are not incremental acts. However, the chair of the evaluation effort can offer regular reports on steps made toward designing and completing the evaluation, and pro-change individuals can support and reinforce the efforts of the working group at each step of the process.

Give People the Tools to Succeed

Board members will need information on current best practices in CEO evaluations, examples of instruments and processes used in analogous organizations, and coaching on how to embrace the role in light of the board's limited observations of the CEO. Sonja should not take a predominant role in this effort. Rather, she should encourage surrogates with expertise and legitimacy on the issues to take visible roles in communication, interim targets, and lead communications.

Solidify Changes

A particular vulnerability for Sonja's change effort is that the proposal for evaluations may be approved, but its execution may be flawed. She and her allies must plan for this possibility from the outset, ensuring that messaging, planning, and success measures emphasize both aspects as essential to the association's success.

Conclusion

Change is hard, and change is inevitable. In contemporary nonprofits, change can be spurred by crises, funding opportunities, innovations, mergers, expansion, risk management, and an array of other causes. Change evokes strong feelings in individuals, and these reactions can put the change effort at risk from neglect or sabotage. Research and resources exist to help change agents anticipate challenges, create coalitions, devise strategies, neutralize opposition, and sustain gains.

Chapter 11

Integration for Action

The preceding chapters of this text have introduced an array of concepts and strategies for good governance. This chapter brings those ideas and models together and applies them to complex cases, examining the ways that nonprofit organizations (NPOs) can utilize sound practices to prevent and address difficult situations and advance beyond them. Through the cases presented and the associated discussions, readers can employ tools presented throughout the book and learn new strategies and resources for ensuring continued success.

Case One: A Woman Scorned

Kayla was the business manager at Alpha Camps, an NPO delivering recreation programs to children with severe medical problems. Last year, Irene was hired to replace the longtime CEO. Almost immediately, Kayla began to experience concerns about Irene's decisions, such as hiring a close friend at a high fee to conduct a strategic plan and inappropriately allocating charges to restricted accounts. Kayla also discovered suspicious charges to the Medicaid program, which is intended to cover health care delivery while the youngsters are at camp.

When the concerns first arose, Kayla raised questions and offered corrections to Irene, presuming that the errors were unintentional. Irene's responses appeared to confirm Kayla's assumptions that the mistakes were innocent oversights ("Oh, yes! Right! Thanks for clarifying.") Recently, however, Irene has become perturbed by Kayla's queries and scrutiny, alluding to her as rigid, uncooperative, and nitpicky. Concerned for the integrity of Alpha Camps, Kayla contacted a veteran board member to share her observations and seek guidance. The board member declined to get involved, citing the division of responsibilities between the board and the CEO. The board member mentioned the conversation to the board president, who raised it with Irene in their weekly phone conference. Irene portrayed Kayla as a disgruntled employee who could

(continued)

(continued)

not get past her loyalty to the former CEO and adjust to a female leader. At the conclusion of the phone call, she summoned Kayla into her office and fired her for insubordination. Today, Alpha Camps received notice that Kayla has filed a complaint with the Equal Employment Opportunity Commission for wrongful termination and has filed an allegation of misuse of funds with the federal agency overseeing Medicaid.

Prevent

What could Alpha Camps have done to prevent the Equal Employment Opportunity Commission and Medicaid complaints? The answer to that question rests on the things Alpha Camps might have done to prevent questionable conduct by Irene, her conflict with Kayla, and Kayla's termination.

The board as a whole, and the president in particular, should have exercised due diligence in selecting and screening Irene for the CEO position and in monitoring her once hired.[1] As noted in chapter 2, boards and management have different responsibilities, and lines of authority, and sometimes the intersection between the two, is not clear. Communication about expectations, policies, anticipated challenges, and the like is vital, particularly during transitions in leadership. Board oversight is not intended to undermine or second-guess the CEO but rather to ensure that the direction provided by the board is being fulfilled and that problems are detected and addressed at an early stage. If the board had monitored executive decisions, financial statements, and other reports, it could have detected disproportionate expenses, conflicts of interest in hiring, and other problems alleged by Kayla. Similarly, Irene should have established regular and forthright conversations with the board chairperson. These would have provided the opportunity to discuss the tensions with the business manager and the accounting disputes.

As discussed in chapter 7, financial mismanagement whether due to fraud or error can be prevented through a number of mechanisms. The control environment, set by the NPO's governing board, sets a tone for integrity and transparency. Did the board understand these responsibilities and act with integrity? Did it promulgate and uphold ethical and professional standards? Did it promote accountability throughout the organization?

Control activities, communications, and monitoring are designed to prevent, detect, and correct specific instances of mismanagement. In the case of Alpha Camps, additional checks and balances would have moved the debate about finances beyond Irene and Kayla and limited the possibility of a management override of Kayla's assiduous bookkeeping. It is easy to misconstrue disagreements such as those between Irene and Kayla as interpersonal matters or differences in interpretation of standards and thereby divert attention from potentially serious risks. Given the small size of the NPO, a board member from Alpha Camps (for example, the treasurer) should have been charged with conducting analytical reviews of the revenues and expenses. Irene, Kayla, and the board representative could have stipulated the decision points for various cost allocations to ensure that they were handled consistently going forward.

---

1 Ram Charan, *Owning Up: The 14 Questions Every Board Member Needs to Ask.* (San Francisco: Jossey-Bass, 2009).

A further device for risk management is the use of a system to facilitate anonymous whistleblower reports. Alpha Camps either had no such mechanism or failed to make Kayla aware of it. When she went to the board member with her concerns, that person erred in refusing to become involved and also in discussing the conversation with the board president. Although the board should not ordinarily be a conduit for complaints from staff about management, fiscal concerns, such as those Kayla shared, are significant enough that they should not be rebuffed when called to a board member's attention. Clearly, Kayla had attempted to address her concerns through the existing chain of command. The board member she approached should have clarified the parameters of confidentiality and sought Kayla's permission to involve or inform the board president. Upon hearing Kayla's concerns, the board member(s) involved should have developed a plan for additional fact-finding and enhanced organizational monitoring without identifying Kayla or her specific allegations to Irene. As it was handled, Kayla was left unheard, her concerns were unaddressed, and she was singled out for retribution by Irene.

Alpha Camps should have had a conflict of interest policy extending beyond the board to include staff financial decisions. In addition, financial policies could have included purchasing thresholds requiring dual signatures and competitive bids, which might have prevented the lucrative strategic planning contract. One could also argue that the board be very involved in strategic planning as an exercise of its duty of obedience. If it had been more involved, the board (not the CEO) may have had final approval on securing a consultant.

Address

Alpha Camps has two immediate responsibilities: (1) manage the crisis created by Kayla's allegations and (2) explore and respond to conditions that gave rise to the complaint. Crisis management will require retaining legal counsel familiar with employment and accounting law. If Alpha Camps currently has a firm on retainer, it may serve in this role or make proper referrals. Otherwise, board members, the local nonprofit association, or other agencies may recommend appropriate counsel. In light of Irene's role in the allegations, a board member or another administrator should be designated as lead contact person in regard to the complaints. This person must organize a team to respond to the complaint, craft internal and external communications about it, and educate staff about proper behaviors in light of the complaint. For example, Alpha Camps supervisors should not attempt in any way to influence or punish staff who might be subpoenaed to testify about the allegations. In addition, as noted in chapter 6, it is possible that the organization will need to deal with a public relations crisis as well. If this dispute becomes public knowledge (and with Kayla as angry as she appears to be, it might), the organization needs to be prepared with an appropriate response. Failure to handle this aspect judiciously could result in a loss of donors and erosion in the support of other stakeholders.

While the allegations are being investigated, the board must decide how it will deal with Irene. Until the charges are addressed, will she be suspended (with or without pay) or be removed from some duties? What succession plan exists to fill all or some of her responsibilities over the coming months? Should a consultant be retained to work with Irene on managerial or financial matters, or should that be deferred pending the outcome of the investigation? And, if the allegations are founded, what conditions for discharge and contractual obligations are spelled out in her employment agreement? Can Irene be discharged if she were found to have wrongfully dismissed Kayla but not to have misappropriated funds? Should she be? If not, then in what circumstance would discharge be warranted for the CEO?

The last element of crisis management involves attending to the functioning of Alpha Camps and the well-being of its employees. It can take a long time to resolve complaints such as those Kayla filed. The work of Alpha Camps can't be put on hold while that happens. It will be important for the lead contact person and the board in general to ensure that core functions such as fund-raising, financial management, programming, and communications go forward seamlessly despite the complaints. They must also be attuned to the morale and needs of the remaining employees. Personnel matters can be divisive and distressing to the workforce. Consistent support and communication can ensure that the collateral damage of allegations and investigations is kept to a minimum.

The board and leadership should also undertake other strategies to remedy any glaring problems revealed by the complaints. Clearly, Alpha Camps needs a process of whistleblower complaints and protections, a code of ethics, and a conflict of interest policy.[2] Because these are developed and instituted, the organization needs a strategy to inform staff about them and to make them living documents that shape organizational behavior. Ethics and conflict of interest standards express an alignment to the organization's beliefs, culture, and value. Beyond these aspirational purposes, standards about ethics and conflicts of interest address common risk factors such as those facing Alpha Camps. Although the CEO is required to exercise reasonable and ordinary care in the performance of his or her duties, exhibiting honesty and good faith, the board is charged with overseeing and scrutinizing all aspects of the organization. "…Actively promoting ethical behavior and practices not only make sense from a customer-relations standpoint, but also represent a better way to run a business. Not only are clients and potential funders pleased when they view an organization as acting in an ethical manner, but employees are more satisfied when dealt with ethically."[3]

The board might also want to contract for an outside audit to independently examine the agency's financial status. This will help detect and remedy financial irregularities and reacquaint the board with the funding streams, cash flow, program performance, and restrictions on spending. Depending on what is found, the auditors can recommend control activities that may be instituted to diminish future risk. The audit and finance committees should work closely with the auditors in reviewing and acting upon the management letter accompanying the audit. At the same time, the board might want to institute occasional inspection reports[4] in which a subset of the board is tasked with examining the agency's operations to ensure that they are aligned with the board's strategic vision.

The board should also strategize about the implications of various outcomes of the allegations and prepare for those possibilities. For example, if financial penalties and repayments

---

2 BoardSource. (2007). *The nonprofit board answer book* (2nd ed.). San Francisco, CA: Jossey-Bass.

3 Duca, D. J. (1996). *Nonprofit boards: roles, responsibilities, and performance.* New York: John Wiley & Sons, Inc.

4 Brown, J. (2006). *The imperfect board member: Discovering the seven disciplines of governance excellence.* San Francisco, CA: Jossey-Bass.

are required by Medicaid, does the agency have sufficient funds in reserve? Can the agency cover back pay or financial damages if Kayla's wrongful termination complaint prevails? Does the organization carry directors and officers insurance, and would Kayla's case constitute a "nonbodily claim?" Would such insurance cover legal expenses incurred by Irene and the organization as a result of Kayla's complaint? Would indemnity clauses negate coverage of Irene's behavior if it were found to be illegal or fraudulent?

Improve

Alpha Camps can grow from the experience, regardless of the outcomes of Kayla's allegations. If shortcomings are identified in CEO hiring and oversight, risk management, internal controls, finance and accounting, transition management, and board leadership, the agency can institute mechanisms to address these. This is not simply a matter of "closing the barn door after the cow escapes" but rather a common model of organizational development wherein challenges and crises spur examination and growth. Because some of these changes may be particularly complex to institute or may engender resistance, tools for negotiation, conversation, and transformation (as discussed in chapters 3, 4, and 10) may be of assistance.

Organizations need not wait until disaster strikes to review and renew their processes. *Learning organizations* anticipate change and have in place the culture, structures, and capacities to detect and react to threats and opportunities.[5] Orthner, et al, identify eight components of organizational learning:[6]

- **Leadership engagement.** Leaders must champion change and embrace the notion that innovation may come from anywhere in the organizational hierarchy.
- **Tolerance for errors.** Humans often learn from mistakes, trial and error, and mid-course corrections. Learning organizations must make it safe to try and fail.
- **Vision sharing.** Learning organizations promote broad "community" involvement in articulating values, creating strategies, resolving problems, and fostering commitment to a shared purpose.
- **Asking learning questions.** Inquiry is a significant element of breaking down hierarchical barriers and facilitating the exchange of information.
- **Use of tacit and practical knowledge.** Learning organizations recognize the existing wisdom held throughout the organization and foster a climate that facilitates open dialogue.
- **Time to reflect on learning.** Second order changes are those that alter the system itself. These transformations occur when people have opportunities to take stock of what has been learned and what new practices can result.
- **Value given to new ideas.** Innovation is engrained into the organizational culture. Employees are encouraged to raise and address issues through team learning processes.

---

5 Yogesh Malhotra, "Organizational Learning and Learning Organizations: An Overview" (Global Risk Management, 1996): www.brint.com/papers/orglrng.htm.

6 Dennis K. Orthner, Patricia Cook, Yekutiel Sabah, and Jona Rosenfeld, "Organizational learning: A cross-national pilot-test of effectiveness in children's services," *Evaluation & Program Planning*, vol. 29, February 2006, p. 70–78.

- **Process driven toward results.** The efforts of the learning organization should be aligned with a vision and directed toward results (better outcomes, increased efficiency, innovative services, and the like).

Another relevant element of learning organizations is the notion of single and double loop learning, wherein the double loop not only identifies the error but also asks deeper questions about the meaning of the error(s) (for example, is this a pattern emblematic of a problem with organizational culture or the business plan).[7] The learning organizations model has been widely applied in the public, corporate, and nonprofit sectors. The framework might improve Alpha Camps' processes and assist in organizational recovery from the challenges posed by Kayla's complaints. Adoption of this philosophy and its practices could also facilitate early detection of problems in the future.

Numerous resources provide guidance and rationales for continuous changes at Alpha Camps. Some of these resources are included at the end of this book.

Case Two: The Indeterminate Sentence

Carl has recently completed a three year term on the board of Acme County Mental Health Services (ACMHS). When he graduated from college and started work with a local real estate firm, Joe, his team leader there, had tapped Carl to succeed him on the board. Joe is invested in quality mental health care in the region, having experienced the challenges of bipolar disorder with his mother and brother.

Over the last three years, Carl has been astonished at the mismanagement of ACMHS and the dysfunction of the board. The agency is in constant financial peril as a result of its poor and unreliable clientele, flawed business model, and laissez faire organizational culture. Staff members are "too busy" to enter data required for reimbursements, and when they finally do, they frequently fail to code services properly for maximum payment. Clinicians constantly miss productivity benchmarks and blame the clients and the economy for the deficits. The CEO is at the end of his career and seems to lack the energy and attentiveness needed to turn around a failing organization. Monthly board meetings are a never-ending cycle of blame and hope: it is the COO's fault, the CFO's fault, or the clinicians' fault; a new program will make a big difference; other agencies have the same difficulties; a change in computer systems will make billing easier; and so on. In his three years of service, Carl has seen a succession of CFOs and COOs move through the organization. He has also seen a board more captivated by possibility than reality. Many of the board members, like Joe, serve because their families have benefited from ACMHS's programs. They believe each month that the financial figures will improve, that the economy will change, and that the new fix will be the magic bullet for solvency. A couple of board members are willing to ask hard questions, but their concerns never hold sway over the debate and decisions.

7 Chris Argyris, *Knowledge for Action: A Guide to Overcoming Barriers to Organizational Change* (San Francisco: Jossey-Bass, 1993).

Carl has found ACMHS a painful and unfulfilling form of service and has decided not to stand for another term, regardless of the possible repercussions from Joe. Today, he attended what he thought would be his final meeting at ACMHS only to find that he had been reelected at the meeting he missed last month to serve another three year term. During the break, he pulled the board president aside and told her that he could not continue on the board unless things change. She replied, "Then I hope you will be part of that change."

Prevent

By almost any measure, ACMHS is an organization at risk. Fundamental elements of sound governance are missing or have fallen into disuse. Attention to several key measures would have helped prevent financial peril, weak board oversight, and ineffective management. These key functions involve board member selection and preparation, governance structure, and board and staff relations, as discussed in subsequent sections.

NPOs must attend to the role, size, composition, leadership, and organization of the board. As noted in chapter 2, boards have several basic responsibilities, including defining the organization's mission and purpose, taking financial and legal accountability, selecting and supporting the CEO, and developing and evaluating the board. Members should be recruited with a clear appreciation of all of these responsibilities, and the boards as a whole should regularly assess the time they are allocating to each of these activities. It is tempting to minimize the demands of board membership in order to attract people to serve. However, a superficial or unrealistic portrayal of the expectations of service is unfair to the individual and to the organization that needs the time, expertise, and attention of its trustees. ACMHS should have had a governance committee to identify and screen prospective board members and evaluate their contributions and suitability for reelection. Such a committee should start with an inventory of the demographic characteristics, skills, and interests of existing members; the rotation of vacancies in upcoming elections; and the needs of the board and the organization.[8] It should constantly solicit suggestions for possible members and initiate discussions with prospects to learn about their interests and educate them about the NPO's mission and strategic direction, financial health, leadership, and the expectations of members (such as time, meetings, and donations). The active governance committee facilitates succession planning for routine elections, officer positions, and filling unplanned vacancies when they arise.

New board members should receive a comprehensive orientation to the staff, structure, and services of the organization; committee assignments; and audits and other reports. This should emphasize the duties of care, loyalty, and obedience embodied in ethics and in laws incorporating NPOs. Periodic evaluations should be carried out by the executive committee or governance committee to examine the performance of board members and the board as a whole. Evaluations can include electronic post-meeting surveys that query members on

---

8 Ram Charan, *Owning Up: The 14 Questions Every Board Member Needs to Ask.* (San Francisco: Jossey-Bass, 2009).

the use of time, quality of discussion, and decision making at the meeting as well as their appraisal of their own contributions. Time can be set aside quarterly or semi-annually for the board to discuss its functioning and evaluate it across benchmarks for good governance. Officers can initiate one-on-one conversations with members to solicit their assessments, and exit interviews can be conducted with outgoing members. Underperforming board members can be dealt with in a variety of ways: outreach from a board designee to determine reasons for poor participation, removal from the board according to bylaws, rotation off the board after one term, or reassignment to another role or subcommittee that is more suited to the person's interests and availability.

The ACMHS board needed to comprise individuals with a broad array of experiences and expertise. Members needed to understand their responsibilities and have the preparation necessary to carry out their fiduciary responsibilities, particularly in nonprofit accounting standards and how to read financial statements. The board needed mechanisms to hold individual members, the board as a whole, and the senior leadership accountable for competent, ethical, and legal decisions. Certain structural changes would have helped the board carry out its roles. For example, meetings need to happen frequently and be led skillfully so that issues are raised in a timely manner, discussions are well-informed and properly targeted, and decisions are well-founded and enduring. Board meetings need to avoid the common dynamic of passively listening to a series of staff reports. The chairperson is in a critical role to facilitate critical discussion about any agenda item; he or she must encourage board members to ask tough questions of staff. Also, board meetings need to include time and space to deepen members' understanding of the problems the NPO is addressing and the effectiveness of the NPO's business model in addressing them; the board should not wait until disaster strikes to have substantive discussion. Occasional retreats and executive sessions (without staff present) might have facilitated board education, relationship building, and the honest airing of concerns. Subcommittee structures can also assist in board functioning. Typical standing committees include the following:

- **Audit.** Selects and works with outside financial and other auditors.
- **Finance.** Oversees budget development, institution of controls, accuracy of financial reports, and adherence to terms of gifts, grants, and contracts.
- **Personnel.** Evaluates the adequacy of personnel policies and practices. May take leadership in CEO evaluation and compensation decisions.
- **Governance/Board development.** Facilitates board functioning and evaluation, nominations, and committee development.
- **Communications and Marketing.** Oversees integrated strategies to brand and advertise the NPO and its services. May constitute response team to address adverse public relations events.
- **Investment.** Sets priorities and monitors investments of the NPO's portfolio.
- **Advancement.** Assists with fundraising, identification of donors, and solicitation and stewardship of major gifts.
- **Membership.** Devises strategies for increasing membership or service utilization.

These committees and other ad hoc groups can comprise board members and board "alumni" or other interested parties as the bylaws permit. Appropriate staff (CFO, COO, and CIO) should be assigned to each committee in ex–officio roles. Officers should also be assigned to each key committee. Typically, the treasurer sits on the finance and audit committees, the secretary may participate in personnel and membership, the past president may lead the advancement committee, and the vice president or president elect chairs the CEO selection and evaluation processes.

With the right people at the board table and the right structures in place to support their success, the final preventive measure focuses on board and staff relations. The depiction of ACMHS reveals deficits in CEO performance, turnover in key management roles, and the CEO as a single information source for the board. Perhaps the single most important role played by NPO boards is the selection and evaluation of the CEO. Yet as illustrated throughout this book, trepidation, misinformation, poor performance criteria, and other factors can stymie boards in executing this responsibility. ACMHS and other NPOs need proper processes and criteria for CEO evaluation. The criteria can be mutually formulated by board members and the CEO based on the job description and performance targets derived from strategic directions, past evaluations, and other benchmarks (staff retention, job satisfaction, productivity measures, and budget adherence). Obviously, the criteria must be specified in advance of the appraisal period (typically a year, but sometimes more frequently for new or underperforming leaders). The subcommittee tasked with the appraisal should solicit a self-evaluation from the CEO and other board members, using organizational data, critical incidents, and other concrete measures to support its conclusions. This evaluation should be shared with the CEO and the board and kept on file. Areas for improvement and related indicators with specific benchmarks should be specified and a corrective action plan developed. These items should be incorporated into evaluation criteria for the year ahead. Typically, the board president would be responsible for monitoring the improvement plan and addressing continued performance problems.

Boards that are mindful of the risks of micromanaging sometimes overcorrect and take an overly hands–off approach, even when organizational problems are apparent. At ACMHS, the retention problems in key management positions, the failure of staff to meet productivity targets, and the persistent financial shortfalls should have served as red flags to the board that their intercession was needed. The board as a whole or the chair on behalf of the board should have asked for frequent, detailed information from the CEO about these developments and convened appropriate subcommittees to work with the CEO to detect and address contributing factors. The board should have been well acquainted with important industry benchmarks; it is critical to examine performance in relation to similar NPOs. If greater objectivity or expertise were required, the board should have retained the services of a consultant to review the issues, report on findings, and recommend changes.

A particular change that would have helped the board detect management problems would have been to open up additional lines of communication with the leadership team.[9] Rather than relying on the CEO's reports and interpretations of ACMHS's functioning, the board could have included key staff in its meetings so that it could hear their financial,

---

9 Jim Brown, *The Imperfect Board Member: Discovering the Seven Disciplines of Governance Excellence* (San Francisco: Jossey-Bass, 2006).

operational, and fundraising reports directly and question responsible staff about opportunities and challenges facing ACMHS. Chapter 2 describes the distinctions and division of roles between board members and paid staff and offers guidance on effectively working in partnership to ensure that the mission and vitality of the organization are maintained.

Address

Although environmental challenges such as the flagging economy or a destitute target population are out of the organization's control, there are a number of steps that the board of ACMHS can take to address the challenges Carl has identified. A starting place would be institution of the strategies described in the preceding section that might have prevented the crisis. These include creation of board committees, board evaluation, education and rejuvenation, specification and implementation of CEO performance criteria, and solicitation of operational reports from key administrators. As needed, external resources or consultants should be retained to address problem areas. Given ACMHS's precarious financial position, they may be able to seek assistance from local volunteers (like Service Corps of Retired Executives or other service organizations), former board members, other agencies, a regional or state council of NPOs, or local foundations that fund NPOs' services.

The board should also embark on a strategic plan to comprehensively examine ACMHS's current strengths, weaknesses, opportunities, and threats and determine whether its current business model is sufficient to meet its mission. NPOs frequently need to examine their funding sources and ensure that they are sufficiently diversified in case one segment experiences financial stress. Donations, fundraisers, fee for service income, government grants, and grants from foundations are all options that can be pursued by an NPO. This evaluation process may conclude that the model used by ACMHS is unsustainable in the absence of structural and procedural changes, or it may recommend closing ACMHS or merging it with another organization. Such possibilities have a profound effect on employees, clients, stakeholders, and the communities served by NPOs. If ACMHS cannot be righted, the board will remain responsible until all legal, financial, and human relations issues are concluded.

Improve

ACMHS needs to turn around its governance practices and its finances. Assuming it is able to take adequate steps to resolve the current crisis and remain solvent, several additional governance strategies can ensure their continued strength. Chapters 3, 4, 9, and 10 address ethics, moral courage, organizational conflict, and change management, respectively. Each area offers strategies for individual and institutional improvement. Strengthened relationships among board members and between the board and CEO, effective communications about difficult issues, clear vision and strategic direction, role clarity, personal and organizational integrity, and appreciation of fiduciary responsibilities must all be cultivated and maintained for ACMHS to thrive.

Policy manuals are essential for risk management and efficient board functioning. "Whenever an issue surfaces, the first question to ask is, 'What do our standing policies say?' If there is nothing in the board policy manual to guide the organization, the next question is, 'What policy should be adopted to cover this and similar situations in the future?'"[10] At ACMHS, an individual or committee should be assigned responsibility for compiling and organizing such a manual, distributing drafts for review by legal counsel and board members, integrating feedback into a final product, distributing it to members, and delegating responsibility for continual renewal and revision. Typically, such manuals include the organization's articles of incorporation and bylaws, its strategic plan and operational benchmarks, standing policies, position descriptions, and resolutions culled from the minutes of past meetings as well as references to relevant laws and IRS regulations. Manuals may be part of a larger handbook for members that also include committee descriptions, charges, terms and membership, biographical and contact information for members of the board, an organizational chart, annual report, audit report, Form 990, and current annual budget. These handbooks (which can be produced and distributed in electronic form) are used in orienting new board members and as resources at and between meetings. The more they are referenced, the more meaningful and relevant they become.

Larger organizations may wish to institute a risk management committee to perform risk assessments as described in chapter 6. Smaller organizations need to assess risk, but it may be performed at the full board level rather than by a designated subcommittee.

Case Three: Your Turn

Carol and Steven are a well-to-do couple in their 50s. Over the last 3 decades, they have devoted themselves to improving the educational opportunities for children with physical and intellectual disabilities. Initially, their efforts were focused on securing adequate public education for their son, who was born with Down syndrome. Through that effort, they became acquainted with other families in the same circumstance and gradually turned their efforts to reforming educational systems and training and supporting parents to be effective advocates. In the past 20 years, they have created a thriving nonprofit agency operated largely by in kind and philanthropic donations. "KidsEd," as the agency is known, employs a full time executive director and a part-time staff member to do accounting and clerical tasks. The board consists of Carol, Steven, eight upper middle class townspeople who joined KidsEd because they are close friends with Carol and Steve, two parents of children with disabilities, and a local college professor who specializes in education policy. Many of the board members have served since the inception of KidsEd.

Recently, the longtime executive director resigned, and the board is undertaking a search for a replacement. The search thus far has been contentious. Initially, the board split on the background required of applicants. Some board members wanted people with advanced degrees and professional experience, and the founders and others wanted applicants with personal experience with disabilities. Ultimately, the position

(continued)

---

10 BoardSource, *The Nonprofit Board Answer Book* (2nd ed.) (San Francisco: Jossey-Bass, 2007) p. 225.

(continued)

description and advertisement were written broadly so that the board could choose the best available person with either route of preparation. KidsEd was inundated with applications. Interviews were conducted with several candidates who later withdrew from consideration because of the broad job demands and the paltry salary. The search is now back at square one. Some board members have suggested engaging a consultant to help carry out a strategic plan. Others want KidsEd to become more active in lobbying and political activity as a force for change. Some want to increase the salary through more aggressive fundraising and new fee-for-service initiatives and then restart the search. One board member has a niece who recently got a degree in organizational behavior who would be willing to for the job for the current salary. Steven and Carol are taking turns filling the executive director role until the hiring mess is sorted out. They despair that all their hard work in creating KidEd is unraveling before their eyes.

This case is offered as an opportunity for readers to put into practice the material covered elsewhere in the book. The case can also be used as part of board development or continuing education or other opportunities for group reflection and discussion. How could KidsEd have prevented the current impasse? How can the current tensions and divisions be addressed? Are any of the ideas now on the table more promising (or riskier) than others? What can KidsEd do going forward to emerge from these difficulties as a stronger and more vibrant entity? What resources exist to help Carol, Steven, and the rest of the board to stabilize and grow KidsEd?

Sustained Success

In life, whether of an individual or an organization, there is no standing still. One is either advancing, improving, and gaining, or one is declining, losing, and regressing. There is no middle ground. The status quo is an illusion.

An organization that has implemented all the best practices and is enjoying their benefits, which is going along smoothly and achieving its vision, is often tempted to rest on its laurels. That is invariably a mistake.

To avoid the common cycle of success ‡ complacency ‡ decline, one must adopt the attitude that continued success requires continual improvement. This attitude is embodied in the Japanese (although it was developed by an American) concept of *kaizen*. This is a system that involves making small improvements frequently. Improve just a little every day, and in a year you will be amazed how much better your organization is fulfilling its mission. *Kaizen* is often thought of as a system for industrial improvement, and it is. However, for the purposes of this discussion, it just means always keeping an attitude of looking for how everything you do can be improved just a tiny bit.

The world is constantly changing. Today's best practice is tomorrow's also-ran. To do the best job of implementing its vision not only today but also in the future, an NPO needs to institutionalize a commitment to continual improvement.

Conclusion

NPOs are complex and dynamic entities. The organizations, their funders, and stakeholders all rely on sound executive and volunteer leadership to steer the organization forward through challenging times. Successful governance requires committed and talented board and executive leadership, adherence to roles and responsibilities, persistent communication, constructive relationships, legal and regulatory compliance, integrity, and evaluative processes. NPOs need the processes in place to maintain and renew these capacities and the foresight to adjust as circumstances demand. Fortunately, abundant expertise and resources exist to help NPOs live these ideals. In doing so, NPOs fulfill their individual missions and the vital roles they play in society.

Glossary

accrual accounting. A basis of accounting in which revenue is recognized when earned and expense is recognized when incurred. Distinct from cash accounting.

accumulated depreciation or **accumulated amortization.** Depreciation is an accounting method by which the cost of a long-lived tangible asset (a fixed asset, typically one with a useful life of more than one year) is spread over its useful life. Each year, a portion of its cost is charged to depreciation expense on the income statement and credited to accumulated depreciation on the balance sheet. Accumulated depreciation reduces the net remaining cost of the asset on the balance sheet, and this process continues until the reported net value has been reduced to a minimum amount, known as *salvage value*. Various methods are used to calculate the portion of cost that is charged to expense in each year, and some tangible assets are not depreciated (notably land). Nonprofits most often use straight line depreciation, in which the asset is depreciated at a uniform rate over its useful life. Accumulated amortization functions similarly for intangible assets.

AGI. adjusted gross income. An intermediate subtotal in the calculation of an individual's taxable income, in which total income is reduced by certain statutory (Internal Revenue Code) deductions. Used as the basis for calculating a number of limitations, including the limitation on the deduction for charitable contributions.

AICPA. American Institute of Certified Public Accountants.

amortization. (See **accumulated depreciation** or **accumulated amortization**.)

annuity. An income payment of a specified amount at specified intervals for a specified period. The period may be fixed or contingent, often continuing for the recipient's life. These annuity payments are made in return for a premium that was paid either in prior installments or in a single payment. The payor is usually an insurance company, but need not be, and is sometimes a large nonprofit.

appreciation. The amount by which an asset has increased in value.

asset. Any item of economic value owned by an individual or organization. Examples include cash, accounts receivable, equipment, buildings, furniture, stocks, and bonds.

audit. An examination of financial statements by CPAs (the auditors), using generally accepted auditing standards. It normally results in the CPAs expressing an opinion on whether the financial statements are fairly stated in all material respects in accordance with generally accepted accounting principles. Audited financial statements are frequently required of a nonprofit by its funders.

board of directors. The part of an organization that is charged with governance. It may have a number of different names, such as *board of trustees* or *board of regents*.

bonded. An insurance contract whereby the insurer agrees to indemnify the policyholder if the bonded individual misappropriates the assets. When an individual has control over or access to significant valuable assets, it may be wise to have that individual bonded.

bylaws. A set of rules adopted by an organization to regulate its affairs and the behavior of its members.

churning. Excessive trading by a broker for the purpose of earning additional commissions. This practice is illegal in most jurisdictions but is often difficult to prove.

cash accounting. A basis of accounting in which revenue is recognized when cash is received for it and expense is recognized when paid. Distinct from accrual accounting.

constituents. The people involved in or served by an organization; stakeholders.

contemporaneous. Documentation is contemporaneous when it is prepared at the same time as the events being documented, rather than later. Those concerned with the reliability of documentation, such as auditors and the IRS, generally value contemporaneous documentation more highly than documentation prepared after the fact.

cutoff. In preparing financial statements, whether on the accrual or cash basis, it is important to ensure that only transactions belonging to the reporting period go into the financial statement preparation and that transactions belonging to a succeeding period are cutoff from the current period and assigned to the next one.

deferred revenue. An organization may receive funds that appear to be revenue but do not pass accounting tests to be recognized as revenue in the financial statements. Such funds are reported on the balance sheet as a liability called *deferred revenue* and are recognized as revenue only when they are subsequently earned.

defraud. To commit an act of fraud.

depreciated value. The net value of fixed assets on the balance sheet after reduction by accumulated depreciation.

diversification. A means of reducing the overall riskiness of an investment portfolio by investing in a variety of different assets so that the failure of any one will not be catastrophic.

diversion. Occurs when a dishonest person takes assets that belong to the organization and diverts them to his or her personal use.

easements. A limited right for another to use an owner's land, usually for a narrowly specified purpose. For example, a nonprofit may acquire a conservation easement to prevent development of a piece of land.

embezzlement. Theft by an employee.

escrow. Assets are in escrow when they are held by a neutral third party until certain contractual obligations are fulfilled.

expense. Money or other thing of value paid or obligated to be paid for goods or services (except goods with a useful life of usually one year or more, which become assets).

fraud. Intentional misrepresentation of a material existing fact with the purpose of inducing another to act in such a way that the perpetrator will receive an unearned benefit at the expense of the one defrauded.

funders. Persons and organizations that provide funds to a nonprofit through contributions and grants.

governance. Consists of the systems by which the board ensures that its policies are being effectively implemented. Usually this includes systems to monitor and record what is happening, to identify instances in which policy is not being followed, and to take corrective action in those cases.

illiquid. An asset is illiquid if it would be difficult or costly to convert it into cash within a short period of time.

imprest. An imprest fund is money given to an employee to make small disbursements; petty cash.

indemnify. To pay or agree to pay losses or expenses that one party may incur because of another. For example, a nonprofit may agree to indemnify members of its board of directors for expenses or judgments resulting from a lawsuit that results from the performance of their duties as board members.

inventory. Items owned that were acquired with the intent of reselling them or of incorporating them into items to be sold.

investor owned. For-profit organizations are owned by investors, who are entitled to share in profits earned. Contrast with nonprofit organizations, which do not have owners.

lessor. One who grants a lease; one who receives rent.

lessee. One to whom a lease is granted; one who pays rent.

levied. Imposed; for example, "additional taxes were levied to cover the city budget deficit."

liability. An obligation for payment; for example, accounts payable (amounts due for goods and services previously purchased), notes payable (money previously borrowed), or accrued payroll (due to employees for time worked but not yet paid for).

liable. Responsible to pay or otherwise fulfill an obligation.

liquidity. The liquidity of an asset is how quickly it can be liquidated (converted into cash). The liquidity of an organization is a measure of the overall balance between current (easily liquidated) assets and current (short term) liabilities.

litigation. A legal proceeding in court; lawsuit.

lobby. To influence a decision by a legislator or other government official. Sometimes extended to mean an informal effort to influence any decision maker.

lockbox. A service offered by a bank whereby a depositor's incoming checks go directly to the bank and are put in the depositor's account without being handled by the depositor's employees.

margin. The excess of revenue over expense.

master file. Files that contain relatively permanent information about items, donors, vendors, employees, and the like. For example, the employee master file may contain an employee's identification number, name, address, social security number, and date of hire. Contrast with transaction file. For example, the employee transaction file may contain an employee's identification number, paycheck number, check date, earnings amount, tax withheld, and net check amount.

maturity. The length of time until a financial asset matures (in other words, until the time specified by contract when it must be repaid). For example, a 2 year loan made 20 months ago now has a 4 month maturity.

median. The middle value in a set of values. Not the same as average. For example, the median number is 11 in this set of numbers: 1, 2, 3, 11, 700, 800, 900.

metrics. Any number (often one calculated using two or more input numbers) used to evaluate some part of an organization's performance.

nonprofit. An entity organized for other than profit making purposes.

orientation. Initial training of new board members, employees, and the like.

oversight. Monitoring of activities and processes by those charged with governance.

payee. One who receives payment from another (the payor).

payor. One who pays to another (the payee).

perpetuity. Forever.

Ponzi Scheme: A fraudulent investment operation in which unrealistically large returns promised to investors are in fact paid out from money that they and other investors paid in. The scheme will collapse soon after the inflow of money from new investors slows because it becomes more and more difficult to pay out the promised rate of return. Named after Charles Ponzi, who did not invent this fraud but made it famous around 1920.

prospectus. A detailed description of any new financial security and its issuer. It must be filed with the Securities and Exchange Commission as part of the process of registering the security, and it must be given to prospective purchasers before the security may be sold to them.

reconcile. To ensure that two separate parts of the financial recordkeeping system are in agreement. For example, reconcile the accounts receivable ledger by determining that its totals are the same as those on the accounts receivable summary page in the general ledger. For example, reconcile a general ledger cash account to its bank statement by preparing a list of outstanding checks and deposits in transit to account for the difference.

recuse. Originally, a judge may recuse (excuse) him- or herself from a case if he or she has a personal interest in the outcome or otherwise lacks impartiality. May apply to anyone in a decision-making role, such as a nonprofit board member.

skimming. A form of embezzlement in which an employee responsible for receiving cash or other easily stolen property steals a portion of it. Because the theft occurs before the property is entered into the financial system, detection is especially difficult.

SSAE. Statement on Standards for Attestation Engagements. Issued by the Auditing Standards Board of the AICPA.

stakeholder. Anyone with an interest in an organization. In the nonprofit world, examples include board members, donors, employees, grantors, vendors, service recipients, and the IRS.

stockholders. In a for-profit organization, the stockholders are the owners. Nonprofit organizations do not have stockholders.

subsidiary organization. An organization that is entirely or mostly owned and controlled by another.

subsidiary ledger. An accounting ledger that contains a particular category of accounts (such as accounts receivable, accounts payable, or payroll) and that is subsidiary (subordinate) to the general ledger, which shows only the totals from the subsidiary ledger.

transparency. Transparent organizations seek to improve their operations by acquiring better feedback and earning greater trust from their stakeholders. They do this by disseminating more information about their operations (sometimes information that in the past may have been considered internal or confidential), and they disseminate this information to a wider audience.

variances. The difference between a budget amount and the corresponding amount actually earned or received or incurred or expended. Analysis of variances can provide valuable information about how the organization is performing.

variance power. The ability to expend funds in a way that is at variance with the donor's instructions. Normally this requires particular legal language in solicitation materials.

whistleblower. An informant who exposes wrongdoing in an organization.

Bibliography

- Nancy E. Algert and Christine A. Stanley, "Conflict Management," *Effective Practices for Academic Leaders*, vol. 2, iss. 9 (Stylus Publishing, 2007) p. 1–16.
- Chris Argyris, *Knowledge for Action: A Guide to Overcoming Barriers to Organizational Change* (San Francisco: Jossey-Bass, 1993).
- Philip Aspden, Julie A. Wolcott, J. Lyle Bootman, and Linda R. Cronenwett (Eds.), *Preventing Medication Errors: Quality Chasm Series*. Institute of Medicine, Board on Health Care Services (Washington DC: National Academies Press, 2006).
- Steven Barth, *Corporate Ethics: How to Update or Develop Your Ethics Code so That it is in Compliance With the New Laws of Corporate Responsibility* (Boston: Aspatore, 2003).
- BoardSource, *The Nonprofit Board Answer Book* (2nd ed.), (San Francisco: Jossey-Bass, 2007).
- George Brager and Stephen Holloway, "Assessing prospects for organizational change: The uses of force field analysis," *Administration in Social Work*, vol. 16, no. 3, 1992, p. 15–28.
- George Brager and Stephen Holloway, "A process model for changing organizations from within," R. M. Kramer &H. Specht (Eds.), *Readings in community organization practice*, Ralph M. Kramer and Harry Specht, eds. (Englewood Cliffs, NJ: Prentice-Hall, 1983) p. 198–208.
- William Bridges, *Managing Transitions: Making the Most of Change* (Philadelphia: Da Capo Lifelong Books, 2009).
- Jim Brown, *The Imperfect Board Member: Discovering the Seven Disciplines of Governance Excellence* (San Francisco: Jossey-Bass, 2006).
- Ron Charan, *Owning Up: The 14 Questions Every Board Member Needs to Ask* (San Francisco: Wiley, 2009).
- Chief Ethics & Compliance Officer (CECO) Definition Working Group, *Leading Corporate Integrity: Defining the Role of the Chief Ethics & Compliance Officer* (CECO) (Washington, DC: Ethics Resource Center, 2007).
- Carlo C. DiClemente, Debra Schlundt, and Leigh Gemmell, "Readiness and stages of change in addiction treatment," *The American Journal on Addictions*, vol. 13, 2004, p. 103–119.
- Diane J. Duca, *Nonprofit Boards: Roles, Responsibilities, and Performance* (New York: John Wiley & Sons, Inc, 1996).
- Roger Fisher, William Ury, and Bruce Patton, B. *Getting to Yes: Negotiating Agreement Without Giving In.* (New York: Penguin, 1991).
- John R. French and Bertam Raven, "The bases of social power," In D. Cartwright (Ed.), *Studies in social power*. Dorwin Cartwright, ed. (Oxford: University of Michigan Press, 1959) p. 150–167.

- Gerald Frey, "Framework for promoting organizational change," *Families in Society*, vol. 7, 1990, p. 142–147.
- Margaret Gibelman and Sheldon R. Gelman, "Very Public Scandals: Nongovernmental Organizations in Trouble," *Voluntas: International Journal of Voluntary and Nonprofit Organizations*, vol. 12, no. 1 (New York: Springer, 2001) p. 49–66.
- Margaret Gibelman and Sheldon R. Gelman, "A Loss of Credibility: Patterns of Wrongdoing Among Nongovernmental Organizations," *Voluntas: International Journal of Voluntary and Nonprofit Organizations*, vol. 15, no. 4 (New York: Springer, 2004) p. 355–381.
- Ann Gilley, Pamela Dixon, and Jerry W. Gilley, "Characteristics of leadership effectiveness: Implementing change and driving innovation in organizations," *Human Resource Development Quarterly*, vol. 19, 2008, p. 153–169.
- Hylton, W. S. (2006, August 18). *Prisoner of conscience.* Retrieved January 23, 2007 from men.style.com/gq/features/landing?id=content_4785
- Independent Sector, *Obedience to the Unenforceable: Ethics and the Nation's Voluntary and Philanthropic Community.* (Washington, DC, 2002).
- Rushworth M. Kidder, *Moral Courage: Taking Action When Your Values are Put to the Test.* (New York; William Morrow, 2005).
- John P. Kotter, *Leading change* (Boston: Harvard Business Press, 1996).
- Richard Lacayo and Amanda Ripley, "Persons of The Year 2002: The Whistleblowers," *Time*, December 30, 2002. Retrieved January 22, 2007, from www.time.com/time/subscriber/personoftheyear/2002/poyintro.html.
- Frederic L. Laughlin and Robert C. Andringa, *Good Governance for Nonprofits: Developing Principles and Policies for an Effective Board* (New York: AMACOM, 2007).
- David A. Lax and James K. Sebenius, *The Manager as Negotiator: Bargaining for Cooperation and Competitive Gain* (New York: Free Press, 1986).
- Kurt Lewin, "Defining the 'field at a given time,'" *Psychological Review*, vol. 50, 1943, p. 292–310.
- Yogesh Malhotra, "Organizational Learning and Learning Organizations: An Overview" (Global Risk Management, 1996): www.brint.com/papers/orglrng.htm.
- John McCain, *Why Courage Matters: The Way to a Braver Life* (New York: Random House, 2004).
- William I. Miller, *The Mystery of Courage* (Cambridge; Harvard University Press, 2000).
- Patrick E. Murphy (Ed.), *Eighty Exemplary Ethics Statements* (Notre Dame: University of Notre Dame Press, 1998).
- Dennis K. Orthner, Patricia Cook, Yekutiel Sabah, and Jona Rosenfeld, "Organizational learning: A cross-national pilot-test of effectiveness in children's services," *Evaluation & Program Planning*, vol. 29, February 2006, p. 70–78.
- Kerry Patterson, Joseph Grenny, David Maxfield, Ron McMillan, Al Switzler, *Influencer: The Power to Change Anything* (New York: McGraw-Hill, 2008).

- Kerry Patterson, Joseph Grenny, Ron McMillan, and Al Switzler, *Crucial confrontations: Tools for talking about broken promises, violated expectations, and bad behavior* (New York: McGraw-Hill, 2004).
- James L. Perry (ed.), *The Jossey-Bass Reader on Nonprofit and Public Leadership* (San Francisco: Jossey-Bass, 2010).
- John Rawls, *A Theory of Justice*, (Cambridge: Belknap, 1971).
- J. K. Rowling, *Harry Potter and the Sorcerer's Stone*. (New York, Scholastic Press, 1997).
- Susan Scott, *Fierce conversations: Achieving Success at Work & in Life, One Conversation at a Time* (New York: Berkeley, 2004).
- "Silence kills," *Nursing*, vol. 35, issue 4 (2005) p. 33.
- Kimberly J. Strom-Gottfried, "The use of conflict resolution techniques in managed care disputes," *Social Work*, vol. 43, 1998, p. 393–401.
- Kim Strom-Gottfried, *The Ethics of Practice with Minors: High Stakes, Hard Choices* (Chicago: Lyceum Books, 2008).
- Kenneth W. Thomas and Ralph H. Kilmann, *The Thomas-Kilmann Conflict Mode Instrument* (Palo Alto: CPP, Inc., 1974).
- Sloan R. Weitzel, *Feedback That Works: How to Build and Deliver Your Message* (Center for Creative Leadership, 2003). Retrieved from www.ccl.org/leadership/pdf/publications/readers/reader405ccl.pdf.

Suggested Reading

- Internal Controls
  — *Guidance on Monitoring Internal Control Systems* (2009): www.cpa2biz.com/.
  — *Internal Control over Financial Reporting—Guidance for Smaller Public Companies* (2006): www.cpa2biz.com/.
- Policies and Procedures
  — *Model Accounting Financial Policies and Procedures for Not-for-Profit Organizations* in electronic form: www.nonprofitresource.com/models/index.cfm.
- Nonprofit Strategy and Leadership
  — Atul Gawande, The Checklist Manifesto: How to Get Things Right (New York: Picador, 2011).
  — Barbara Kellerman, Followership: How Followers Are Creating Change and Changing Leaders (Boston: Harvard Business School Press, 2008).
  — Bill George, Authentic Leadership: Rediscovering the Secrets to Creating Lasting Value (New York: Jossey-Bass, 2003).
  — Ira Chaleff, The Courageous Follower: Standing Up to and for Our Leaders (San Francisco: Berrett-Koehler, 2009).
  — James L. Perry (ed.), *The Jossey-Bass Reader on Nonprofit and Public Leadership* (San Francisco: Jossey-Bass, 2010).
  — Jim Collins, Good to Great: Why Some Companies Make the Leap … And Others Don't (Dunmore: Harper Business, 2001).
  — Leslie R. Crutchfield and Heather McLeod Grant, Forces for Good: The Six Practices of High-Impact Nonprofit. (San Francisco: Jossey-Bass, 2007).
  — Peter F. Drucker, Managing the Non-Profit Organization: Principles and Practices (New York: Harper Paperbacks, 2006).
- Learning Organizations
  — Peter M. Senge, Nelda H. Cambron-McCabe, Timothy Lucas, Art Kleiner, Janis Dutton, and Bryan Smith, *Schools that Learn* (New York: Doubleday, 2000).
  — Bill Byron Concevich (Ed.), *The Learning Leaders Fieldbook* (Saratoga Springs: Masie Center, 2009).
- Ethics
  — *Obedience to the Unenforceable*, (Washington, DC: Independent Sector, 2002).
  — Rushworth M. Kidder, *How Good People Make Tough Choices: Resolving the Dilemmas of Ethical Living.* (New York: Simon and Schuster, 1995).
- BoardSource, *The Nonprofit Board Answer Book* (2nd ed.), (San Francisco: Jossey-Bass, 2007).

- Frederic L. Laughlin and Robert C. Andringa, *Good Governance for Nonprofits: Developing Principles and Policies for an Effective Board* (New York: AMACOM, 2007).
- Carter McNamara, *Field Guide to Developing, Operating and Restoring Your Nonprofit Board* (Minneapolis: Authenticity Consulting, 2008).